# FINDING FUNDING

## The Comprehensive Guide to

# GRANT WRITING

## DANIEL M. BARBER

Graduate Center for Public Policy and Administration
California State University, Long Beach

Bond Street Publishers
Long Beach, Californ

FINDING FUNDING: The Comprehensive Guide to Grant Writing
SECOND EDITION
Copyright 2002 Daniel M. Barber

Library of Congress cataloging -in-Publication Data

Barber, Daniel M.
Finding Funding: The Comprehensive Guide to Grant Writing
p.288 cm.

1. Proposal Writing for Grants-United States. 2. Grants-in-aid-United States. 3. Fund Raising. 4. Proposal writing in education and social services. 5. Intergovernmental relations. 6. Funding Sources-United States-Directories. 7. With Document Diskette I. Title.

Published By
Bond Street Publishers

1261 Hackett Avenue
Long Beach, CA 90815-4636
www.grantwriters.com


Cover Design by George Olarte
Graphics/Book Design by Michelle Glush

ISBN 0-9638091-1-3
Printed in the United States

# Table of Contents

# List of Figures

# Acknowledgements

A new edition of a book is a most satisfying time for an author. It signifies, to at least some extent, that the ideas and presentation have passed the test of time. Ideas without merit, or those that spawn indifference or confusion are not the stuff of which new editions are born. When the author launched the first edition I was pleased to acknowledge the assistance and interest of a number of individuals. Since then I can add to that thank you list literally thousands of readers from all walks of life, ranging from leaders of prestigious foundations, college and university faculty, community based and nonprofit organization staff, and simple folk with a singular cause and purpose. They have all contributed greatly to the substantial revisions in this latest edition. This effort is the culmination of over 30 years of studying the intergovernmental process, teaching, consulting, research and of course, writing grants. All of this made possible and generally pleasurable because of the opportunity to work alongside tremendously talented friends and colleagues.

In the early days individuals such as Professors R. H. Kite of Florida Atlantic University, and Carl E. B. McKenry of the University of Miami, were inspiring. They and other colleagues had the wisdom to see a problem early on, the creativity to develop a solution, and the energy and perseverance to create and conduct successful grant projects.

In more recent times, I owe a considerable debt of gratitude to my students at California State University, and around the world in our web based courses who have given generously of their time and criticism to make this a better book. I also thank my associates at Bond Street Publishing and Grantwriters.com. Included in this latter group are talented persons such as Mike Netter, who has grown from a curious student to professional grant writer, Marvin Wolf, an author and expert writer himself, and a host of others who have given wit and wisdom along the way. Finally, it goes without saying that beyond funding of any sort or any amount, the foundation of our lives is our families. To Mom and Dad, Andy, Betsy and Jim, and the other apples shining on my family tree, thanks.

Daniel M. Barber
Long Beach, California
January 2002

# Preface

Any successful grant writer must master various techniques, processes and procedures. It is extremely likely that the strategies and tactics for obtaining external support for one's field or specialty was not a part of traditional educational experiences. Scientists know science, artists know art, teachers know education, etc. but the reality of many endeavors is that there is a need, or at least a desire, to obtain extra or external financial support for a project or organization. This book and diskette is designed to assist individuals of varied backgrounds in obtaining the external support needed in today's complicated and changing fiscal and organizational environment. My intent is to provide readers with strategies and tactics to improve their chances of being awarded a grant and administering it in a successful manner.

Like any new endeavor, writing grants and proposals is challenging and this latest edition, with considerable attention to using the Internet, is a testament to that fact. There are thousands of federal, state, and local programs, and almost an equal number of foundations and corporations. It can be confusing. The Federal Register is published daily just to try and keep up with regulatory additions, deletions, and revisions. Yet, the process can also be rewarding. With hundreds of billions in public and private funding available and the established trend toward contracting out, joint ventures, and shared programming, the time has never been better for finding funding.

Successful grant writers must learn a new vocabulary, recognize new players, and develop a variety of relationships to consider individually, and in combination, against a background of deadlines, pressure, and public interest. The chapters to follow contain a general discussion of what grants are, the problems they can help solve, and a sample of the vocabulary used by grant writers and grant administrators.

It is important to realize that grants are not the solution to all administrative and societal problems. They are merely a bridge between resources and a problem to be solved. In the best of times though, grants provide models for long-range improvement and a solution to pressing social dilemmas. In the worst of times, they may give false hope, raise unrealistic expectations and stifle local effort.

Grants, most often, but not always, come in the form of money, usually on a year-to-year basis. Money pays salaries, buys equipment, and builds buildings, funds travel, and an assortment of other items of interest to most humans, including administrators. Grants have become associated with (1) improving the human condition in general, and at times, (2) improving the fiscal health of individuals and organizations and (3) raising citizen expectations.

As a grant writer, it may be that your goal is to address one or all of these areas. Let the words and ideas that follow blend with your own experience and lead you to doing good work and enjoying success in finding funding.

# 1

# Welcome and Why We Are Meeting?

♦ *I keep hearing different expressions about finding funding. Some people say it's a grant, some say a proposal, and somebody else says they got a contract. What's the difference?*

♦ *When do I write and present a "short or letter proposal" to a funding source?*

♦ *Why should I be interested in grant writing?*

With the commitment you have made to open the cover of this book, you have entered a grant writers zone with as much musical background and character foreground as that old Rod Sterling series, "The Twilight Zone." The big difference is that by the time you finish reading this book, you will have moved that much closer to finding the funding you need to advance an issue, cause, or concern that is on the top of your own, or your organization's, wish list. For some that will be a consistent and lifelong passion. For others, particularly the aspiring professional grant writer or the administrator of a public or private organization, it is tackling current needs as identified by your clients, your city council, county commission, or your check book.

This book, and the templates on the accompanying diskette

Grantwriters Diskette, are designed to get you thinking like a grant writer. More importantly this book will help you to anticipate the questions that will be in the mind of a funding source, when you examine the needs of your program. While you can use this book for reading and thinking, you will also be invited to take a more active role by preparing some of the standardized written materials which we call templates and can be incorporated into the working parts of your next (or first) grant proposal. Like all good computing work habits, you should save these new documents on another disk or the hard drive of your computer; later to be modified and used over and over again in future proposals.

# Creating Comfort and Confidence

## What's the difference between a grant, a proposal, and a contract?

This is a very common question with a somewhat complex answer since there are several very different terminologies, yet are all similar in meaning, that relate to this field. The most generic and widely used term in this field is "grant." The origins of that word and a brief account of the notion of one party giving or "granting" to another dates back to ancient Egypt. Chapter 3 has background on that interesting historical time and those events; suffice it to say that the word has been around for a long time.

The funding source, be it public or private, may title their overall initiative or program as a "grant program" but likely what they will be actually requesting from you a "proposal." Thus you will often see the acronym RFP; this is how the funding source says we are issuing a "Request For Proposals." In reality, it is more precise to say that you are not as much writing a grant as you are writing a proposal to receive grant funding.

Now that we've established that we are actually seeking a "grant" of funds, (sometimes with so many strings attached that the grant actually looks more like a loan), we need to begin by preparing a proposal. As thousands of readers from our earlier editions, and students in our workshops and on-line courses have testified, proposal writing in and of itself is perhaps the fastest growing topic in public administration management education. To close the loop, after you have written your proposal, and a grant of money (or permission to proceed) is offered, the next step is probably to convert the promise of your proposal into a contract, formal or informal. Thus some in this field would say that they really aren't writing grants, or proposals, but preparing contracts. The good news is that everybody is right. You hear about money being available because someone says they are "giving grants," you prepare a "proposal," which, after approval (and sometimes re-negotiation) becomes a contract.

*The contract... is the point at which the "sport" of grant writing turns into the business of grant management.*

The contract, however, is the point at which the "sport" of grant writing turns into the business of grant management. After all a contract is a legal agreement that both parties sign and indicates that each side has the capacity to provide what they say they will. Money in the amount agreed upon from the grant source and services, in the exact detail, as stated in the proposal from the requesting organization. This notion of mutual consent is the heart of the business we are about and the outcome, meeting the pre-stated goals and objectives, is critical to all parties. Critical to the funding source, who wants to brag about the worthwhile projects they have supported, and to the fund recipient, whose reputation is enhanced by the needs and problems they have successfully addressed. Sometimes there is actual and lifelong change; sometimes it is a pilot program, an experiment, an innovation or variation on past practices. Seldom will one grant sure anything, let alone world, hunger, eliminate any disease let alone the common cold, stop some injustice, certainly not world peace but by trying, and effectively disseminating the results of our efforts the planet surely will be a better place.

Next up in our "comfort and confidence tour of grant writing," let's take an overview of the typical elements of your grant proposal. For our expert source we will cite the guidelines from the prestigious Ford Foundation, found on the Internet at: http://www.fordfound.org, although every funding source will have its own particular preferences and process.

# Grants and Program-Related Investments to Organizations

The Ford Foundation, and many other similar foundations, often use a two part process, an initial letter or pre-proposal then a longer full proposal. This smaller first step saves time for both the foundation staff who will give the funds as well as the staff of the organization seeking funding.

## When do I write and present a short or letter proposal to a funding source?

Before a request is made for a grant or program-related investment, a brief letter of inquiry is advisable to determine whether the Foundation's present interests and funds permit consideration of the request.

### The letter should include:
- The purpose of the project for which funds are being requested
- Problems and issues the proposed project will address
- Information about the organization conducting the project
- Estimated overall budget for the project
- Period of time for which funds are requested
- Qualifications of those who will be engaged in the project

After receiving the letter foundation staff members may ask the grant seeker to submit a formal proposal. There is no grant application form.

## The proposal should include:

- The organization's current budget
- A description of the proposed work and how it will be conducted
- The names and curriculum vitae of those engaged in the project
- A detailed project budget
- Present means of support and status of applications to other funding sources
- Legal and tax status

In some instances, the Ford Foundation requires the grantee organization to match the Foundation's grant with funds from other sources.

The Ford Foundation, as do many other funding sources with similar funding interests, supports pluralism and equal opportunity in its grant making and in its internal policies. The opportunities that prospective grantee organizations provide for minorities and women are considered in evaluating proposals and are worthy of special emphasis and inclusion in your proposal.

Applications are considered throughout the year. Normally applicants may expect to receive within six weeks an indication of whether their proposals are within the Foundation's program interests and budget limitations. Activities supported by grants and program-related investments must be charitable, educational or scientific, as defined under the appropriate provisions of the U.S. Internal Revenue Code and Treasury Regulations. The Foundation monitors grants through regular financial and narrative reports submitted by the grantee.

The Foundation's funds are limited in relation to the great number of worthwhile proposals received. (Note a award from the Ford Foundation is extremely prized and hence highly competitive. You will find a much higher percentage of applicants funded in less well known foundations. As an example in a recent year the Ford Foundation received 38,200 grant requests and funded 2,252 grants. Of that number, 22 percent were first-time grant recipients. The Foundation directs its support to activities that are within its current range of interests and are likely to have wide or long-term impact.

Support is not normally given for routine operating costs of institutions or for religious activities. Except in rare cases, funding is not available for the construction or maintenance of buildings.

By now you have probably decided that you probably want to learn how to write proposals and receive grants that will bring your organization funding. That's great. The rest of this book describes step by step the ways that you can make this happen.

The first and perhaps most important phase is finding the money. In Chapter 2, you will learn, among other things, how to use the Internet to create a broad list of funding sources that are most likely to approve your type of grant applications, including tips on how to search efficiently, when to submit proposals, and how to find granting organizations that are currently accepting proposals. Because of the dynamic nature of the Internet, this new section has the most up-to-date information regarding the Internet as a tremendous resource for the different aspects of grant writing research and follow-up. In Chapter 3 you will find techniques to help you zero in on funding sources from local, state and federal governments. You may be surprised to learn, for example, that over 1500 government agencies have earmarked millions of dollars specifically for grants to worthy organizations and individuals. In Chapter 4, you will see how to focus your funding search on foundations and other private-sector sources. These are establishments whose only purpose is to give their money away—but they are always most particular about to whom it goes and what for what it will be used.

*Since writing a successful grant proposal is a process involving consistent effort and not magic, these skills can be learned and adapted to a variety of funding and organizational needs.*

Since writing a successful grant proposal is a process involving consistent effort and not magic, these skills can be learned and adapted to a variety of funding and organizational needs. In Chapter 5 you will find the manager's overview, including learning how to think and write within this particular arena of grant proposals and effectively manage internal and external individuals and groups throughout the critical stage of the information gathering phase of your proposal writing. Chapter 5 also includes an overview of the budgeting process, shows you how t o administer grant funds and how to prepare for and survive an audit—all essential if you ever hope to get a second grant.

Chapter 6 describes the steps required to prepare your organization to enter the grant arena by taking stock of its present situation, including a thorough review of institutional history. In Chapter 7, you will learn how to read the coded messages every grant maker inserts in its request for proposal. To those who know these ciphers, RFP's provide a blueprint describing each grantor's most fervent desires, including all the "hot buttons" that a successful applicant must push.

The proposal writing detail starts in Chapter 8, where you will find an explanation and rationale for each element of the proposal, as well as a raft of timesaving tips. On the accompanying diskette you will find worksheet templates, boilerplate texts, timelines, and a myriad of other forms to help simplify and de-mystify the process. Since not every grantor requires a lengthy proposal, and some funding sources expect a letter of inquiry to precede the actual grant proposal, you will learn how to create these brief applications in Chapter 9.

Chapter 10 focuses on creating budgets to accompany your grant—including the cost of paying for the services of the grant writer. Chapter 11 describes the requirements for administering the grant, including a section of frequently asked questions. Because funding is in the details, this chapter also deals with ways to ensure that every proposal you write is correct down to the last detail, including methods of self-review and evaluation by outside agencies and you will learn how to prepare the proposal for submission. To conclude your journey throughout the universe of grant writing, Chapter 12 closes with the importance of securing future funding and the ways in which you ask for it. Additionally, this chapter discloses some problems which nearly all grant writers encounter and how to manage them.

# The Grant Proposal Overview: A Few Basics

**A brief review of the grant universe reveals that nearly every proposal requires:**

- Executive summary / Introduction;
- Qualifications to do the task,
- History of the organization and identification of program organizational chart;
- Problem statement and/or needs assessment;
- Program(s) goals and objectives;
- Methodology for funding implementation;
- Evaluation criteria;
- Itemized budget to implement funded program(s)
- Long-term funding needs

As you read this book, you will learn not only about asking for money, but also about those from whom you will be asking, including how to evaluate a private foundation's Request For Proposals in terms of what the giver needs to make a favorable funding decision for you. You will also discover some virtually universal truths about foundations and other private organizations that are in the business of giving away money. For example, you will learn that the ways in which they operate are different than government granting authorities thus allowing foundations to behave differently when grant funding proposals. While government agencies support mostly traditional and widely accepted projects and programs, private funding sources—foundations, corporations and individual—are generally open to innovative and virtually unimaginable projects and more likely than a government agency have a specific set of guidelines and questions different than government funding sources.

# Why Study Grant Writing?

Many different types of organizations may apply for grants from an ever-expanding cosmos of funding sources, including governments (federal, state, county, municipal), private foundations and corporations. In addition, over the last several decades, as tax sources dried up or were reallocated, government has begun to look for ways to make itself smaller and more efficient, and one way of accomplishing this is to fund private organizations to carry out programs that government finds desirable. These grants range in scope from a few hundred dollars to multiple millions. The demonstrated ability to bring in that sort of funding to any nonprofit organization will boost any career, and successful grant writers, especially those whose title may be anything but, are in great demand. Beyond the obvious satisfaction of landing grants themselves, however, learning how to write proposals hones and refines both critical thinking and writing skills, which have enduring value in nearly every discipline.

Not every grant proposal is funded, however, including many that display outstanding creativity and are finely focused on highly worthwhile goals. And most problems are not completely solved simply because a grant proposal is funded. The final chapter of this book describes how to find new sources of funding, how to re-fund a project whose grant has been expended, and how to transform a proposal from a failure in one venue to a winner in another.

Grant writing can be dauntingly frustrating or highly rewarding. Often it is both. Like so many things in life, it often depends on how much intelligent effort is expended. Above all else, this book will help you turn your creative energy and ideals into a soundly written proposal. In buying this book you have shown the desire to succeed. The next step begins when you turn the page.

# 2

# Locating and Connecting with Funding Sources

u **Who gives out the most money?**

u **Is funding virtually all from the federal government?**

u **Where is funding easiest and faster to obtain, with little or no "strings" attached?**

In planning to carry out virtually any human endeavor, it's essential to understand all of the parties, places and things that you could reasonably expect to encounter. If you extend that notion to include interacting with, influencing or persuading those parties, places and things, then the case for understanding the grant writing and funding working environment becomes even more compelling for the emerging grant writer.

A grant writer's knowledge of the working environment of funding sources is especially important and, in this era of easy access to vast streams of information via the Internet, it is far easier to access than ever before. With that it mind, let's begin with a valuable admonition from a veteran grants administrator who cautions grant and proposal writers, "Don't forget the phone call." His experience indicates that a many grant seekers have grown so attached to the anonymity of the Internet and the efficacy of email that they act as if they can find everything they need to know without ever leaving the virtual comfort of their office, living room or laptop. But forgetting to develop your own network using good old personality and ambition with similar organizations or miss making a live connection to the program officer of your fund source(s) is to never understand the subtle nuances and future direction of that source. Additionally, you won't be successful in building and maintaining your own programs because you will lack the political savvy and interpersonal relationship building so important to the successful grant writer.

You won't be able to understand how to ask or get the answers to these types of pertinent questions: How the direction of your funding source will be changing in the next three to five years? Who else funds this type of project? Is there some type of agency or organizations that we could, or should, collaborate with? None of the answers to these questions can be discovered on the Internet at the crack of noon or the gong of midnight. And frank answers are not likely to come via an email query even if you have a most engaging cyber-style. But in a phone conversation or if possible in person, you will be pleasantly surprised to find out how much more you can learn.

*None of the answers to these questions can be discovered on the internet at the crack of noon or the gong of midnight.*

The information in Chapter 2 identifies the prominent actors in the public grant funding environment such as federal, state and local government funding sources; (private funding sources are covered in Chapter 3). While techniques for gaining background information on these parties will be imparted in this chapter, it should be noted that the topic of grant funding sources is sufficient for much longer study and will only be touched upon briefly here. Grant writers are encouraged to do additional research, reading and most importantly, networking, since the changing nature of grant funding, the people involved and their roles greatly affects the funding sources and amounts of funding from year to year. Lastly, this chapter discusses techniques successfully used for locating and connecting with identified funding sources.

# *Understanding the Faces Behind the Forms*

## Federal Actors And Roles

The scope and size of the federal government is almost too large to comprehend. Careful examination of this level of government, with the specific goal of finding funding sources, makes the process of understanding a bit simpler. The key actors at the Federal level are the President, the Congress, the Supreme Court, administrative agencies, political parties, and public interest groups. The following is a discussion of each of these "key actors" with some analysis of the trends or recent developments in each actor's arena. While we hope that you will find this information useful, never stop collecting information on your own, from agency newsletters, professional and general circulation publications, and from your networking with partner organizations.

## The Chief Executive

As an individual, most grant writers have a better chance of being hit by lightning than making personal contact with the President. Perhaps the best one could hope for is to be updated by an aide as to the President's preferences for solving society's current ills, and those of the future. Most observers feel that the President's attention to matters of intergovernmental relations (and the resulting grant funds available each fiscal year) is at best cyclical and erratic due to the political nature of developing, and passing through Congress a federal budget. Much of the budgeting process of which government programs get funding and how much is dependent on global and domestic situations, especially the influence of Interest Groups and other governmental actors. While the President listens very closely to his closest, hand-picked White House advisory staff, increasingly the influence of Interest Groups on the budget process, the glare of media coverage bent on increasing ratings and the importance of public opinion have made the President less insulated than ever before and more aware of public perceptions.

The President does have at his disposal a staff of Intergovernmental Relations (IGR) experts. The IGR process began around 1953 with the Kestenbaum Commission on Intergovernmental Relations which recommended the staffing of a unit within the President's Office to attend to IGR matters. Since then the concerns and power of these staff members have changed, but due to the tendency of bureaucracies to grow instead of decline, this IGR staff has grown in line with the number of governmental departments and programs in existence, their budgeted amounts and complexity of the IGR's expanded role in today's political environment.

> "...it is Congress—not the courts—that makes most of the major decisions concerning the allocation of power within the federal system..."

Several executive staff units deserve attention because of the roles they play. Foremost are the Office of Management and Budget (OMB), which is the executive staff unit with the longest track record in the IGR, and the Advisory Commission on Intergovernmental Relations (ACIR) which has the general mandate to study, review, evaluate, and recommend IGR policies to all levels of local officials. The ACIR is broadly representative of the whole country with 26 bi-partisan members and a highly trained staff. They regularly publish on the entire range of grant making and grant management topics.

The General Accounting Office (GAO) also plays a role of importance, particularly after a grant program is underway. The GAO reviews performance in terms of adherence to fiscal guidelines and program goals and directives. Reviewing GAO reports will help grant seekers fine tune proposals to avoid potential problems. Cynics would add the initials FBI—as in Federal Bureau of Investigation—as an "ultimate" evaluator of grant programs gone wrong.

## The Legislature

The Congress has a role of the arbitrator of the Federal System.

Professor George Brown, writing in the *Harvard Journal on Legislation*, commented:

*"...it is Congress—not the courts—that makes most of the major decisions concerning the allocation of power within the federal system; and, increasingly, Congress exercise this choice when it shapes the contours of federal grant-in-aid programs."*

Although he wrote those words over a quarter century ago, the situation remains the same today. Every grant program on the books today was placed there by an act of Congress. Although the Congress, is made up of directly elected representatives, congressional staff members are at least as important for the grants persons, since the staffs often remain in their offices long after an individual Congressional seat has turned. Staff members are also much easier to contact and work with than a busy elected official who, while being a tremendous referral source, generally has little to do with the grant program in question except for long range funding matters. Typically these staff can be contacted either at the Washington office, or more conveniently, at a local district office. When you work with them be a specific as you can, perhaps with a reference to the Catalog of Federal Domestic Assistance (CFDA) which lists programs by a discreet and unique numbering system. Being informed when you work with Congres-sional staff is essential even though they are trained to be friendly to one and all. Is your funding source a formula or project grant, there is a big difference and you should be knowledgeable about this matter.

## The Judiciary

The role of the federal courts is clearly one of dispensing just findings on a broad matter of disputes that come before the court, including those with intergovernmental overtones. The implication of these decisions for most grant seekers is mild, to say the least, but in the case of larger cities and states their findings can be most important. Particularly at the Supreme Court level, legal decisions can and have made social policy, and thus provided new ground-breaking programs especially in the areas of education, employment and housing.

In the matter of interest groups, i.e. parents of handicapped children, the attention they receive from the courts, which in turn, became the impetus for a legislatively mandated grant program has had a profound impact on society. More recently the Americans with Disability Act (ADA), prompted in part by court decisions, has become a highly significant source of funds and important programmatic activity.

## The Bureaucracy

Executive agencies are, generally speaking, the most important to the grant writer. The executive agencies administer federal assistance programs in a policy-making environment and are usually the direct source of funds. In many cases the grant funds will flow through a specific Federal institute such as the National Institute of Education (NIE), or the National Institute of Mental Health (NIMH). Likewise, in some cases the agency's dollars will first go the States for subsequent redistribution to sub-state agencies. The top executive staff (i.e. the Agency Secretary) is appointed by the president and will change from time to time, but many career specialists will stay on through these presidential changes. Like the Congressional staffs, middle level agency staff are dependable, regular, easily located (i.e., you can look them up in staff directories) and are interested in seeing that the intent of Congress is carried out. These agencies are outlined in great detail in a number of publications but, as noted above, perhaps the single best reference for grant programs is the Catalog of Federal Domestic Assistance (CFDA).

# Political Parties and Public Interest Groups

For a number of reasons the influence of political parties on the IGR network has declined in recent times. There has, however, been a rise in the activities of public interest groups (and industry/trade associations) who actually help design and monitor a number of grant-in-aid programs administered by the federal agencies. The so-called Iron Triangle of interest groups, bureaucratic agencies, and Congress, is hard to penetrate if they choose to close ranks on a particular issue or point of view. Fund seekers need to carefully assess the positions of interest groups, and would be wise to cite them as sources in needs statements and other parts of the grant proposal.

As the world becomes more complex, and business increases its role with public affairs, it is not unexpected that these interest groups would have an increased role in our daily life. The groups number in the tens of thousands and range from ultra powerful lobbies such as the National Rifle Association, the U.S. Chamber of Commerce, and the National Association of Manufacturers to very small single issue groups that have a small agenda and budget to match. The Internet however has given virtually everyone (at least those with a computer) a voice and the email blitz from a ten-person organization may look as imposing in the in-basket of an elected official as does the heavy pressure of a traditional mover and shaker.

## The Media

Traditionally the American media have served as watchdogs to curb government excesses and to expose unprincipled conduct. Over the last few decades, however, the media have often seemed more like attack dogs. This is because the media are now Big Business: Newspapers and broadcasting stations are increasingly part of national enterprises—fewer and fewer are locally-owned and controlled entities. Because many of these huge companies own a newspaper, magazine, radio and television station in the same city, and because they too often view their corporate mission as making money, their interests and concerns may seem closer to those of their corporate leadership than to their readers or viewers. Nonetheless, to find readers and capture audiences, the media must provide something of value, and that is what is presented as "news." It is in your interest to cultivate good relations with local and national media representatives, both because a good reporter may be able to save you days or weeks of research by sharing information, and because there will likely come a day when you want them to tell your story.

Remember, however, that electronic media value brevity over precision: They want you to answer their questions with a snappy 20-second sound bite. In dealing with print media, remember that although they have more time to prepare stories and more room to display them, they are prone to choosing bits and pieces of interview material and shaping these selected tidbits to suit their story's slant. Make good friends among the media, but remember that their job, in the end, is to sell papers and capture viewers, and that most everything else is secondary. To better illustrate these federal actors and their roles take a moment to examine the following figure "Policy Actions on the National Level."

## Policy Actors on the National Level

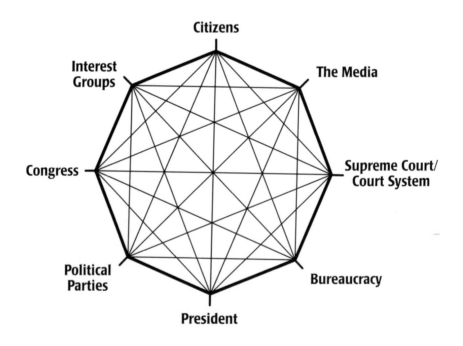

*Finding Funding:*
*The Comprehensive Guide to Grant Writing*

Figure 1

## State Actors and Roles

Like the federal level, state government has a chief executive, a legislative body, administrative agencies, political parties, and interest groups. However, a number of significant differences exist. The first is that you must view them, like the message in your rear view mirror, "objects may be closer than they look!" States play the important pass-through role for federal ideas and initiatives and often mimic the feds in the title of and purpose for a program. Another major difference is that your state may actually create a program if there is enough widespread interest and effective politicking!

Overall the major difference is that while the federal government and its actors have a primary role and responsibility in designing grant programs, states without the initiative process rarely originate such efforts. Theirs is often called the "pass through" role; the funds (most of which actually originate as taxes from the local level) are merely passed through the state on their way to local organizations or agencies.

The second difference is a geographic one. Obviously, any state capitol is closer to the people than is Washington, D.C. unless one lives in certain geographical corners of Virginia, Maryland, or West Virginia.

A third difference is that state government officials are politically closer to the local conditions and can be expected to have a better understanding of local affairs. In fact, state politicians will often run for office based on these roles. The state role is best described as facilitative and instrumental rather than forceful and integrative.

The term sub-state refers to the situation whereby states will divide themselves for the delivery of services along some traditional geographical boundaries, by urban and rural centers, or by similar ways. The importance of this to the grant seeker is in knowing how their state is divided and how to explore and exploit the possibilities of a grant program designed for a larger area than a single city or county, but less than one with statewide implications.

In some cases, a state government will be the direct program operator in what has been called the "balance of state region." This means that smaller rural counties are grouped together because

independently they do not have the administrative structure to operate a particular service or grant program. Further, it should be noted
that while, on paper, each rural county may seem similar; they should
be treated as individually as possible. Finally, in many states the grant
seeker can work through a council of governments or regional planning council, however, these councils are sometimes fiscally fragile
with a less-than-firm political base.

## Cities and Counties

The main distinctions that funding from cities and counties enjoy
is that this level is relatively close to the average citizen, it offers
many joint venture possibilities, applicants usually face less competition, and if it is a locally originated grant program, you can more easily impact the RFP guidelines and the evaluation standards.

Cities and counties are frequently a prime recipient of grant
funds, and very often dependent on federal and state funds for
day-to-day program operations. Usually they have an appointed
administrator or manager, an elected mayor and council in the case
of cities, or a board of supervisors or commission in the case of counties. Up-to-date knowledge of the financial condition of the city or
county is essential.

Also imperative for grant seekers is knowledge of the city or
county's power brokers, both positional (meaning they have a ranking job title) and personal (they earn attention through a charismatic
style and force of personality). In general it is sometimes easier to
deal with the local level because of the close proximity, the fact that
one can lobby personally for the approval of a grant or contract, and,
if the grant is rejected initially, first-hand feedback and critique is
more readily available. With diligence an once-rejected program may
be resubmitted in a subsequent period and be successful. In addition,
very large cities may be part of a Standard Metropolitan Statistical
Area (SMSA) and funds could be sought for projects within the SMSA
boundaries as opposed to just the city or county boundary.

In summary, after examining in detail the major aspects of the
federal and state levels and their organizational arrangements and

personnel patterns, the following points can be made about grant writing for the local level.

## Characacteristics of Local Funders:

- Obviously the local level is simply much closer and this physical proximity has both good and bad aspects. Good in that visits are usually in person and can be fairly frequent, bad in that the old adage "familiarity breeds contempt" may apply.
- The local agency is usually under heavy in-person pressure to apply political weighting to the grant selection process, a condition that the sheer distance makes less burdensome at state and federal levels.
- The depth of professionalism will be much more varied at the local level, strong in some cases and weak in others. Thus the potential for collaboration or joint venturing is mixed at best and the talent to review highly technical approaches may be limited or delayed.
- Funding at the local level usually does allow for a greater level of creativity and ingenuity in proposals and for periodic modifications to meet changing local conditions. Funding from the local level usually is more flexible but usually almost always will result in a smaller grant award than from a state, federal or major foundation source.

## Community-Based And Non-Profit Organizations

Community-based and non-profit organizations (CBO'S and NPO'S) are, in the minds of many, the third sector of administration, one neither private nor public. These organizations are usually organized around either neighborhood or geographical lines or with respect to a special interest, such as employment, youth, or health. These outfits often have very special interests, and will do the sort of work that government may not want to do!

Many cities and counties have turned to these community-based groups for the delivery of services because of their special insights with the target population, low overhead and the fact that they do not add permanently to the city or county payroll. The disadvantage to established governments of the CBO/NPO network is that they do not cover all needs or areas, they have independent boards of directors and are subject to more internal turmoil, staff changes and redirection of mission, than a comparable government agency. However, these organizations are a vital link between the community and the grant seekers and, with the current state of government finances, may well be even more important in the future.

## Neighborhoods

As public policy has evolved in the last decade, we have previously noted an interest in reducing the overall size of the government staff. A second trend is to decentralize decision-making to levels closer to the citizen. In some large cites (and even in medium to small cities) the use of neighborhood associations, neighborhood watches, homeowner associations, block leaders, etc. has gained in popularity and use. These generally informal organizations have leaders selected on a less formal basis than an traditional elected official, and often they are one of a few in that area willing to take the job. Notwithstanding that fact, the organizations often grow the next generation of elected officials. You may want to cultivate, consider and consult this level when you are working on a project in their sphere of interest and influence. Remembering that "people tend to support what they help to create" this is an excellent source of volunteers and also a means of avoiding potential conflict with folks who feel they have been left out of the loop.

## Corporate Faces and Places

Just as the previous section identifying key actors and roles is important to beginning to understand the complexity and diversity of federal, state and local government funding sources, insight of the corporate and business world is critical to your understanding of the types of major players in the private sector.

The first assumption that most people make about the private sector is that corporations have an overwhelming single-mindedness about the bottom line—making a profit. While it may take some effort to convince public sector and community-based organizations that profit is not a four-letter word, it's important to note here that in the past century of American economic growth and development, very little human improvement could occur without the private sector. Since World War II, corporations have provided for an increasingly higher standard of living for many Americans. In part based on federal policies developed as a result of The Great Depression, corporations have been at the forefront of the U.S. economy, driving the economic engine on which our domestic and foreign economic policies are based. Leaders of corporations, especially large multi-national organizations, have a desire to show themselves as being a "good corporate citizen"; proving these leaders have egos that need feeding as well as their corporation's balance sheet. And they have to develop a climate in which they can be successful. Targeting these three variables— helping stabilize or increase profits, enlarging or stroking the corporate ego and helping to build a favorable business climate makes a powerful

> *While it may take some effort to convince public sector and community-based organizations that profit is not a four-letter word…*

case for funding support. A combination of these conditions allows the fund seeker to address the corporate fund source at a level of mutual gain, although certainly the direct corporate gain may be comparatively modest or long term.

As to faces and places, the corporate organization chart is sometimes difficult to decipher. Do you deal only at the highest level, the highest local level, the friendliest level, or make an end run to a major stockholder or member of the board of directors? The recommendation is to develop an individual strategy that is specific to each corporation and its leaders. If you have a genuine and real contact use it, if not, try and research who generally handles similar requests and find some background on that person. Stress the relationship of your project to the profit, ego, or climate concept. Demonstrate the impact of your project on the community and neighborhoods where the workers live, shop, play and receive services. This factor may in fact be among the most important single aspect of dealing with the private sector.

Finally, as you would with a private foundation, be ready to prove that you must have their help. That you have responsibly used what ever else you have or have access too, and only then are you coming to them for assistance. Write and talk in their terms, show the "return on investment" and you will be cable to capture and keep corporate interest and principal.

## Foundation Faces and Places

If there is a degree of complexity that increases when a grant seeker tries to understand government funders, and then corporations, perhaps the whole process reaches its most complex level when foundations are being considered.

The reason for this is rooted in the fact that the foundations themselves differ so greatly, in size, sophistication of staff, and in the circumstances in which one makes contact with them. If you know the funding source, or have a board, commission, council or committee member who does, then contact may be only as complicated as deciding where to go for lunch. At the other extreme, if the foundation is located in a distant city and is relatively unknown or unfamiliar to you, it is often a real challenge to the grant seeker.

There is also a challenge in dealing with tens of thousands of smaller foundations, especially family foundations, that make only sporadic, and hard-to-track, grants. Here you must carefully research what ever they have done, and gently probe, through an intriguing inquiry, letter or visit (if possible). Larger and more active foundations may be tracked via the Internet, through their own publications, or through one of the several national data books on foundations.

As a rule, foundations insist that you prove, if nothing else, that you have an absolute need for their limited resources, and that your normal funding, from taxes, subscriptions, etc., is not sufficient. Like corporations, foundations have recently become more active in funding government-based programs; usually avoiding it on the basis that access to public funds is or should be sufficient to fill the need.

Foundations also tend to be somewhat more politically and socially conservative (with notable exceptions) and grant seekers should be mindful of this condition. The originators of these foundations usually have several common characteristics, namely the topical areas from which their fortunes came, i.e. real estate, mining, manufacturing; often a keen interest in health since as one's own mortality approaches they become increasingly interested in like subjects; and for many of the same reasons, a.k.a. mortality, programs of a religious nature or those that support or reinforce a certain set of beliefs or values.

In summary, hearken to the wisdom of Campagne Associates, a leading provider of fundraising software. They suggest that in evaluating a potential funding source, use the three Cs of fundraising: Connection, Concern, and Capacity. These are the specific attributes that determine a donor's level of motivation to give to any particular organization. Grant applicants should spend time up front to identify, qualify and understand all prospective fund sources, public or private, foundation or individuals.

Connection is often the strongest factor in determining the likelihood of a gift; it is the emotional link to a specific organization. Concern is the tie between the granting agency and the mission of the organization seeking support, and reflects shared institutional values. Capacity is the financial ability of the prospect, and while it is often critical to determining the size of the gift requested, it is the least important to predicting a prospective giver's inclinations.

Now that we have a better understanding of the people and players essential to our task, let us spend some time with the printed, paper and digital documents that are needed for our proposal. In the following section you will find: strategies of locating printed materials, Internet documents and other archival data, along with tips and techniques for networking to locate the most current information and that which is hard to find.

# *Finding the Best Funding Source*

One of the most important steps in the grant process is identifying the full range of available funding sources and identifying them in a timely manner thorough understanding of the range of available funding sources is a critical first step since this world is generally much larger than most grant seekers realize and it changes from time to time as agencies expand and contract.

Keeping tabs with the current regulations of an agency becomes crucial when the agency has set different application deadlines for its various programs. A missed deadline is, in effect, a non-existent program. If your proposal is too late or beyond the deadline, it is the same as not having a program to apply to in the first place.

Here we present the best methodology for searching sources. It is tempting to say that the new technologies available mean that source-searching can be done exclusively from the friendly confines of the computer keyboard. Experienced grant writers understand that while the Internet is a powerful database capable of searching for a myriad of funding sources, however successful grant writers still rely on the time-tested manual research of printed materials and regularly read newspapers, professional journals and newsletters, and spend many hours on the telephone and in meetings making contacts with key informants.

# *A Simple Methodology for Searching Printed Materials*

The art of searching for data in printed materials is usually slightly more difficult than would first appear. However, a good research plan will be of great importance in accomplishing this task with efficiency and effectiveness. Although your collection may appear to be "a mile wide and an inch deep," you must be open to a wide selection of materials. This search is also known as a review of the literature or a literature review.

## Descriptors and Key Terms

Determining key terms, or descriptors, is a classical early step that is very much like finding the right key to open a door. Without the correct key, or in this case, key term or terms, the grant writer is doomed to a long session of fumbling for entry. Several ways to develop your descriptors are as follows.

The thesaurus or subject vocabulary exists in various different forms. Most databases, whether print or electronic, use a limited vocabulary so that the researcher does not have to use a million synonyms in the search process.

The first step may be to consult the Library of Congress Subject Headings, the vocabulary used for most library card catalogs, even the electronic versions. From here the grant seeker may consult more specific sources such as *The Thesaurus of ERIC Descriptors* (education), *The Thesaurus of Psychological Index Terms*, and *Medical Subject Headings*. The catalog of Federal Domestic Assistance itself is an excellent source of descriptors and the creative use of the index of such publications as the Foundation Centers' *The Foundation Grants Index* or Oryx Press's *Directory of Research Grants* will also greatly speed up your building of a complete list of descriptors that is both efficient and effective. Oryk also publishes directories in such specialized fields as biomedical and health, and, like the above example, their index is an excellent source of descriptors. Whatever path you choose, how you go about searching, and how effective you are, will be a major determinant in your ultimate success.

## Specific steps to help you develop a grant writer's vocabulary include:

* Identify the major concepts in your topic. The concepts are the keywords you want to search. For example, in the topic "low cost housing for the elderly," the key words are "housing," "low-cost," and "elderly."
* List synonyms for each concept. Often, a key concept can be stated using two or more synonyms, for example "women" and "females." Some databases have thesauri, or dictionaries, of

terms, which accompany them. If the list of databases indicates a thesaurus is available (as discussed above) check at the reference desk. It is essential for an efficient and effective search that you use a thesaurus to develop vocabulary. Ask a librarian for assistance if you have questions concerning use of the thesauri. Of course regular reading of journals and publications in the field will also yield up-to-date descriptors. Keep good notes as you go along and keep them in a section of your project development workbook (Chapter Eight).

- Write concisely. Truncate (make shorter and crisper) the word in your descriptors and eliminate any "stop" words from your search plan. Again librarians will get you started and then the rest just takes effort.

## Common Errors in Reviewing the Literature

The following are a list of common errors and mistakes that are made in reviewing literature, both for the purpose of applying for grants and for writing the needs statement that is a part of the grant application. Here are some tips to help you avoid the most common mistakes in proposal development.

- Come to work prepared. Have a diskette handy to "cut and paste" the nuggets of information you mine and also have some 3 x 5 or 5 x 7 cards to take notes that you can not collect electronically.
- Do not carry out a hurried review of the literature in order to get started on the project. This usually results in overlooking sources and previous studies containing ideas that might improve your proposal. Take enough time to research this mother lode thoroughly.
- Use primary source data and do not rely too heavily on secondary sources. Get the most current data you can.
- Don't overlook sources such as newspapers and popular magazines that often contain articles on or about potential grant topics.
- Be sure to define the topic limits of your review of the literature. Searching too broad an area often makes the grant writers discouraged and leads to a slipshod job. By the same token, searching too narrow an area may cause you to overlook many articles

that are peripheral to the research topic but contain information that would help design a better study.

- Copy bibliographic data correctly or you will be unable to locate the reference needed.
- Do not copy too much material onto one note card. This often indicates that you do not have a clear understanding of the project.

# *Form of Published Materials*

This section contains brief description of the major forms of published material that are, or should be, found in a basic grantsmanship library, either in your or at a nearby public or college library.

## Computer Databases and Internet Resources

A relatively new friend of the grant writer is the computer and its database information, including your set of bookmarks, favorite web sites and Internet addresses. You probably have some of this already at your fingertips on your own computer but don't forget to make an occasional visit to a local college, university or one of the larger public libraries for more resources to search from. When you select even a very broad term like "grantsmanship", the computer will share with you related descriptors that the system has used to locate relevant material through that computer's network access. You will also want to build a list of descriptors for the possible content of your proposal, such as juvenile delinquency, environmental protection, or small town economic development. In any event, carefully note these descriptors and build your own specialized lists. You can then examine literally thousands of abstracts and titles. Once you have a targeted list based on your program funding descriptors you can print from the computer what you've located, and/or download from the library computer on to your own disk. When you return to your own computer system, you will be able to quickly access this custom list of full citations, abstracts, and other data that you can then edit or use for your immediate needs.

## Essays

Collections of essays on broad or related topics (very useful in writing a needs or background of the problem statement) are generally published in monograph format. Most libraries do not catalog every essay in a collection. Access to these publications must be obtained through a specialized index such as Public Affairs Information Service (specifically on government issues) or the Essay and general literature index, a semiannual publication with annual and five-year accumulations. Indexes by subject and author; mostly humanities with some social science publications. The important idea to take from this note is that you need to broadly understand your topic and the arguments that have made it both important and fund-able.

## Government Publications

These include the publications of governmental agencies at the federal, state, and local levels as well as those of foreign governments and international agencies. Look especially for annual reports of government agencies as a clue to the type of funding they offer and the type of recipients. As just mentioned above, these publications are critical for understanding the background and recent activities of the government as they have impacted on your subject area, particularly if you will be asking the agency involved for future support.

## Newspapers

Newspapers are important sources of information and often they are the only available documentation of a particular event. With the advent of micro cards and microfilm, most libraries can keep a good collection of newspapers and many have Internet based archives. Such indexes as the Newspaper Index, Newsbank, The New York Times, Wall Street Journal and other similar indexes are very helpful. Moreover, most libraries can arrange to borrow microfilm of out-of-town newspapers, even those from former decades if you cannot successfully search them on the web.

## Pamphlets, Proceedings, Yearbooks and Annual Reviews

Distributed to a narrow audience after a usually limited press run, these items can be worthy of search if you need a certain piece of data. These are often kept in vertical files and/or are only available from the source. Proceedings, the records of a particular conference, meeting, short course, etc, are found in a similar way. Two guides of use in this area are the Conference Publications Guide published by Hall, and the Proceedings in Print, a bimonthly publication. Proceedings often include priority topics for the upcoming year and can be extremely valuable. Don't forget that in most disciplines there are annual and/or bi-annual reviews which serve as guides to major events in that area or by that federal or state department of government. They give a condensed view of the activity and usually list the contact persons who can provide more information. Add those contact persons to your Grant Action Files as discussed in Chapter 8.

## Indexes and Abstracts

Most journals do not provide an index to their articles; hence you will find it useful to consult one of the many indexes or abstracts. These special publications list the pertinent bibliographic information and in some case a synopsis or brief summary of the articles. Each index may be limited to a specific field but may work from several hundred periodicals. These publications may be published as frequently as weekly and some offer an electronic searching service for a fee. A fairly new and interesting publication of this type is Current Contents, which is published weekly and ingeniously reproduces the table of contents of hundreds of journals in a wide variety of fields.

## Periodicals

Periodicals are a major and most familiar source of information for grant seekers. They are published in every possible field, by private and public sources and depending on format, may be weekly, monthly or quarterly. Inter-library loan services can help you acquire the article from an obscure journal if it is not in your library or is too expensive to subscribe to.

## Folder of Web Site Bookmarks

A computer file folder of bookmarks is another useful tool. When viewed through your Internet browser software such as Netscape or Microsoft Internet Explorer, these "book marked" sites are located under a pull-down menu known as "Favorites. They provide links to useful websites and may be compiled on an ongoing basis by drag-and-drop of URLs into a folder, or by clicking "Add to Favorites" on your taskbar. The information in this folder may be shared with colleagues and supervisors, and should be constantly updated to reflect new Websites.

### Useful Web page URL categories:
- General Information
- Similar Organizations
- Funding Sources

## Searching Internet Databases

Although the World Wide Web contains millions of pages of documents, a great wealth of information can only be found inside the four walls of the library. However, there are some basic library reference tools on the Internet; sources where you can find factual answers to simple questions, look up the definition of a word, or read the text of historical documents such as the Constitution of the United States. Most university libraries have a Virtual Reference Collection, allowing you to read the text of certain books as though you had the actual volume.

To search for information on the Internet beyond the subjects in a university or college library requires an Internet search engine. These tools comb through hundreds of millions of pages of Web documents to identify text that matches your search. Search engines work in different ways, so it is important to understand their differences and select the one, which works best for you. Later in this chapter are links to web documents which describe and compare search engines and that may help you decide which is the best for you. There are also links to lists of major search engines in case you already know which search engine you prefer. A note of caution, the information that follows is fairly technical and if you are currently satisfied with how you search skip forward to the next section "Techniques for Networking."

## News and Current Events

In recent years, the information world has grown from a few free news sources—local radio and television stations—to the World Wide Web, which presents a cornucopia of international, national, and even local news, all free, including current stories from hundreds of periodicals. Major US news media update important breaking stories on their Web sites, and many community-based media offer daily local coverage. In addition, most Internet Service Providers, search engines, and directories offer headlines sports scores, stock quotes, and other news items. Finding breaking news and popular topics on the Web is now routine.

Less complete, and more difficult to use effectively, are searchable news databases. Searching beyond current headlines requires searchable databases. Experts recommend TotalNEWS, News Index, Excite's NewsTracker, Northern Light's Current News. The news sections on Yahoo!, HotBot, and Infoseek are also good. These databases index news stories published on the Web by newspapers, television networks, and other news sources. Current editions of actual newspapers, domestic and foreign, can be found at www.newspapers.com.

## Other Archives and Databases

Literally thousands of archives and databases are scattered throughout academia and government, many accessible by outsiders, even those without any reasonable justification for viewing them. Many colleges and universities offer access to both their own and other database archives, and will entertain requests from outsiders, whether they are alumni or not. A good place to start to gain access is to contact the institution's research librarian. Similarly, government agencies at every level may allow outsiders to access their data, or they may be willing to do the search and provide you with results for a modest fee.

## Advanced Web Search Terms

**Audio, Video, and other Page Content:** Handled in several different ways, they relate to the types of files and programming included in a page. Applets and objects, for example are of primary interest to programmers or page designers looking at ways that devices are used.

Date of a Web page does not necessarily refer to the publication date of the material on the page, but usually to the creation date given in the page's HTML or the last date the page was modified. When neither is available, it is the date the search engine found the page.

**Images:** Finding images is approached differently by different engines. These divergent approaches can make a big difference. In HotBot, for example, specify a subject, such as "camel," in the query box, then specify that you want only pages with images. You will probably find most pages with a camel image, but also get pages mentioning camel in the text but with unrelated images, including logos and word images used as directory buttons. AltaVista, however, allows a search within the file name for an image (image:camel). You have a very high probability that the camels found are those you seek. File names for many camel images, however, will not include the word "camel," and you may miss many good pictures.

**Links:** The capability to search for links is useful in a relatively small number of searches. AltaVista, HotBot, and Infoseek allow searching this field for pages that link to a specified URL or portion of same. If you are looking for an obscure or a hard-to-define topic, and have located one relevant page, it might be useful to identify other pages linked to it. For example, If you are tracking a small company, you might want to know who is linked to its page.

**Title:** The word or phrase that appears in the blue banner at the top of the browser window. Often it seems unrelated to the page content. Title phrases cited on the chart means that phrases in a title are searchable in that engine. If the example given is one word, this engine does not effectively search title phrases.

**URL:** URLs are searched to varying degrees of detail and with various approaches. Often you may distinguish between domain, host, and overall URL. AltaVista and Infoseek are among the most flexible,

allowing searches of contiguous segments of the URL, including directories and file names to the right of the domain portion of the URL. The
Continent field In HotBot is a derivation of URL country domain
names, bringing together country codes for each continent.

## Characteristics of Search Engines
- Locate full-text of selected Web pages
- Search by keyword, trying to match exactly the words in the pages.
- No browsing
- No subject categories.
- Compiled by computer-robot programs ("spiders") with minimal
  human oversight
- Size of search: ranges from small and specialized over 90+ percent
  of indexable Web

Meta-Search Engines quickly but superficially search several individual search engines at once and return results compiled into a
somewhat convenient format. They catch only about ten percent of
search results in any search engine visited.

## Basic Search Engines
- Alta Vista
- Infoseek
- Google
- Lycos
- Excite
- Netscape
- Northern Light
- Fast Search
- Yahoo
- Hotbot
- Inktomi

## Meta-Search Engines
- Metacrawler
- Dogpile
- Ask Jeeves
- Inference Find
- Metafind
- 37.com

## Subject Directories
- Hand-selected sites picked by editors

- Organized into hierarchical subject categories
- Often annotated with descriptions
- Browse subject categories or search using broad, general terms
- NO full-text of documents.
- Searches only subject categories and descriptions.

## Others

- Librarians' Index
- Infomine
- Britannica's Internet Guide
- Lycos'A2Z and top 5 percent
- Galaxy
- Scout Report Signpost,
- Looksmart
- Yahoo!
- Excite
- Infoseek

## Subject Guides

- Web page collections of hypertext links on a subject
- Compiled by "expert" subject specialists, agencies, associations, and hobbyists
- Locate through special guides to guides or subject directories or search engine keyword search

## Guides to Guides

- Argus Clearinghouse
- Virtual Library
- WWW

## Specialized Databases

These provide access through a search box into the contents of a database in a computer somewhere. They may include any topic: trivial, commercial, task-specific, or a rich treasure devoted to your subject. You may locate these by accessing special guides to databases in Librarian's Index and Yahoo! and sometimes by keyword searching general search engines.

Searching the Internet means primarily relying on search engines that are remarkably useful for tracking down information on one of nearly a billion Web pages around the world. Don't expect perfection:

even with advanced search features, including Boolean operators, field searching, limits, and date sorting. search engines do not always behave as expected.

# Search Strategies

## What are you really searching?

Unlike a library catalog, which assign Library of Congress or some other widely accepted standardized subject descriptors to their documents, or journal-article indexes which uses standardized subject descriptors, the Web is not indexed in any standard vocabulary. Moreover, when you "search the Web," you are NOT searching it directly; your computer cannot find or go to all or even most of the Web pages residing on computers (called "servers") all over the world. What you can do is access one of several intermediate databases and/or web-pages which contains selections of other web pages organized to allow you to find other web pages and sometimes other databases. Searching these intermediate "search tools" can provide you with hypertext links (URLs) to other pages around the world.

## Search strategies to avoid:

Because they are inefficient and often yield haphazard and frustrating results, these approaches for finding Web documents are not recommended:

- Browsing searchable subject directories. Sometimes this is fun, but it is not an efficient way to use Subject Directories. You locate documents by trying to match your topic in first the top, broadest layer of a subject hierarchy, then by choosing narrower sub-subject-categories in the hierarchy that you hope will lead to your target. Browsing usually fails because of the difficulty of guessing the subject category of your topic. Worse, each subject directory uses different taxonomy, making browsing inconsistent from one search engine or database to another. "Simple" keyword searching accepts the system's defaults, usually retrieves irrelevant documents or too many of them to usefully consider. For larger Web databases, we recommend using more advanced techniques from the outset. In smaller databases and in subject directories, their size makes complex searching unnecessary and may exclude documents you want. "Simple" keyword searching is usually the best approach.

- Following links to sites recommended by popular vote or commercial interest. Search results often display links to sites that are selected from your search results based on their traffic volume, or on fees paid to the browser. Other searches recommended "cool" sites. Because there is no way to know who visits a site for what reason, the sites best suited to your quest may be largely undiscovered by the vast public. Make your own evaluations.

## News Groups

If you have exhausted the search options above and still lack information, consider posting a message to a news group. There are tens of thousands of these forums, most of them highly specialized. If you find the right newsgroup, chances are good that someone will have the answers to your questions. Most Web browsers, such as Microsoft Internet Explorer and Netscape, have the capability to receive from and post to news groups. For extended searches of multiple newsgroups, you may wish to download software that automates this task. One of the best is called Newshound, but there are many others, mostly very inexpensive or free for downloading.

## Tips for Finding Statistics Online:

- Favor sources consisting primarily of statistics, including almanacs, statistical compendia, and numeric databases.
- Look for at Web sites links to areas named Statistics; Publications, Reports, or Bulletins; Library or Archive(s); Data or Databases; and Press Releases.
- In full text, look for statistics-indicating word patterns, such as: "According to a study/survey/report…" or "32 percent of Americans polled by Roper…"

- Look for data presented as figures, tables, charts, graphs, "info-boxes", and captions.
- Use numbers-indicating index terms, such as Statistics, Market share, Numeric, Demographics, Industry overview, and Forecasts.

# Techniques for Networking

Another effective way to find funding is through organized networking. More than merely a list of phone calls, networking of this kind involves brainstorming with one or more associates and building a list of possible key informants, contacts, and sources.

During the call to each person, make notes on a 3 x 5 card of their pertinent information, address, phones, fax numbers, current and recent projects and then close by asking each person to name two other parties that would be good for you to contact. Repeat this exercise at high or low power lunches, in the lobby of a convention, wherever you meet the right people. Writing down the information at the time will build their confidence and interest in your project and also be a safety net for your own memory. Try and return the favor to particularly helpful contacts by clipping and sending them an article or notice of interest to them. They will particularly value a clipping of a story about your successful grant application that they helped you to win.

# Summary

While not everyone will agree, for many folks one of the most satisfying aspects of writing a grant is in searching the printed materials, networking ideas, mining the library for nuggets of data, and eventually finding a list of good sources of funding. That is what this chapter has been all about. In the Appendix at the end of the book you will find the reference information necessary to locate basic materials useful to grant seekers. The accompanying document diskette has been carefully loaded with the largest and most frequently used funding sources, public, private and corporate, While every effort has been made to include the most current information and publications, some editions may have been updated since these lists were prepared. Always look for the latest edition, address and or working URL web addresses.

The bibliography you have just made is a good starting point for moving onto the next step in getting a grant. Do not assume that this list is everything worthwhile, but by example it includes a wide range of materials that have proven to be useful in the past. You might want to take the time right now to skim through the list and make of note of items of interest, then consider adding your own favorite sources and more recent materials that will be of help in present and future projects.

# CHAPTER 3

# Public Money: Federal, State, and Local

◆ *How can I find sources of public monies?*

◆ *Do public monies come with strings attached?*

◆ *Is public money available for private purposes?*

Throughout Chapter 2 we identified and discussed who the "players" are in the world of grant giving and how we can visit them on paper or on the Web. In this chapter we'll focus on public sources of grant funding, from the largest, federally controlled revenue-sharing programs to mini-grants made by neighborhood associations.

Public grants are usually given to find solutions to public issues. Sometimes the grants are awarded because the grantseeker either invents a specific solution to the problem or figures out a way to achieve the result government wants. Often grants are awarded because the grantseeker has a particular expertise in a given area.

Grants may be awarded from agencies at any level of government, from the federal level right down to neighborhood associations. Where these grants originate has changed over time, based on the political tenor of the time, and may change again. So that you will understand this better, we'll briefly discuss next the history of grantmaking.

Often, grant monies go unawarded because a connection is not made between the grantseeker and the funding source. This chapter will show you where to look for funds on the public side of things and the following chapter, chapter 4, will do the same for the private funding sources.

Government also can give assistance other than money, including both goods and services, to assist in the completion of worthwhile projects and services. Those services will be discussed briefly in this chapter although you will want to look at Chapter Six for a full discussion of mission statements which are also a good clue to what kind of assistance, monetary and otherwise, that you can expect from an organization. Next, however, is a discussion of what government wants, followed by a brief history of government grants, an examination of the "bible of government funding"—The Catalog of Federal Domestic Assistance (CFDA), the classical advantages and disadvantages of the current grant-in-aid systems and finally (at last) the most widely used types of government assistance.

## *What Government Wants*

Actually, the public funds in terms of the number of grants awarded are greater than those awarded by private sources such as foundations, corporations and individuals. The gross dollar amount, however, is often greater from the private side than the public side, but that is not an issue for us at this point.

To start with, you should know that grants are generally associated with the creative task of drawing up a novel solution to a pressing problem. In recent years there has been an increase in the number of categorical and formula grants, sole source grants and similar other funding patterns. Thus, it is fair to say that grants now include both new approaches and ideas and "qualified" efforts that meet the rules of a prescribed formula.

A solution may be one suggested by government, or one you are suggesting yourself. Either top down or bottom up.

Creative when the purpose of the grant is to invent "a better mousetrap." Qualified when the grant recipient gets the money because of some pre-qualifying condition or formula, i.e., population, percent of citizens unemployed, or some other variable

The mix of organizations receiving government funds also has expanded in recent times, in part because of a widespread public desire to limit the size of government. From a time when government money almost exclusively went to recipients also in "government" we now see funding patterns as follows:

- Government to government funding, sometimes using "pass-through" from the federal via the states to local governments
- Federal government funding directly to states only
- Federal funding to only large cities, counties or sub-state regions
- Federal funding via states (passing through) to community-based and non-profit organizations (CBOs and NPOs)
- Federal and/or state funding directly to (CBOs and NPOs)
- Cities funding directly to (CBOs and NPOs) and local government or neighborhood associations

## *Grants: A Brief History*

The recent resurgence of grants in the United States, in the mind of many experts, dates back at least to 1837, when the federal treasury was too full and the government distributed some surplus revenue to the states. Today, the types of grants are many and varied. Simply stated, government grants are usually classified as either block or categorical, and project-oriented or formula-oriented. Some grant programs have requirements for matching funds, while others are restricted (via eligibility standards) to a specific type of qualifying recipient agency and/or group or individual.

Historically, grants have been as varied as their sources. Deil S. Wright writes that a review of the origins and justifications for grants shows no single or simple cause for their development. The presence of scores of very different grant programs is indicative of their diversity, the notion of pluralism found in the USA and the fragmented character of our political process. Add to this condition the expansion funding to the widening list of CBOs and NPOs and you can envision the somewhat complicated environment faced by grant givers and grant seekers. Under these conditions, it is not surprising, then, that the fiscal and policy effects of grants-in-aid on recipients are diverse, varied and not amenable to easy explanation.

On a more positive note, grants may be viewed as funds that are supplemental, thereby allowing jurisdictions, agencies and individuals to provide services or offer programs which might otherwise not be available. Most people would agree this is good. Conversely, the presence or absence of grant monies may serve to skew the priorities of elected officials, figuratively or literally, making them seem to jump through hoops for projects where funding exists, while ignoring, or paying insufficient attention to legitimate problems that do not seem to have the ability to attract external support.

Grants also affect policy-making and administration through the conflict between the local policy preference and those of the granting agency and through procedural, compliance and reporting requirements. These latter three points, the rules and regulations or "strings" attached to grants, often are seen as so severe that some agencies actually pass up grant funds rather than be constrained, in a real or imagined way, by these conditions.

Because of the delicate balance between the requirements and the benefits, some agencies apply for and utilize grants, others do not. The following section provides a historical perspective of the effects that grants have on local government, community-based and non-profit organizations.

## The Age of Grantsmanship Begins

Consultants, researchers and students of grants administration have debated for some time a calendar year or event that would serve as the benchmark for the beginning of the age of active grantsmanship in the United States as opposed to the matter of redistribution of federal dollars in 1987.

For the purpose of getting to the starting line, a reasonable event would be the passage of the Vocational Education Act of 1917 (The Smith-Hughes Act.) This important piece of legislation was the first time that the federal government became active in the process of sending money to the states based on state plans and applications, and according to at least a primitive formula.

Through this piece of legislation (which still provides considerable funding today) states were asked to do something they had never done: prepare a proposal and make it fit into one or more of several categories (i.e., vocational, agriculture, home economics, industrial arts, teacher training). Create a plan and timetable to execute the proposal plan. Request a budget and later spend money. And, to some degree, devise a plan to evaluate their work. For their part, the federal government had to receive and roughly evaluate the proposals, send the money and receive and file (very unlikely that they critically studied) the final reports.

*...grants may be viewed as funds that are supplemental, thereby allowing jurisdictions, agencies, and individuals to provide services or offer programs which might otherwise not be available.*

While the nation went off to World War I, the movement toward grants slowed considerably and it wasn't until Franklin Roosevelt and the New Deal, starting in 1933, that the next set of grant activities would appear. This incredible explosion of government activity, centered around the three R's of reform, relief and recovery, saw the birth of over 40 new agencies, many of which began to test the embryonic proposal writing skills of state and local officials in such diverse areas as rural electrification, flood control, agriculture, conservation, emergency relief, housing and many other similar topics. The scale of these programs was impressive. In the Civilian Conservation Corps alone some 2.5 million young men and women were put to work.

After the veritable explosion of new agencies and their varied proposal requirements in the New Deal, the grant landscape became relatively calm until the turbulent 1960s opened a new age of inter-governmental activity pre-shadowed by the Area Redevelopment Act of 1961 and then Lyndon Johnson's "Great Society" War on Poverty (formalized with the passage of the Economic Opportunity Act of 1964). This massive effort was spawned somewhat by John Kennedy's unfinished work with the New Society. The sum and sub-stance of this period was an attempt to use categorical funding to iso-late and solve national problems, principally those associated with the urban and rural poor.

While citizen participation and economic development were major thrusts, the largest and most complicated of the grant-related efforts were in the area of employment and training. The first of a series of such programs was the Manpower Development and Training Act (MDTA) of 1962, which was followed by the Work Incentive Program (WIN) of 1968 and the Comprehensive Employment and Training Act of 1973. Interestingly, these programs were the foundation and precursors for the widely estab-lished Job Training Partnership Act (JTPA) passed in 1982 in effect well into the new millennium.

*...federal assistance to the states and localities in recent decades has both enlarged and shrunk.*

In summary, federal assistance to the states and localities in recent decades has both enlarged and shrunk. In the 1970s and early 80s federal aid proliferated and expanded to include over 1,000 pro-grams and sub-programs. By the beginning of the new millennium such grant programs were usually categorical (i.e. transportation, health, public safety...) and were administered on an individual basis by the granting agencies. There has even been a movement toward funding faith-based organizations, however, there will be guidelines in place to insure that government monies go only to human servic-es and not church services! While certain general regulatory require-ments were carried over from agency to agency (due largely to the enabling legislation), the plethora of application and reporting requirements created opposition to the entire grants award process.

However, as the decade of the 90's began, the residual reaction to government regulation combined with serious attempts to control government spending resulted in more precise and targeted federal and state funding programs. Since then, every new administration in Washington has tinkered with the sharing of federal money (and the accompanying duties) with states, localities and CBOs and NPOs. However, despite the overall budget concerns and the elimination of some programs, most experts agree that total dollars available are up, perhaps as high as $100 billion annually for the largest 200 federal government programs. In addition, new program areas such as drug abuse, AIDS, child abuse, juvenile crime and related topics exist today where little or no programs (and funding) existed before. Currently, the Foundation Center estimates that there are more than 50,000 active independent, corporate, community, and grantmaking operating foundations in the U.S.

Finally, in an effort to persuade taxpayers that they are managing efficiently, governments have recently been cutting full-time payrolls and job slots in favor of contracting out to community-based, non-profit and private concerns, thus in effect expanding, through a re-granting process, the total dollars available.

Originally, many of the programs created were direct federal to local grants, bypassing the states. This meant that local governments were required to initiate grant proposals and work their way through the difficulties of filling out the forms and complying, via long distance communication, with federal regulations. Governors were disturbed because they had been bypassed in many of the new programs. They found the matching requirements too expensive and the regulations too burdensome. Meanwhile, smaller or "poorer" cities lacked the expertise to make a successful proposal and to perform the work required. Numerous studies also have shown that many cities in the 2,000 to 5,000-size class could not afford to apply for federal grants since the administrative costs (and/or matching requirements) were too great.

As a reaction to this opposition and to exclusionary factors inherent in the grant process, many categorical grant programs were consolidated into what became known as 'block' programs. In 1972, the Nixon budget included block grants for education, community development, rural development and manpower. In October 1972, the State and Local Federal Assistance Act, known as "general revenue sharing," was signed into law. This Act was an attempt to remedy through compromise many of the problems found in the categorical grant processes and programs.No applications were required for general revenue sharing, and funds were distributed to the states based on formulas determined by the U.S. Treasury's Office of Revenue Sharing.

The change in emphasis from categorical programs to block grants and revenue sharing served to provide local governments with federal money largely without strings attached. Administrative requirements have been simplified and local governments have acquired more authority in the selection of projects and programs within the general functional areas.

The movement from categorical grants, in which the local agency applied for its own grant monies, toward block programs, in which states often acted as "pass-through," or funding conduits did little to alleviate the debate over whether federal money should be given directly to localities or disbursed by the states. The positions of both sides had positive and negative aspects, and historically the federal grant-awarding agencies have shown no preference for one over the other. Some authorities pointed out that the public assistance program was founded on the theory that the federal administration should have no direct relations with local governments, only with states.

An argument for dealing directly with localities is that it enhances federal control of the use of funds by avoiding dependence upon intermediary agencies (state governments) which may not share federally defined purposes and which may lack the administrative capacity to supervise local governments, especially big city governments.

More recently, experts feel that the tendency of the federal government has been to channel funds to the states for those activities that are universally engaged in, or in which state governments were already involved at the time the federal program got underway, such as highway construction, public assistance, and elementary and secondary education. In education the federal administration has in the past dealt with local districts as well as state governments for new programs. The federal government has also dealt directly with local agencies for those programs directed primarily to cities, such as public housing, urban renewal and the anti-poverty program. General revenue sharing has continued this tendency, with funds allocated to both state and local governments. The most recent turn in the funding highway is the new direction by all levels of government to fund CBOs and NPOs. In some cases they do this to control the numbers of persons on the permanent "government" payroll, in some cases to control costs because these organizations have lower-paid staff and volunteers, and in still other cases, to take sensitive service delivery out of "city hall" to these types of organizations. An example of this latter point would be programs caring for high-risk populations such as persons involved with substance abuse, chronically dehabilitated individuals, senior citizens and similar. Faith-based funding is also somewhat cyclical and at the outset of the George W. Bush administration is beginning to be back in vogue. A review of the CFDA using their keyword searching is a good way to begin an understanding of this relatively new or at least "re-born" federal funding interest.

## The Catalog of Federal Domestic Assistance

The Catalog of Federal Domestic Assistance is a government-wide compendium of Federal programs, projects, services, and activities which provide assistance or benefits to the American public. It contains financial and nonfinancial assistance programs administered by departments and establishments of the Federal government.

As the basic reference source of Federal programs, the primary purpose of In 1984, Public Law 98-169 authorized the transfer of responsibilities of the Federal Program Information Act from the

Office of Management and Budget to the General Services Administration (GSA). The transfer took place in July 1984. These responsibilities include the dissemination of Federal domestic assistance program information through the Catalog of Federal Domestic Assistance, pursuant to the Federal Program Information Act, Public Law 95-220, as amended by Public Law 98-169. GSA now maintains the Federal assistance information data base from which program information is obtained. The Office of Management and Budget serves as an intermediary agent between the Federal agencies and GSA, thus providing oversight to the necessary collection of Federal domestic assistance program data.

The catalog is to assist users in identifying programs that meet specific objectives of the potential applicant, and to obtain general information on Federal assistance programs. In addition, the intent of the catalog is to improve coordination and communication between the Federal government and State and local governments.

The catalog provides the user with access to programs administered by Federal departments and agencies in a single publication. Program information is cross referenced by functional classification (Functional Index), subject (Subject Index), applicant (Applicant Index), deadline(s) for program application submission (Deadlines Index), and authorizing legislation (Authorization Index). These are valuable resource tools which, if used carefully, can make it easier to identify specific areas of program interest more efficiently.

Other sections of the catalog provide users with information on programs added and deleted since the last edition of the Catalog, a crosswalk of program numbers and title changes, regional and local offices, intergovernmental review requirements, definitions of the types of assistance under which programs are administered, proposal writing, grant application procedures, and additional sources of information on Federal programs and services. Also included are two charts on how to use the catalog to locate programs of interest.

Programs selected for inclusion in the Federal assistance data base are defined as any function of a Federal agency that provides assistance or benefits for a State or States, territorial possession, county, city, other political subdivision, grouping, or instrumentality thereof; any domestic profit or nonprofit corporation, institution, or individual, other than an agency of the Federal government.

A "Federal domestic assistance program" may in practice be called a program, an activity, a service, a project, a process, or some other name, regardless of whether it is identified as a separate program by statute or regulation. It will be identified in terms of its legal authority, administering office, funding, purpose, benefits and beneficiaries.

"Assistance" or "benefits" refers to the transfer of money, property, services, or anything of value, the principal purpose of which is to accomplish a public purpose of support or stimulation authorized by Federal statute. Assistance includes, but is not limited to, grants, loans, loan guarantees, scholarships, mortgage loans, insurance and other types of financial assistance, including cooperative agreements; property, technical assistance, counseling, statistical and other expert information; and service activities of regulatory agencies. It does not include the provision of conventional public information services.

The catalog is published annually in two editions using the most current data available at the time either edition of the catalog is compiled. The basic edition of the catalog, usually published in June, reflects completed congressional action on program legislation. The Update, usually published in December, reflects completed congressional action on the President's budget proposals and on substantive legislation as of the date of compilation, and includes information on Federal programs that was not available at the time the latest edition of the Catalog was compiled. It is suggested that the Update be retained and used along with the basic edition in order to obtain the most current information on program revisions.

# *Benefits and Restrictions of Grants: The Overall Philosophy*

As a reader of this book, you are likely to be somewhat committed to the grant and proposal process. However, not everybody is. Remember the adage "to be forewarned is to be forearmed." As the section title indicates, there are arguments for and against the grant process and a good bit of that critique, that pro and con, follows.

Whether government agencies have applied for and received categorical grants or block grant funds, they have always been required to comply with federal regulations. In the case of categorical grants, the regulatory constraints and restrictions were often different from granting agency to granting agency, as were the application processes, forms and requirements. This practice in diversity diminished with the advent of the block or formula grants, though some funding retained restrictions for use.

There has been much debate over whether grant money actually provides beneficial results. Methods of measuring dependence on grant money have been devised, though opinions still vary on what constitutes dependence and how state and local governments can avoid it while still getting the money. Clearly, grants must have some benefits or no one would apply for categoricals and receiving agencies would refuse their portion of revenue sharing funds. Since neither case is true, the positive aspects must outweigh those perceived as negative.

## Purposes of Federal Grants

Although some might dispute his view, Professor Deil Wright suggests that *"...the purpose of federal grants is to help solve particular public problems with a minimum of disturbance to our established political framework."* Wright listed the purposes of grants under seven categories, including:

• Stimulation (encourage new activities/services or enhance existing ones);

- Minimum service level (basic funding levels);
- Equalization (more funds to those less able to pay);
- Economic stabilization and development (product-oriented vs. process-oriented effects);
- Special hardship (disaster relief, "impacted areas");
- Experimental or demonstration ("seed money" or pilot projects) and;
- Planning and coordination (attempt to standardize and reduce conflicting requirements).

The advantages and disadvantages of grants are numerous. They were first listed by the 1958 House Subcommittee on Intergovernmental Relations. Since that time, the granting structure of the federal government has changed, to be sure, but the "good news, bad news" aspects of grants remain. The disadvantages listed point directly to those areas later emphasized in the change from categorical to block grants. The arguments for and against grants-in-aid are listed in three categories.

# Advantages or Arguments for Grants-in-Aid

## A. Philosophical and legal considerations:

- The grant is a valuable device for forging cooperative effort among the levels of government in solving cooperative problems.
- By avoiding the alternative of complete nationalization of activities, grants ...help preserve State and local government.
- Grants are necessary in a humane, increasingly interdependent nation to assure all individuals a minimum level of essential public services.
- Federal grant programs have developed because of the failure of the states to meet pressing public needs of national concern.

- Grants have developed principally not as the result of failures at any level, but rather because problems of national importance have emerged that require cooperation among all three levels of government.
- To interest groups and minorities it may appear that the Federal Government is more representative of and hence closer to the people than many State governments.
- The Congress is more representative of urban citizens, and therefore majority interests, than most State legislatures.
- Restrictions on local home rule and detailed State constitutional and statutory control of local affairs have forced the cities to seek assistance from the Federal government.
- Withdrawal of Federal aid, even with the release of some revenue sources, would result in the termination of programs in many areas.

## B. Financial considerations:

- The most productive tax sources can only be reached equitably and efficiently by the Federal government.
- Most tax resources are distributed among the States in a manner that differs from the distribution of need for public services.
- Federal aid draws heavily upon "progressive" national taxes to support activities which otherwise would be financed primarily by "regressive" State and local taxes.
- Federal aid is necessary to help municipalities meet their essential needs.
- The grant is useful in stimulating activities for which State and local governments have a primary responsibility and in which there is a special national interest.

## C. Administrative Considerations:

- Federal supervision of aided programs has been an important factor for improving State and local standards of administrative performance.
- Federal participation in programs administered by the States

and localities has provided a valuable medium for the exchange of information and ideas and the provision of Federal technical assistance.

# Disadvantages or Arguments Opposed to Grants-in-Aid

## A. Philosophical and legal considerations:

- Grants have been used by the Federal government to enter fields of activity reserved by the Constitution for the States.
- The use of grants involves the danger that too much authority will be concentrated in the Federal government. The expansion of Federal power at the expense of State and local government is inherent in the grant mechanism.
- Grant programs substitute the policies and decisions of Federal bureaucrats for the control of government by elected State and local officials.
- The establishment of a grant program coerces a State into participating in an activity it otherwise would not undertake or would perform in a manner more in keeping with local attitudes and preferences.
- Grants weaken initiative in the States, and have detracted from the incentive of State and local governments to solve their own problems.
- Although the growth of Federal grants has resulted to some extent from the failure of States to meet their responsibilities, other factors have been of major significance.
- A lasting solution (to state government weakness) can be achieved only through encouragement and faith in the philosophy that the government which is best for the people is that which is closest to them.

## B. Financial considerations:

- States lack the necessary revenues because the Federal government has preempted the most productive tax sources.

- The absence of a direct connection between the taxing and spending authority encourages financial extravagance and irresponsibility.
- Grants distort State budgets since the States are tempted to provide matching funds for the aided programs, sometimes to the disadvantage or neglect of other State activities.
- programs once started are difficult, if not impossible, to terminate, both because the recipient governments become dependent upon this source of revenue and because the programs tend to build up political interest groups.
- The elimination of the Federal cost of administering grant programs—the "freight charges" on money being hauled from the States to Washington and back—would save the American taxpayers a tidy sum.
- The grant system has gained its popularity from the illusion that Federal money is free money.
- Federal grants place unfair burden on some States because their citizens are taxed to support public services in other States.
- A continuous dependence on Federal assistance postpones necessary economic and social readjustments and tends to perpetuate communities not facing fiscal realities.
- The great need of States is not for Federal grants but for more capital to develop their own resources.

## C.  Administrative considerations:

- If given access to adequate revenue sources, States would perform most grant-in-aid activities more efficiently and economically.
- By involving the participation of two or more levels of government in a single activity, the grant divides responsibility and diffuses accountability.
- Grants tend to be limited to fairly narrow categories of a general activity.

- State financial planning is made more difficult by the timing and uncertainty of Federal appropriations.

# Some Philosophical Points and Counterpoints

Grants used in a particular area or to satisfy a particular need or objective may deny state or local officials the flexibility to shift funds to reflect changing needs, while frequent requirements for matching funds siphons money from more pressing needs. Often the funding agency's requirements become a higher priority than the overall objectives of a funded agency, which leads to department heads favoring the objectives of a national agency over those of the state and/or local agencies.

In recent years state and local governments have begun to examine their dependence on federal money in the light of financial need and willingness to assume political risks that may accompany such handouts. Historically, "basic" services have been paid for by locally raised revenue and administered by local officials. Many in local government have voiced concerns about: unstructured support from overlying governments; using federal funds to pay for functions for which a city is responsible; federal funding determining the level of service that a city provides; the price of providing a given level of service; and the proportion of federal funds a city uses to support its own agencies.

Uncertainty about the level and form of federal aid makes local officials hesitant to use substantial amounts of federal money in the city's operating budget. In the event of funding cutbacks or significant rule changes, local officials would be forced to choose between raising taxes or reducing services, thus alienating either local taxpayers or recipients of federally funded services.

Every grantee faces a set of administrative provisions to ensure that grant funds are spent and accounted for in a business-like manner. Strict federal standards are established for virtually every dimension of funds use and accountability. Further restrictions arise from the statute establishing the grant program under which funds are awarded. These often include so-called "matching" funds, where Congress not only requires a local contribution, but also forbids grantees from lowering fiscal support provided for the activity before receiving federal funds, a stipulation sometimes called "maintenance-of-effort."

Another common requirement is citizen participation, which demands that individuals directly affected by the grant activity participate in its planning and execution, including public hearings, advisory committees, citizen involvement on grantee policy making boards, and employment in the grant program.

Congress may also create new governmental bodies, or force modifications in existing agencies and organizations as a condition of funding. Another standard condition is regular self-evaluations; performance review is often transferred to grantees with government review.

Along with grants for a specific purpose, the receiving agency may also be forced to embrace a plethora of national policies including, special procurement procedures, personnel promotion systems based on merit; environmental protection; procedures for acquisition of real property; confidentiality protection for personal information; payment of competitive wages; non-displacement of workers; and protection of private businesses from federally financed competitors.

While grants proponents say that those who not wish to be restricted by federal policies need not accept grant money, there is strong pressure to do so. Special interest groups continue to view grants as "free money" and lobby for its acceptance.

# Final Reflections on the History of Grants

What can be understood from the above discussion is that the rise and development of grants and intergovernmental relations has in most ways mirrored the rise and development of the American administrative state. As citizens increase their trust of leadership, government decreases the amount of rules, regulations and restrictions on programs and funding. They decentralize, de-categorize and delegate. When distrust and alienation increases, the life and times of federally funded programs are marked by a similar increase in restrictions, in categories, in qualifications and formulas. The best example to follow in this area is that of the pendulum in Figure 2 below. Using the employment and training programs as an example, during times of high trust the pendulum is farther to the right, into the area where the private sector would call the shots, where block grants rule and few strings are attached. In times where the public wants an assurance that various significant segments are being properly courted, looked after, and paid homage to, then the more restrictive programs

## Pendulum

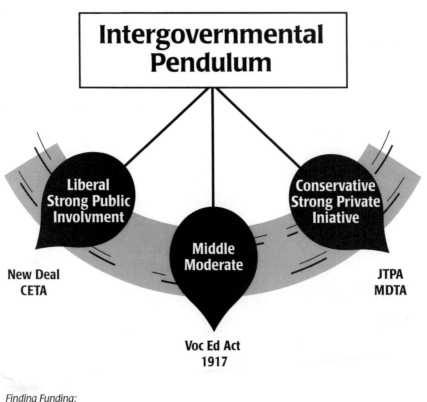

with a heavier federal and state hand are evident.

There is, of course a middle ground in all of this, but one could argue that like the pendulum, the politics of grants and intergovernmental relations are always in motion, and it is for the savvy and smart grant writer to find the direction, predict the speed and present a persuasive proposal appropriate to the current climate.

As we head into the next chapter discussing funding from private sources, plan on reflecting back upon this discussion of the pros and cons of the grant process in general and government funding in particular. You will also want to become familiar with some of the key terms, acronyms and agencies (new ones are invented every day) that are commonly used in grants and contracts, regulations, and announcements. Please consult the Appendix for a comprehensive list of terms and definitions that are located in the Glossary. Now let's take a detailed look at government funding.

# *Fourteen Sources of Government Assistance*

Following the style of the Catalog of Federal Domestic Assistance one could find 14 types of "assistance" available through existing federal, state, regional and even local government programs. This list goes beyond the pure scope of "grants", but serves as a useful reminder of the extent of support available beyond cash the support seeker might benefit from a technical service, free supplies or the complimentary use of a facility. All of these actions will save an organization real dollars of their own. (See Figure 3, opposite page)

1.  Formula grants including funds distributed by a predetermined manner, i.e., via population as determined through the Census.
2.  Project or categorical grants, the typical and familiar process of funding for research, planning, surveys, products and publications.
3.  Advisory services and counseling, including direct consulting and technical assistance.

4. Direct loans, often for public works projects, and to repair services in the event of disasters or emergencies.
5. Direct payments for specified use such as operating subsidies or services in the federal interest. No repayment is expected.
6. Direct payments for unrestricted use such as found in many entitlement programs like Social Security.
7. Guaranteed and insured loans similar to programs offered by the Department of Housing and Urban Development.
8. Insurance, sometimes routine, sometimes more exotic, such as Foreign Investment Insurance.
9. Disposal of property and goods through sale, exchange or gift, the more frequently seen practice as military bases are closed and property transferred to local jurisdictions.
10. Specialized services whereby federal personnel come on-site to give assistance in highly technical matters such as flood control.

## Sources of Government Assistance

1. Advisory Services and Counseling
2. Direct Loans
3. Direct Payments for Specified Use
4. Direct Payments for Unrestricted Use
5. Formula Grants
6. Guaranteed and Insured Loans
7. Insurance
8. Project Grants
9. Surplus Property
10. Technical Assistance
11. Training Programs
12. Use of Equipment
13. Reduction of Fees
14. Asset Forfeiture (Criminal or Civil)

*Finding Funding:*
*The Comprehensive Guide to Grant Writing*                     Figure 3

11. Sponsor organization training programs that reduce the financial burden on recipient organizations by allowing the recipient organization the opportunity to send their employees for specialized training at no cost.
12. Use of equipment, facilities and property without charge.
13. Obtaining discounts on charges such as a reduced water or electrical rate from a central utility during times of surplus in exchange for extra conservation measures during a time of drought or peak use.
14 Acquisition of money and property through seizure of assets as is the current practice by various law enforcement agencies and courts.

# *Project Grants or Categorical Grants*

At the risk of repeating the history of grants just presented it is useful to note that the growth in grants, as we know them, received the greatest impetus as late as the 1960s under the Kennedy and Johnson administrations' "New Frontier" and "Great Society" programs. These grants were primarily administered on the federal level with some passed down or "passed through" the state level. Most were of the project-grant type and followed definite categories of funding. In the 1970s a growing trend toward local and regional distribution of federal government grant dollars began. This phenomenon is most often called "Revenue Sharing" and is the basis for formula or block grants. As a reminder the CFDA is the largest directory of federal grants, and a excellent tool for collecting key terms and up-to-date.

Today, there seems to be a shift in the balance from fund distribution via block grants to distribution through categorical grants. In practical terms, this shifting means there are more local political considerations to take into account when applying for federal grant dollars. For this reason, it is a very good idea to get to know not only the funding officials in Washington but also in the state capital and regional, county and local government offices. Non-profit and community based organizations (NPOs and CBOs) should also meet periodically in round table discussions to consider common interests and possibilities of joint proposals, linkages, etc. These agencies have taken on greater roles since the "tax revolt" of the late 70's and early 1980's made governments interested in cutting payrolls and contracting out with specialized agencies. Whether it is in regard to governmental agencies or NPO's and CBO's, the greatest amount of funding has in the recent past been for "secondary services"—health, job-training, social services and housing—and largely to persons in the lower income groups, and the bulk of this money has been in project or categorical grants.

This genre of funding, the project or categorical grant, is designed to promote proposals within narrow government guidelines that describe the area that a government program deals with. Examples include topics such as drug abuse prevention, nutrition education for the elderly, gangs and community violence, research on AIDS and other types of disease, and so on. The government decides the general area and the proposer designs a specific approach to the problem or responds to a list of "priorities" that have been developed by the agency staff, its advisory commission or in some other way.

Project grants are given out by various agencies under legislatively authorized programs. Grants are awarded to the organizations that submit the best proposals to meet announced program guidelines. Most programs require outside review panels to evaluate the project. Because project design is often left to the grant seekers, this has been the most popular kind of government grant. A whole series of categorical grants has been developed, with each grant category having its own federal office to administer it.

Most categorical grants are announced in the Federal Register and by the agencies themselves through news releases, conferences and mailing lists. It is extremely important for prospective grantseekers to get on the various mailing lists in order to have timely notice of potential funding. Descriptors are key words used for searching library sources, are invaluable for inclusion in proposals, and can be found in the Catalog of Federal Domestic Assistance (CFDA). The CFDA is updated regularly, widely available and can be searched manually in a library or electronically via computers. Build your own list of key word descriptors for your grant topics and up date that list regularly.

# *Federal Block Grants*

Block grants at the state and federal level are perhaps the least understood of all entities in the world of grants, since, in a nutshell, only those levels of government who are pre-determined to get a block grant need bother to apply. This excludes individuals, community agencies and like organizations from large federal or state block grants.

Many of the older categorical funding programs have been consolidated and the money given to the states in the form of a lump sum payment called a "block grant." The states then redistribute the monies for whichever priorities and using the methods they see fit under broad guidelines provided by federal regulations. This follows the trend begun in the early 1970s.

For example, not too long ago 21 separate categorical health grants were combined into block grants and given to states for distribution. Monies like these are distributed using demographic variables which may include population, number of elderly, number of employed, minority populations, or number of welfare recipients. The states then award the grants—theoretically reducing the number of federal employees that would have been needed to oversee the 21 categorical grants.

The movement toward block grants started when the federal government wanted to pass more program control over monies to the states and at the same time trim their own federal payroll and deal with a decline in revenues. Remember the popular joke around Washington of "good news and bad news from the White House"? The good news is that the block grants are coming and local government will be able to decide what to do with tax dollars—the bad news is that everyone will only get 80 percent of what they got last year!

Federal block grant monies passed on to the local level provide that the final recipient abide by the appropriate federal regulations and rules. The state may sign an assurance that all grants will abide by federal rules but, ultimately, the local grantee assumes all responsibility in complying with the rules. This often leads to the state or local governmental agency adding on more requirements to insure that they have complied with the federal requirements. One expert put it this way, " Goals and priorities related to federal grant programs are not determined by government agencies; they are assigned to them!"

## From Block Grants to Sub-Contracting: Some New Trends

From what was formerly called "pass through funding" to the more modern public-private partnering, sourcing and the like, a phenomenal amount of grant and contract business is actually simple sub-contracting. Interestingly, this trend to cut responsibility and staff by "passing the bucks" to a lower level of government is now being considered by many big cities facing financial difficulties. Some cities, wanting to get out from under the expensive and labor intensive administration of programs, have taken money they used for their own direct staff services in a particular area, for example in human services, and have begun distributing them to competing community-based and non-profit organizations. This theoretically results in total dollar savings to the city by reducing the bureaucratic staff needed to administer, operate and monitor the formerly city hall based programs.

This is a developing area for grantseekers to closely monitor since new opportunities to deliver previously restricted and exclusive "government" services may now be available to outside parties. In general the important elements to look for are prime funding sources that are attempting to reduce their own staffing levels or want to see work done by less expensive outside sources. They then seek out, in an almost consulting manner, others who can perform work in one or more of the following four categories:

- tasks requiring genuine and unique expertise
- tasks requiring simple staff extension
- tasks requiring independence or objectivity
- tasks so sensitive that the prime agency wishes to distance itself

from a controversial issue or duty such as services to populations having sexually transmitted diseases, HIV/AIDS, substance abusers, ex-offenders and citizens with various mental health conditions.

A final aspect of sub-contracting that is worthy of note is that smaller community based and non-profit organizations, associations and even individuals can help write a proposal and put themselves in a preferred position for a sub-contract, which in actual dollars and responsibilities is every bit as good as a direct contract. In fact, the dollars may come with considerably less responsibility than if one is the original funding recipient.

## State Government Grants

The movement toward elimination of categorical grants and the shift of block grants to states has led to an increase in state government grants. This puts grant funds closer to the ultimate recipient, requires less long distance travel and often allows you to use local authorities to make your case. This is a double-edged sword, however, because the state may now set its own priorities for the grants, add additional restrictions and bring in to play a review system by state agencies and, often, political appointees.

Sometimes this new system may prove a blessing, and other times you will not fare well. Your choice is to (1) try to impact the political process on the state level, (2) adapt to the state policies, or (3) move to another state with priorities more in line with yours!

## Contracts

In recent years the distinction between grants and contracts has become harder to define. Indeed, after hours of negotiation with a federal agency on your grant, you may end up with a contract officer to finalize your budget. The basic difference between a grant and a contract is that a contract tells you precisely what the government wants done and you bid on accomplishing that task. You must prove that you have the ability to perform and to do so at the lowest price. The flexibility in deciding the approach to the problem is decidedly less with a contract than with a grant.

Contracts are publicized differently, are governed by different OMB circulars and rules and are awarded on a lower bidder basis from those contractors deemed qualified to do the specified work. Federal contract opportunities are publicized in the Commerce Business Daily or sent directly to individuals and firms who ask to be on the appropriate mailing list. Similar publications are available from states and even larger counties and cities.

Being a contractor requires, besides necessary permits, having a track record and expertise in the area you are contracting for. The best way to start is to look for a successful bidder and approach them as a possible sub-contractor, as a participant in a joint venture, or merely as an interested observer. Often the contacts you make while learning as an apprentice will lead to your own government contract in the future.

# *Summary*

What you have just read should have fairly well explained the various types of government support and the difference between project and categorical grants. Clearly most grant writers know, and unjustifiably may fear, that these government funding agencies usually require grant seekers to fill out long standardized applications rather than submit personally prepared requests. A fast glance at a fully packed set of government forms is often enough to frighten away a potential grant seeker, but do not let the mass of paperwork diminish your hopes. All that is needed, besides a good pen and lots of patience, is pre-planning and organization.

It may be difficult, but it is not impossible, to tailor proposal contents to the needs of the grant seeking or grant giving agency. These applications differ in format from agency to agency and they are tedious, complicated and time-consuming, but they will frequently use the same or slightly modified information in different places. Grant writers need to stay calm, cool, collected and determined when facing a stack of government forms.

To keep frustration to a minimum, it is a good idea to keep a photocopy of a long application to be used as a sample for other similar forms. Searching for agency budget information, tax exempt numbers, names, dates, and addresses at the last minute will be easier if you have this information already on hand in a special file. Sometimes demographic information is "guarded" by accountants/managers and the like and is difficult to get on short notice even with a legitimate and/or desperate need. Plan ahead.

Maintaining "boilerplate" data in your computer files—i.e., history of the organization/agency, major promotions and events, demographic data as well as a description of programs, short biographies of key staff, etc. will also be an important part of your application backup file.

After you have filled out the forms and mailed the proposal package, don't expect instant gratification. Usually proposals go through an intensive and lengthy multi-stage review process, sometimes even involving regional appraisal in a "regional clearinghouse," staff review for mechanical details, and peer review of proposal content. This can last from four weeks to six months, during which time the grant seeker can do little to aid their own cause. Repeated inquiries rarely do more than give the funding source the impression that yours would be a difficult grant to monitor and supervise and in reality, lessen your chances of finding funding.

In reality, public money is really more plentiful today than many believe, and the rules and regulations restricting it can be both a blessing and a curse. A curse no doubt in terms of the time and exactness preparing a proposal takes, but a blessing in that all parties have that "level playing field" where, in most cases, decisions are made based on merit.

# CHAPTER 4

# Private Money: Foundations, Corporations, and Individuals

- ◆ **What sources of private funding are available?**

- ◆ **What are the trends in grant funding from the private sector?**

- ◆ **How do I find the right match for my grant need?**

**W**hen the average person begins to imagine possible sources of grant funds, their first thoughts usually turn to government as the grant giver of public funds. Without a doubt as we have already explored, public funds are well known and substantial. However, private funds are considerable and often easier to obtain and private funds have less strings attached, meaning more flexibility for you, the grant recipient. Following is a detailed overview identifying categories of the largest private organizations operating today in the United States and their impact in the universe of grant funding.

## Identifying Private Funding

According to the prestigious Foundation Center, there are approximately 32,000 active grant-making private foundations in the

United States, plus hundreds of community foundations. Another 10,000 to 15,000 foundations remain on the books, but are inactive. Taken together, these numbers may seem staggering to the beginning grant seeker. A more realistic appraisal, however, should include the fact that approximately 2,500 foundations make 80 percent of all grants. The size of the average grant by a foundation with $20 million to $100 million in assets is $20,000. Libraries are loaded with thousands of reference books that list grants awarded. While these directories are helpful tools most sophisticated grant writers use the Internet to get the most current profiles of specific private organizations providing grants, and interested in the activities of either major or minor program implementation or support.

*A more realistic appraisal, however, should include the fact that approximately 2,500 foundations make 80 percent of all grants.*

Interestingly, but perhaps to be expected, only a small percentage of foundations control most of the assets and bestow grants that are relatively high in dollar amount size. Because of considerations demanded by the Internal Revenue Service, nearly all foundations, private or public community-based, have a common denominator, 501 (c) (3) status. This numerical nametag for part the IRS code simply allows all the funds these organizations receive to be tax deductible for the giver. Additionally, this 501 (c) (3) tax status also provides federal tax-exempt status for these organizations thus providing more capital to be available for grants.

The systematic grant-seeker needs a quick reference to select the most logical type of foundation to approach with his or her proposal and should research enough background information to know why this funding source may be interested in their proposal. Grant-seekers must also be aware that most foundations are not interested in funding programs for which government funds or private-sector venture capital are available. Thus, an exhaustive effort should be made, or a logical explanation ready, to prove to the foundation that public or other private funds are not a possibility for funding your idea.

## Sources of Private Funding Assistance

1. Community Foundations
2. National General Purpose Foundations
3. Special Purpose Foundations
4. Family Foundations
5. Corporate Foundations
6. Corporations
7. Individual Sources

Finding Funding:
The Comprehensive Guide to Grant Writing

Figure 4

# Private Funding Sources

## Community Foundations

Since the early 1980s, increases in privately held wealth and subsequent increases in private funding has led to the establishment of new community foundations and the growth and sophistication of older established community foundations. In a nutshell, most community foundations are a meeting point for gifts and bequests of persons wanting to maintain and improve the health and welfare of a geographical area, city, town, county, or even a state. This is different than other types of foundations that have a particular focus on a certain problem, groups of citizens, or the service areas of their business, etc.

There are thousands of community foundations in the United States. Because of their regional focus, they are primarily interested in the local needs of the community they have been created to promote. This is the fastest growing area in the foundation marketplace.

Assets in community foundations are vast—in the billions of dollars and growing. The primary beneficiaries of community foundations are organizations concerned with health, welfare, education, arts and culture, and increasingly technology and science. Most community foundations begin with contributions by public-spirited citizens who want to support specific types of local projects. Since the monies are held separately for donor interests, most of these groups are technically classified as public charities.

Because community foundations exist to deal with local needs, they will often fund causes that other foundations would not even think of funding, and fund them for relatively long periods. Because it is a local need, even your agency's last year operating deficit may be fundable. You can approach these foundations with the argument that a good needs assessment will result in monies from other resources being attracted to the community. A modest needs assessment grant from them could be parlayed into substantial additional funding from a variety of sources. Overall, the community foundation model is being replicated throughout the country. One of the several reasons for this is that the two decades between 1990 and 2010 will include the largest inter-generational transfer of wealth in the history of mankind. Not all of that money will go to traditional heirs. Much of it will go to support the causes and concerns that wealthy individuals felt were important during their lifetimes. Modern estate planning also figures into this trend, in that there are now many tax-smart strategies that provide for heirs while also funding charitable gifts. Additionally, because government and particularly local agencies find it increasingly difficult to fund desired levels of social, cultural and community services, the role of the community foundation is highly important and doubtless will become more so.

> *...the two decades between 1990 and 2010 will include the largest inter-generational transfer of wealth in the history of mankind.*

To determine whether a community foundation exists in your area search the Internet using the tips and tools in Chapter Two, or write: Council on Foundations, 1828 L Street N.W., Washington, DC 20036. For quick reference, visit their website: http://www.cof.org . If there is no foundation in your town, check their website to determine how to start your own foundation. They have a wealth of information about foundations start-ups and can provide you with the resources appropriate for you and your organization.

## National General Purpose Foundations

When you think of foundations, the names usually heard are Rockefeller, Ford, Carnegie, and so forth-the great names of American capitalism. The foundation center reports that there are now 50,000 active foundations with their assets growing by almost 20 per cent per year at the close of the decade. These private funding sources are making gifts that fluctuate due to business cycles but usually account for between $27 to $35 billion per year. The larger foundations number only a few hundred, but control two-thirds of all assets and account for 50 percent of private grants. While some of the foundations in this group may have more of a philanthropic interest in one or more areas, they give on a national and international scale, and the general scope of their giving patterns and interests is broader than many of the other foundations.

General-purpose foundations prefer proposals with the potential of making an impact on the nation. They want model, creative, innovative projects that can demonstrate ways for other groups to solve their problems. Since they like to be in the forefront as a force behind change, they don't fund deficits, operating income, or the many necessary but not highly visible functions of your organization. Again, the most accessible source of current information from a foundation is the Internet. You may also find information in the publications or libraries of the Foundation Center, which publishes both The National Data Book of Foundations and the Foundation Grants Index. The Index is updated quarterly; the Data Book may be searched online, and of course The Foundation Center web site is excellent and regularly updated.

## Special Purpose Foundations

Several hundred organizations fall into this category. They include foundations whose funding record supports a specific area of funding and their funding represents a significant contribution in that specific area. For example, the Robert Wood Johnson Foundation specializes in grants to improve health. The key is to fit your proposal into their area of specialization. This group evaluates your request in light of its potential impact on their special interest. With the advent of the Internet, support for these "niche" foundations has grown tremendously as individuals who had little contact with each other previously can now link efficiently and effectively electronically with others of their kind throughout the nation, or worldwide.

## Family Foundations

There are over 20,000 foundations in this category. Hard to categorize, they represent the interests of family groups, living and deceased. Many have geographic preferences, and may act as small-scale, special-purpose foundations. Family foundations whose governing boards include family members are more flexible than those that were formed as a memorial to someone now deceased, and are governed by independent trustees. Ghoulish as it may seem, this is important to know when approaching a family foundation with new ideas or a proposal. No detail about a funding source should be overlooked by serious grant seekers.

## Corporate Foundations

Generally an auxiliary activity of a for-profit company, they tend to view the world the way a business enterprise does. Many fund projects only in communities where they have facilities, or maintain some special interest. The corporation must envision some benefit, tangible or intangible, in funding your project. Making the grant benefit the corporation, its workers, or the ability of the corporation to attract quality personnel to the community are some of the concerns that corporate foundations may exhibit in making grant choices. In addition, some corporations have a special program for the geographical region in which their employees live, (e.g., allowing the corporate foundation to leave a lasting "footprint" in the communities in which they're best known).

Beyond the foundation types just described, the grantseeker may find it necessary or beneficial to directly solicit a corporation, company, or similar private enterprise.

Many people are under the impression that the majority of the over 3 million United States corporations engage in philanthropy. This area of private giving, full of controversy, contradiction and potential, is probably the least understood and the least used of all potential funding sources. Some corporations make gifts outright to agencies, and want no publicity. Others will fund equipment or training programs for their employees or dependents. Obtaining corporate funding almost always requires knowing someone high in the management structure and soliciting their assistance.

For corporations with strictly regional or local bases, solicitations by regional or local groups dealing with pertinent and timely issues to their employees, stockholders, customers or communities may be particularly appealing. As is the case with national corporations, getting to know corporate officers and staff is critical. Later in this book you will find a useful discussion about determining local interests and needs, as well as techniques for building support and lobbying.

## Corporations

Beyond funds given by corporations through their foundations, considerable monies are available from companies for one-time, ad hoc purposes. If the corporation has a foundation, obviously they usually prefer to channel their generosity through this entity. Under certain conditions, however, they will provide funds directly. Some of these circumstances might include the aftermath of a disaster, a tragedy or emergency: A school building burns down, families lose their homes in a hurricane, etc. Support for a project of particular interest to a corporate officer, or to their spouse, may often be funneled through the corporation.

Programs that may benefit a corporation indirectly or in the future may also be of interest to management. One of those benefits might be the restoration of the company's good name after a spate of negative publicity; in fact, we say that the Scarlet Letter of grant writing is "G," as in Guilt. If you want absolution from some corporate gaffe, giving money will show at least enough penance or remorse to distract, disarm or confuse critics. Finally, corporations may choose to fund through the corporation and not through the foundation programs that the foundation may not fully support, or that might jeopardize the foundation's tax-exempt status.

For corporations and businesses without a foundation a direct approach is warranted—although the very fact that they do not have a foundation may warn the fund seeker that the reception could be cool or at least require a considerable amount of time. The approach is similar to that of contacting the corporate foundation, except that the grant seeker must carefully research the organizational structure to determine the correct person to contact. Sending a beautifully prepared program to the wrong person may mean that it decorates the bottom of a wastebasket rather than getting the consideration it deserves. The time invested in personal visits or telephone calls to people in the corporation to get the name of the best person to contact may reap great dividends.

*...the grant seeker must carefully research the organizational structure to determine the correct person to contact.*

Another way of researching corporate interest is to see to whom they give political contributions, and particularly with what causes they align themselves. Many states have a nonpartisan guide that serves as a one-stop shop for anyone searching for election-related information on the Internet. These voter guides allow you to follow the money including the Top Ten donors for and against various propositions and candidates. For example, the California Voter Project tracks hundreds of California campaign web sites at

http://www.calvoter.org /home.html, with other sites tracking donations at the national level as well.

The smaller the enterprise approached, the more time must be
spent selling the advantages of donating money: tax deductions,
increased community or industry name recognition, the benefits of
projecting a positive corporate image, and other rewards of sponsoring a program. The fund-seeker must also be able to coherently
explain how money will be transmitted from the business to the program, and how the program managers will account for it. This is a
good place for a well-formed support group of community members.
A fellow business owner who belongs to your group may be invaluable as just the person to explain and sell your program. Charity loves
company. And now a final point on corporate giving. Whether a corporation is inclined to grant funds based on mutually-beneficial altru-
ism, flat-out monetary interests in receiving tax deductions or tax
credits, or somewhere in between, corporate foundations are a growing source of grants and should not be overlooked.

## Individual Sources

While foundation and corporate sources are vital to any fund
seekers search, individual or unaffiliated donors should not be
ignored. In most communities wealthy individuals can be found who
are more than willing to contribute to a worthy cause for their community. The nameplates on city cultural centers and university buildings bear witness to the generosity of these individuals.

# *Trends in Non-governmental Funding*

To put some numbers with the above sentiment we look again to
a recent report of the Foundation Center who said that by the turn of
the century foundations gave an estimated $27.6 billion annually a
number that rises faster with a stronger economy but generally always
moves forward. Community foundations are experiencing the fastest
growth in giving followed closely by independent foundations. With an

uneven economic climate growth in corporate foundation giving has slowed, reflecting declining corporate profits and stock values.

New foundations have been a key factor in increased grantmaking. Between 1985 and 2001 the number of grantmaking foundations more than doubled-from about 25,600 to over 53,000 but many of these are fairly small and limited in their impact. Since 1995, the number of active foundations has risen by just over 10,000, or 5.8% a year.

Realizing the above to be perceived as more than one more out-stretched hand, however, a fund seeker must offer a potential donor a crisp, organized idea of what it is that the donor can do for his community. The idea should be local and timely, and it must appeal to an interest that the donor already has—or one that you can develop through a reasonable educational campaign. It is your responsibility as a fund seeker to conduct background research on possible donors, and then select individuals most likely to respond to your plea. Approaching a devout Catholic, for example, with a plan for a "family planning" clinic is not merely unwise, it is poisonous, and will quickly mark you and your organization with unwelcome controversy in the very small world of the wealthy. On the other hand, the same donor may be the ideal candidate with whom to discuss a home for unwed mothers, adoption services or a foster care program. Plan before you act, and think before you speak. Invest some of your up-front time in knowing as much as you can about the potential donor, where they got their money, other gifts and bequests, their personal issues and social activities.

It is also your responsibility to succinctly present your program to the potential donor, and to evaluate when to leave him or her with a neat package explaining what it is that would be accomplished with his money, and why it is that he or she should give their money to your cause. A warm smile and handshake may open the door to a donor's heart, but it is the lasting impression of a well-planned, easy-to-understand project presentation that will open wallets and purses, treasuries and trust funds. The timing of the actual request for funds, with its attendant numbers and details of recognition in exchange for generosity, varies from individual to individual.

As important as it is not to rush a donor or under-whelm a prospect, it is of equal consequence not to let the request go unanswered indefinitely. Unlike the government or foundation grant with a specific deadline for a proposal and awarding dates, gifts from individuals oftentimes, but not always, depend on deadlines set by the fund seeker.

Another relatively new and fast-growing private source is IRS approved mutual funds that allow individual donors to allocate funds that are then distributed as grants to a pre-determined set of causes. Among the major players is Fidelity Investments' Charitable Gift Fund, which awarded $146 million in grants to 18,000 charities recently.

On a smaller scale, some cities have created "human services" or "park and recreation funds" to which employees in local businesses agree to payroll deductions of a certain amount per month, typically to fund one or two items on a city's "wish list," including scholarships for a child's summer camp, playground equipment, a parkway tree, etc. From large and sophisticated to small and simple, individuals play a tremendously important role in providing funding to meritorious causes and concerns. Be ready with your wish list and be persistent in getting all that you can that's on the list!

Another technique for use when considering foundation funding sources is to use the Grant Action Files explained in Chapter 8. Several special characteristics of foundations prompt questions you may wish to pose to yourself when deciding which of your several leads you will want to pursue.

- Does this foundation fund programs in my city or county or state?
- Is this a national foundation which funds programs in my state?
- Does this source have a past history of funding my type of organization?
- Do our project objectives match the funders objectives?
- Does the average award from this foundation match our desired level of support?
- Is this foundation heading into a future direction in the areas we specialize?

# *Summary*

Looking outside the government loop to private funding is unquestionably a wise move, and some organizations NEVER seek government funds at all, even though they are clearly eligible. You will recall from what you have just read that there are upwards to 1500 assistance programs administered by over 60 Federal agencies. As a potential applicant, always contact the agency information sources in the program descriptions for the latest information concerning assistance programs.

Looking at the private funders at the beginning of the new millennium, the total given was just over $200 billion coming form four main sources. The largest single source was from individual (75%) totaling $152 billion but this largely one time giving. The more renewable sources are from foundations (12% and $25 billion), bequests (generally all from estates of recently deceased persons) $16 billion and corporations $11 billion.

As with almost every request for external support, the private funding challenge is to package your proposal then market it to more exacting and often far narrower standards, and usually for somewhat smaller dollar amounts. The advantage of private funding sources also lies in the speed in which they generally accept (or reject) an idea, and the creativity and willingness that foundation officers have in trying new and novel ideas. Clearly, they are a significant source of money and display many virtues that, regrettably, the public sector seldom or never displays.

As we have said before, don't be obsessed with building the perfect plan of approach. You really need what works for you since there are obviously many ways to accomplish worthwhile goals. The key is to keep the idea, the problem, at the forefront of all your efforts. While there are times when a funding source merely wants to financially help an organization, a sort of middleclass welfare, generally grant writing is linking documented problems to workable solutions and bridging the gap between people with ideas and people with money.

# CHAPTER 5

# Organizing and Managing the Grant Writing Team

◆ **How can I get help from my colleagues who I am seeking to find funding for important programs?**

◆ **How important is it to manage my organization's expectation throughout the grant-writing process?**

◆ **What internal and external resources can I use to help with the grant-writing process?**

**A**s enthusiastic as any grant writer might be about the value of the proposal they are working on, managers, department heads and other organizational leaders often have a more considered, measured, and at times, narrower viewpoint.

This chapter addresses issues of concern to these managers, and therefore of even greater concern to the grant writer who needs to "sell" their own manager on supporting both the grant-seeking process and ultimately, in making good on the promises made in the grant proposal.

Here are some useful ways to explain the overall grant writing process to a third party; those people inside or outside your organization who can become part of your grant-seeking coalition. (A detailed discussion on joint ventures is featured in Chapter 6.) The following steps will help you gain support from others through clear and consistent communication.

# Grant Writing Is...

## Idea Generation

As discussed throughout the book, determining needs is a necessary first step, whether it be through a formal, academic needs-assessment using surveys, focus groups and the like, or merely a good brainstorming session around the lunch room, coffee pot or water cooler. Somehow, you must have an idea at work. An example of this process:

"Well, we all agree that housing is the most important issue for us. What do each of you mean by "housing"?

- Group one responds that they mean more housing for low-income persons.
- Group two says that their idea is earthquake-safe housing.
- Group three is interested in accessible housing for the handicapped.
- Group four wants to end landlord discrimination in housing.
- Group five wants to help poor people close the gap between what they can afford to pay as rent and what the actual rents are in their town.

You are left with a single overall goal: HOUSING, with five special objectives or sub topics. This is the first step along the trial to finding funding-understanding the idea and refining it.

## Resource Identification and Allocation

As managers begin to understand, and concur with, original ideas, you might be well served to solicit their input on what sources of funding you should seek. While many web sites offer keyword searching, the good old boy and good old girl networks that leaders travel often offers some excellent funding source information.

Moreover, involving managers and supervisors in the process almost invariably energizes the grant writer because effective managers who offer their advice and contacts will seek commitments and concurrences, which motivates both parties.

If your leader's first response is to say they don't know, in a gentle, non- confrontational way, interview them and ask pertinent screening questions:

- Do any of the national associations and groups that we belong to have a summary of grants and funding that folks like us have received?
- Who are the most admired organizations like ours, and whom might I contact in that organization to find out what they think the issues are and what they are doing about it?
- Who is operating a good program similar to those that we are interested in—regardless of where it is located? (You want good role models and you don't care who funded them!)
- Do we have friends in high places, i.e., Congress, the State House, etc., who will refer us, or even just point us, to possible sources?
- Do we want to spend some up-front money and hire an outside consultant to build a customized list of funding sources? One example of a provider who does excellent work in this area is an affiliate of our publisher, www.grantwriters.com.

## Completing Forms

Once the preferred sources have been contacted and their guidelines received, the next step in the grant writing process is to dissect the proposal and begin to fill out the forms. Always make copies of the forms and put the originals in a safe place, since you don't want to white out and erase while the UPS truck idles outside your door. As you turn the pages on the proposal guidelines, quite often you will realize that not every need you have can be fulfilled by this funding source. Likewise, you might not have anticipated all the "work elements" or services that the funding source expects. Make a list of all areas in which your idea list fits, where it doesn't and what else you must include. This process then leads to the next step, refining your original idea.

## Refining Ideas

At this juncture you, and your significant others—direct supervisors, council, commission and, of course, consortium and/or joint venture partners, need to have a serious chat about what you will do about the "fit" between your original ideas and needs and what a given source offers. One alternative you may wish to consider is to break your "wish list" into several smaller fund requests to several different sources. In any event the outcome of this idea-refinement meeting should be a plan of action, including work assignments and deadlines.

## Writing "Inside Out," and Pre-writing

Now it's time for the fingers to hit the keyboard. A noted author once described writing as "very simple, you just sit down and sweat blood." Another noted, and as yet unpublished, author, Snoopy from the late Charles Shultz's comic strip Peanuts, never seems to get past page one, line one, "It was a dark and stormy night..". Our advice for grant writers seeking to avoid writers block comes in two parts: write from the "inside out," and "pre-write."

Writing from the inside out means picking any part of the proposal requirements (we suggest that you pass out sections to your colleagues), ignore page one line one and write the selected section. Eventually all the sections can be joined and their writing styles homogenized and smoothed into a clear and consistent format. Meanwhile, nobody is stymied by waiting for the other party. If NASA had not simultaneously worked on communications, propulsion, spacecraft guidance and astronaut training, the U.S. space program would still be on the launch pad. To meet deadlines, work on various parts of a proposal must be undertaken at the same time. Writing from the inside out removes barriers and bottlenecks.

Pre-writing means creation of basic or "boiler-plate" materials before the application deadline looms around the corner. Virtually all grant applications require an organization history and sometimes a description of key features such as laboratories, libraries, parks, centers and the like. Build these paragraphs before deadline pressure arrives and save them as a "template" on your hard drive and your back-up floppy disks. Other information to pre-write includes resumes and thumbnail bios of key personnel and the organization's funding history: Who gives you how much and for what purpose. Details should be offered on external grants and contracts, since that is what you will be seeking. Include the outcomes of all previously funded projects, including honors, awards and acknowledgements. These data are always useful and often required. Similarly, pre-write your organizational affiliations, accreditations and licenses that outsiders might need to know about. By creating this material in advance of the deadline, a great deal of useful and required proposal elements will be available, with only slight modification, and maybe dropped in to your final proposal. This saves time and anxiety for the more specialized sections.

# Approval, Packaging, Politicking, and Re-funding

## Approvals

The "last" major step in the grant-writing process is actually a step that needs to be examined early on to see if your organization has special timelines, rules or regulations that might affect the end of the process. One of these items is approval. Different administrators have different styles about how and when they wish to be consulted regarding a proposed grant process. It is hoped they are already engaged in the idea- generating process, because, following the axiom, "people tend to support what they help create" they will have already bought into your idea. If they haven't, or others must also approve and "sign off" on a project, you need to know how this approval is obtained and the time required to get the critical signatures. If your project is a joint venture, allow extra time for transferring these documents between organizations and sorting out who signs first.

## Packaging

As you'll read in Chapter 7 "Dissecting the RFP," careful dissection of the RFP yields the instructions for proper packaging of your proposal and organizational information. This is minutia, but often critically important: How many copies, single or double sided, how fastened—stapled, bound, etc.,—how organized, budget separate or included, allowable page length, mailing addresses, copy to a clearing house, etc. Following is a seven step checklist of the packaging requirements and elements requested by a typical funder. This handy checklist is also available on the accompanying document diskette.

## Proposal Check List

o  Organize carefully your material from your needs assessment and align it with the funding source's expressed guidelines and their more subtle preferences, as in key words used throughout the RFP materials or on their website, indicating to you their "hot buttons."

o  Ensure that a thorough outline of the funder's requirements for the proposal content has been written and double-checked by a second person.

o  Develop your problem statement and your methodology so that you can deliver on your promises in the time allowed with the money offered.

o  Prepare background information on all key personnel as well as your organization's funding history, including non-cash gifts, for at least the past three years.

o  Identify and confirm your joint venture partners and document their involvement.

o  Obtain supplementary documentation required for such things as: tax status letter (501(c) tax exempt status), annual report, annual budget, etc.

o  Develop the budget for the entire project and include summary figures as well as a complete itemization for each budget line item, including item justification. Be sure to identify which items being requested by the funder will be provided by your organization and which items will be supplied by other organizations.

# Lobbying, Politicking, and Friend-Raising before Fund-Raising

In the hundreds of books and articles published about grant writing, one of the least covered topics is how to lobby others on behalf of your organization's proposal that has just been, or is soon to be, submitted. For many it may seem unethical, offensive or even frightening. For others, they may actually enjoy the arm-twisting, cajoling and ear-whispering more than the actual proposal preparation process. So is there a middle ground, something between submitting your proposal and doing nothing, and doing "nothing" in the submitting and everything in the post-submission lobbying? Of course there is.

> *Studies of successful grant organizations… is that they make friends first and raise funds second.*

Studies of successful grant organizations—and that may be defined as having received a funded grant on say four out of 10 applications—is that they make friends first and raise funds second. It is important whenever possible to build a foundation of understanding, support or at least basic recognition in the hearts and minds of the funding source. They may not know you by name, but funding sources should at least be aware in general of your deeds or approach to problem solving. This is almost essential when requesting external support from a local community foundation, corporation or individual benefactor. This may seem like a long term and somewhat slow approach but the history of this field indicates it may take up to two years, or at least a couple of repeated asks, to find the initial funding. After that it does become easier as you build a track record of responsible spending your benefactors money. Finally, you always want to keep your organizations good works in the mind, or at least on the radar screen, of your targeted funding sources during the "off-season," not just the "ask-season."

Assuming that you have built, or have under construction, the foundation of "friend raising," we can come back more directly to the question of politicking and lobbying.

## Re-funding

The final question to be addressed before your proposal can go out the door is whether your project could be funded for a second, third or fourth year. If so, will it be funded at the same dollar level? More money or less? Will any matching requirements change or be added, i.e., you must come up with 25% cash match for year one, 50% for year two and so on.

These major steps and grant-writing elements provide a fast summary for managers and grant writers to consider before they embark on a journey to find funding. Having the broader picture in mind is critical to staying the course, working within organization rules and constraints and ultimately being successful in securing external support.

### Tips for organizing your organization

Ideas are the first step in finding funding. Create an environment in which ideas are encouraged and rewarded.

- Consider a needs assessment-formal or informal—but be aware that asking questions raises expectations. Become sincerely ready for change.
- One of the most significant funding trends in recent years is joint ventures. They raise the power of your proposal and reduce competition for the same funds. Joint ventures, however, add a few wrinkles to administration, such as shared program and fiscal responsibilities.
- Consider using volunteers. Many new programs mandate a volunteer element as a form of both cost-saving and citizen empowerment (the citizen technique of the '90s). You might even use volunteers as grant writers: After all, they often have the time and single-minded dedication to stick with a task, play telephone tag and work on building outside support.

- Encourage your staff and help them by prewriting grant "boiler-plate." Store it on your computers for easy access and editing. Organizational charts, staff and organizational bios, evaluation plans, a list of previous funding, an inventory of resources, etc., can be prepared well in advance and modified as required.
- Establish procedures for internal and external clearance of proposals for both quality-control and for legal reasons.
- Be sure the RFPs and program announcements are promptly shared by all appropriate staff and that you are on the mailing list of prospective funding sources.
- Plan for periodic staff training on effective proposal preparation. You may discover that some of your best writers are at the middle or bottom of the organizational chart.
- Ensure that your staff has both adequate time and the requisite supplies to complete grant projects.
- Time your organization and organize your time. Even the greatest of ideas won't get funded if nobody hears about it. To meet the deadline, make sure you don't let colleagues (or managers) slow you down.
- Teach your grant-writing team to think sideways, which is to say: Analyze complex situations by deciding not just what is wrong, but what can be fixed to bring about the desired change. Then examine all solutions, including those that may not involve the department or agency that is to benefit from them. For example: High absentee rates in a welfare-to-work job training program for single parents limit the number of graduates. Providing an on-site child care facility, however, may dramatically reduce absenteeism.

## Brainstorming: No Need To Rain On The Parade

While many folks would assume that the brainstorming process is always a positive and affirmative experience, in reality it can cause problems for some organizations. People adopt, hold and defend their ideas because in truth, people's ideas are part of their identity.

In a group they sometimes make selecting the grant idea a competition with one winner and a bunch of losers. Good brainstorming allows for a multitude of ideas to be considered without bias or fear of rejection. Creating an open-discussion environment is key to soliciting good ideas without self-censorship. Brainstorming is essentially when a group of folks think out loud and a facilitator writes down the group's ideas. Then, the group through the facilitator reviews the ideas generated and tries to eliminate those ideas that are outside the scope or don't have a good "fit" with the task at hand. The group should have appropriate people for the general area of the topic under review for that brainstorming session.

## Brainstorming: Developing And Evaluating Proposal Ideas

Most experts agree that one of the best techniques for developing sound proposal ideas is to brainstorm the idea with your staff and your colleagues. This process gives you the added benefit of using their collective genius. In the brainstorming process you build support for the proposal since you invited your staff to share in the idea generation. The project then becomes "our" project and the staff will be more willing to work at night and on weekends to meet the deadlines (when a lot of proposals are worked on).

Brainstorming is a technique for quickly generating a long list of creative ideas from a group of individuals from both inside and outside the fund-seeking organization.

### This is how it works:
- Develop groups of five to eight individuals.
- Appoint a neutral group leader to facilitate the process (encouraging and prodding other members, checking the time).
- Appoint a recorder.
- Set a time limit (Ten minutes per question or topic will be plenty).
- State one question (direct or in-direct) or problem (e.g., reducing student drop-outs, increasing attendance at mental health

forums, keeping pregnant teenagers in school, increasing citizen interest in an environmental issue).

- Ask group members to generate as many answers to the questions as they can within the time limit.
- Encourage group members to "piggyback" on each other's ideas (clarifying, suggesting or augmenting new ideas that add to ones already given).
- Record all answers; combine those that are similar but beware of the jealousy that can tear asunder the most delicately assembled joint venture.

### The Single Most Important and Overriding Rule for Brainstorming

Never make a premature evaluation of an idea. Avoid discussion of ideas until the process is over. The recorder can ask to have an idea repeated but no comments by others (e.g., "We can't do that... " or "That's a dumb idea, stupid, etc..."). Sharing is risk taking, so never punish those parties who play the game by the rules and take the risk of sharing a new or novel idea.

## *Summary*

Clear and consistent communication with key stakeholders in the grantseeking process and building coalitions with internal and external individuals and organizations will go a long way toward ensuring success for getting funded and re-funded. Because the grantseeking process can be time consuming and ask much time and energy of others, identifying and managing your internal organization's expectations throughout the grantseeking process is vital to maintaining internal stakeholder's expectations. The same is true with joint venture coalition partners' momentum and managing the grant funding support. Each internal and external actor has much to gain in the funding process. Your job is to ensure that your grant is funded and administered successfully in all the intended ways. Clearly identifying the intended funding to key stakeholders and getting joint venture coalition members active and behind your grant effort will be an important factor your success.

# CHAPTER 6

# Mission Statements, Needs Assessments, and Joint Ventures

◆ *I have done my basic research on sources, what is the next step?*

◆ *What is this stuff about mission statements and should my organization have one?*

◆ *What is a needs assessment and how are they completed?*

After the advice just given (and the calm, cool, calculated chapters one through five), this chapter marks the time for you to begin to put your ideas into action. One of the first steps is to whip your own organization into shape if it isn't already, or to compare what you say you want to do with what funders say they want to fund. The first step in that process is to examine and compare mission statements including those of your regular, or potential, joint venture partners.

The following is a selection from real operating and funding organizations. See how they see themselves and then see how you compare with the funding sources you have uncovered for your own use.

As a second step, it is always helpful, and sometimes required, that you have recently completed a needs assessment. We offer a couple of models from formal (which could mean time consuming and expensive), to informal, fast and obviously more subjective. In either event it is important that you have a clear understanding of what your clients, constituents and leaders want before you begin a journey to find it for them.

# Typical Mission Statements from the Organizations Perspective

## Southern Environmental Law Center (SELC)

SELC is the only environmental organization dedicated solely to protecting the natural resources of the southeastern United States. Founded in 1986 as a small group of attorneys working on strategic cases to enforce environmental laws, SELC has grown into a multi-faceted organization that is leading several broad-based, regional conservation initiatives to strengthen environmental protection laws and policies. Through direct legal action, policy reform, public education and partnerships with other groups, SELC is playing a major role in setting the agenda for the environmental future of the South.

SELC's mission is to restore and safeguard the quality of the region's air, water, forests, wildlife habitat, rural landscapes and other critical resources. Our work is multi-faceted, encompassing the judicial, legislative and administrative branches of government at the local, state and federal levels. SELC provides legal expertise and services to other organizations to enable them to more effectively achieve specific environmental protections. We also take direct legal actions in the courts to stop immediate threats to outstanding resources.

## Children Now (CN)

Children Now is a nonpartisan, independent voice for children, working to translate the nation's commitment to children and families into action. Recognized nationally for its policy expertise and up-to-date information on the status of children, Children Now uses communications strategies to reach parents, lawmakers, citizens, business, media and community leaders, creating attention and generating positive change on behalf of children. With particular concern for those who are poor or at risk, Children Now is committed to improving conditions for all children.

## National Network for Immigrant and Refugee Rights (NNIRR)

The National Network for Immigrant and Refugee Rights (NNIRR) is a national organization composed of local coalitions and immigrant, refugee, community, religious, civil rights and labor organizations and activists. It serves as a forum to share information and analysis, to educate communities and the general public, and to develop and coordinate plans of action on important immigrant and refugee issues. We work to promote a just immigration and refugee policy in the United States and to defend and expand the rights of all immigrants and refugees, regardless of immigration status. The NNIRR bases its efforts in the principles of equality and justice, and seeks the enfranchisement of all immigrant and refugee communities in the United States through organizing and advocating for their full labor, environmental, civil and human rights. We further recognize the unparalleled change in global, political and economic structures that has exacerbated regional, national and international patterns of migration, and emphasize the need to build international support and cooperation to strengthen the rights, welfare and safety of migrants and refugees.

## Kankakee, Illinois Police Department

The mission statement of this department is so straightforward that we offer it verbatim. Not much missing but worth remembering is that if you make such sweeping promises you better be prepared to keep them.

*"We, the Kankakee City Police Department are committed to serving all people with respect, fairness and compassion. Acting in partnership with the community, we strive to prevent crime and help preserve peace, order and safety. With community service as our foundation, we will address problems and seek solutions with honesty and integrity. We shall maintain public respect by holding ourselves to the highest standards of performance and ethics. The Kankakee City Police Department is dedi-*

*cated to providing a quality work environment by promoting the positive development of its members through effective training, education and leadership. We encourage, expect and need community involvement to work toward a mutual goal of enhancing the quality of life within the community."*

In summary what you are working for is an "Ideal Vision," a measurable statement of the kind of world we want to create together. While it may not be achieved in our lifetime, it is any organization's common guiding star for thinking, planning, doing and continuously improving. One such "Ideal Vision" for an agency concerned with children states as follows:

All people will live in a healthy, positive, safe and satisfying environment where all things both survive and thrive. There will be no losses of life or elimination or reduction of levels of well-being, survival, self-sufficiency, quality of life, livelihood, or loss of property from any source. Poverty will not exist, and every person will earn at least as much as it costs to live unless they are progressing toward being self-sufficient and self-reliant). No adult will be under the care, custody, or control of another person, agency, or substance. All adult citizens will be self sufficient and self-reliant as minimally indicated by their consumption being equal to or less than their production.

Having determined a mission, we now use objectives and this is where your formal or informal needs assessment and planning comes into play. For example, you might say that an agency will realize its vision through the success of its clients as indicated by the reduction or elimination of societal-level needs for which responsibility is assumed. To achieve this the agency would say, "We assist leaders in designing and delivering positive societal impact using their organization and its resources as a primary vehicle. Measurably assisting our clients to improve effectiveness requires that the means for performance improvement be based on the ends of simultaneously achieving positive societal consequences and organizational success.

# *Typical Mission Statements from the Funding Source Perspective*

Just as organizations have missions so do funding sources. While your own organization should not change its mission to meet the likes and dislikes of every funding source, it is useful to periodically examine how close your mission is to that of leading funders in your field. Here are six typical mission statements ranging from a major community foundation to large and small private foundations.

## California Community Foundation

Through its funding initiative "Nurturing Neighborhoods/Building Community," the California Community Foundation addresses the essential elements to maintaining healthy and independent lives for at-risk populations in Los Angeles, particularly those who face barriers and discrimination due to language, economics, culture or sexual orientation. The community foundation recognizes that all aspects of a person's life are linked to their community—including personal health, economic stability, living conditions and learning opportunities. Our intention is to fund programs that can make a permanent difference in the lives of the people they serve.

Crucial to meeting the community foundation's goals is the understanding that Los Angeles County is a diverse community comprising many cultures. The California Community Foundation is committed to creating one harmonious community and supporting programs which will not only strengthen individuals and neighborhoods, but the relationships between them.

The primary goals of the California Community Foundation are to build self-reliance among individuals and their communities through four main strategies outlined below in the description of our program areas.

## Herb Alpert Foundation

In the 1980s, musician and painter Herb Alpert established the Herb Alpert Foundation, which funds projects in education, the arts and the environment. Instead of responding to grant proposals, it is "more typical" of the foundation to "focus on a social need, find qualified organizations that can respond in a healing manner to that need and then creatively join in the development of responsive programs." The majority of their funding is directed toward the youngest members of American society, "in hopes that the future for them, and for the world, can be improved by an earlier intervention."

## The Century Foundation

The Century Foundation (formerly the Twentieth Century Fund) was founded in 1919 and endowed by Edward A. Filene to "undertake timely and critical analyses of major economic, political, and social institutions and issues." The foundation is an operating rather than grantmaking foundation and does not award fellowships or scholarships, support dissertation research, or make grants to individuals or institutions. Similarly, it almost never supports large-scale data-gathering efforts or research designed primarily to develop theory or methodology. Currently, it welcomes proposals in four areas: improving living standards, restoring civil society and respect for government, reinvigorating the media and identifying new foundations for American foreign policy.

## The Kresge Foundation

Sebastian S. Kresge, founder of the S.S. Kresge Company that is now known as Kmart, established the Kresge Foundation in 1924. Its mission statement is simple: "to promote the well-being of mankind." The Kresge Foundation makes grants to build and renovate facilities, challenge private giving and build institutional capacity among nonprofits, with goals of strengthening the capacity of charitable organizations to provide effective programs of quality.

## Albert and Mary Lasker Foundation

For 53 years The Albert Lasker Medical Research Awards have celebrated scientists, physicians and public servants who have made major advances in the understanding, diagnosis, treatment, prevention, and cure of human disease. The awards are made by the Albert and Mary Lasker Foundation, whose mission is to elevate and to sustain medical research as a universal priority so that the foundation's goals—to eradicate life threatening diseases and disabilities and to improve health standards—are strongly supported by national and international policies and resources.

## Marion Foundation

Established in 1993 by Marion Sue Kauffman, the Marion Foundation "strives to improve communications and relationships among youth and parents by implementing innovative programs that address the social, emotional and educational issues of our ever changing society." Among other activities, the Arizona-based operating foundation lends financial support to teachers and schools, operates a peer counseling phone line and sponsors a number of youth-related activities.

# Doing A Needs Assessment

The "problem statement" or "needs assessment" is most often the critical part of your project or grant plan. It represents the reason behind the proposal and must bring into sharp focus those conditions in the lives of your clients or constituents that you wish to change. This brief narrative looks at that particular situation, relates it to similar situations that exist in other communities and shows the broader implications of your program. The needs assessment should:

- Be clearly related to the purposes and goals of your organization. Include at least one stated objective for each problem statement.
- Be supported by evidence drawn from your experience, from statistics derived from authoritative sources and/or from the testimony of persons and credible organizations known to be knowledgeable about the situation.
- Be of reasonable dimensions, i.e., describe something that you can realistically remedy over the course of a grant.

- Be stated in terms of clients or constituents, rather than the needs or problems of your organization. Statistics are preferred, but if they are not available, at least provide good anecdotal data or narrative.

## An Example:

**Objective:** to examine variations in the needs assessment policies and practices of social services departments in Vermont and Virginia in dealing with elderly people who have mental illness.

**Design:** postal questionnaire survey.

**Subjects:** a random sample of 61 of 119 social services departments in Vermont and Virginia. Main outcome measure: 99-item questionnaire.

**Results:** 40 responses were received (66%). There were substantial differences in the way referrals were screened before needs assessment and in the design of needs assessment procedures. Disagreements between health and social services were common and, although mechanisms existed to respond to urgent needs, almost one-third found such responses difficult to make.

**Conclusions:** There are national variations in the way needs assessments are performed by social services, which may lead to inequalities in provision of care to individuals. The lack of a standardized approach impedes comparisons of need between areas which might aid in the distribution of resources at a national level.

## The Internet Opinion Poll

Having a feel for what your organization really needs is important. The formal needs assessment detailed above is one such process to get to that point. Another is the realization that the Internet makes it extremely easy to find opinions and request feedback. The folks that use the Web are givers and not just takers and these "netizens" come from a wide and important cross section of every interest area, topic, cause or concern. A number of these web sites have guest books that are a very basic, but effective, tool for gathering opinions. Certainly you should be careful when you read the comments of the more outspoken and vocal segment of your respondents since they are not necessarily representative of the population as a whole.

Experts suggest that you can often get feedback that would be difficult to find expressed elsewhere, including anecdotal evidence, experience with specific services and individual citizen or client reviews. There are several computer tools to assist in this task such as the "listserves" (Usenet is one major source) but remember that e-mail lists from organizations that you belong to or affiliate with can also be very helpful when you are ready to conduct an opinion poll. You may wish to do this surveying anonymously or state your affiliation and do it in such a manner that you accept the advice without knowing who gave it, or with the idea that you want to know whose advice it is so you can properly acknowledge or cite that in your needs statement.

Whether your survey or poll is truly anonymous, confidential or "with credit as due," you should first develop it in a short form and pilot test it with individuals who have a similar background to those you hope will participate. In addition to this electronic survey, you can also have a printed version and, of course, enter a professional chat room with your questions. No matter what format you use, your response rate will improve when you offer to share a summary of your results to all those who participate.

Be sure to include the Internet in your search for sites on a specific topic. Anyone can usually browse the information in a guest book or chat archives. If it is an online survey, contact the Webmaster for that site to see if they are willing to share their data. Finally, recognize that surveys and polls conducted on the Internet have limitations, particularly the fact that only "self-selected people" participate in these sessions and participants are not a perfectly reliable cross-section.

# A Closer Look at Joint and Cooperative Ventures

Most local government agencies, particularly those in the human service field, are facing a period of declining resources and conflicting demands. The various "taxpayer' revolts" of recent years underscore the limits of tax-supported services, but many special interest groups are organizing constituencies to lobby for their needs. With less money for funding available, all grant-funded agencies and governing funding authorities must seek to cooperate with other agencies whenever possible. Further, agency cooperation should focus on priority community goals. Successful cooperative arrangements tend to occur when the cooperative activity is a priority for both agencies. As public resources decline, new ways must be found to match needs and resources.

## Philosophical Premise

Throughout American communities worthwhile activities contribute to the well-being of individuals, and thus to the health of society. The provision of opportunities for those services are properly recognized as a governmental obligation. All public agencies are delegated the responsibility for providing communities with health, learning, leisure and other social welfare opportunities.

Thus, agencies are committed to cooperate because of the need to maximize the quality and quantity of programs. Communication and open dialogue in planning, implementing and evaluating the cooperative effort leads to effective programs.

## Legal Provisions

Education and other public and social welfare agencies are authorized by government codes of individual states to organize, promote and conduct programs. These agencies are further authorized to enter into agreements with each other, and to do what is necessary to aid and cooperate in carrying out these purposes.

In summary, the landscape is fairly clear for the joint venture and alliance, however, all parties may have to check their organizational egos at the door, if they are to have a successful and long-running relationship. Legal, payroll and operational questions can be sorted out, but only if the atmosphere allows a frank and friendly exchange, dialogue and partnership.

## How To Structure Cooperative Ventures

It is widely agreed that most cooperative efforts are based on personal relationships between personnel of the different agencies. Although these arrangements often produce short-term results, the cooperative efforts are often discontinued when one of the key personalities leaves. Thus, organizational structures in support of cooperative efforts are highly desirable in addition to, or instead of, reliance on personal relationships.

In some cases model or demonstration projects begun by staff or initiated by "grassroots" involvement are also found useful for pointing out the benefits of cooperative arrangements. However, these cooperative efforts of agency staff must be supported by agency/organizational commitment if long-term results are desired.

## The Fiscal Implications Of Joint Ventures

We will start this discussion with a short guide of the ways that the grant writer can analyze various local situations. These steps, toward establishing a level playing field, enhance the possibility of success in cooperative undertakings. You will want to add other items and topics to this list to take into consideration along with your estimate of local conditions.

## Develop Cooperative Budgeting and Administrative Techniques

One of the chief barriers to interagency cooperation is that agencies do business separately and differently. But many such differences may be compensated for, overcome, or minimized. Here are a few suggestions:

- Determine the budget format. Do they use performance or program budgeting. That way both agencies will be addressing the same or similar budget items and in the same budget style.
- Consider joint recommendations to governing boards of both agencies. Minimize differences in business transactions and procedures, especially where shared staff are concerned.
- Whenever possible, share staff to maximize use of available

resources. Avoid duplicate program administration. Whenever possible, delegate supervision of a joint activity to one agency or the other.

- Use joint assessment and evaluation techniques, especially in establishing cost-benefit determinations.
- Provide for communication among agency staff responsible for fiscal management.

## Prepare Plans for Cooperative Activities

It's a good idea to be open about prospective plans involving interagency cooperation. Plans should be in writing, and information on plans should be available to staff and other interested people. Up to a point, having the most information available before a joint commitment of resources is recommended or made will be better for everyone. Besides giving fiscal data, budget information and cost benefits, cooperative plans should contain such features as:

- Data on assessed needs and interests
- Identification of existing duplication to be eliminated
- Analysis of costs of independent operation vs. costs of cooperation
- A summary of existing cooperative efforts
- The effect on community groups
- Future possibilities related to present plans

## Establish a Common Ground for Fiscal Planning

Mutual benefits and needs should be explored before either agency presents strategies or plans. A common practice is to set up a joint staff committee charged with developing joint recommendations to agency boards or directors. Care should be taken to ensure that:

- Staff and community involvement is encouraged
- Data on needs assessment are shared
- A joint review of community needs, programs and resources is conducted
- The group concentrates on items of joint priority
- Vital fiscal information is shared

## Marshall Resources Needed for Agreed-on Cooperative Activities

It is quite possible that when resources for joint projects are shared, more resources will become available than if the two agencies try separately to obtain resources for similar activities. The social and operational chemistry is different when two agencies jointly accept responsibility to meet a given need, and then treat existing resources as cooperative. This practice is in sharp contrast with that of administrators who agree to cooperate in order that "I can meet my responsibilities to administer my program" in a more effective manner.

Remember also that many resources are the domain of either agency, but can be marshaled to a common cause for community improvement. Community organizations such as Rotary are examples of such outside resources. Outside funding is more possible through cooperative efforts.

## Be Aware of Barriers to Cooperation as Well as Opportunities to Cooperate

Lack of surplus or available resources is not necessarily a barrier to sharing and cooperation. Rather, it may be one of the most telling arguments for cooperation. But there are real barriers. For example:

- Up-front costs often have priority over long-term savings;
- Insurance restrictions and liability problems frighten some administrators;
- Competition for scarce resources and clients creates a climate of distrust;
- Differing agency priorities for use of resources cause misunderstandings;
- Conflicting state, federal and local regulations and policies create frustrations;
- Personal detachment from shared goals or responsibilities hampers effectiveness; and
- Organizational patterns of program planning and budgeting differ.

## Identify Common Priorities for Existing and Needed Resources

Cooperation often occurs spontaneously, for example, when a local recreation director and school superintendent agree to jointly build, maintain, or use an expensive facility such as a swimming pool. Less obvious opportunities for sharing will emerge when joint staff planning committees are brought together.

For example, one of the schools in a low-income area lacked funds and staff to develop or use surrounding land for recreation purposes. Community members in that neighborhood expressed the need for more recreational activities. To meet that need, the city contributed CETA money to the Recreation District, which in turn hired staff for an activities program to be conducted on school grounds. Thus, a three-way cooperative agreement enabled the community agencies to meet the community needs.

## Final Reminders About Cooperative Ventures

- Cooperation begins with motivation. Why are we cooperating? What's in it for us? What's in it for the others?

- Cooperation requires authorization. Who says we can? Who says we should? Is anyone saying we should not, or cannot? Why?

- Cooperation requires common goals. What are we supposed to achieve? Are specific objectives defined in terms all parties fully understand? Are the criteria for success spelled out in language all parties understand?

- Cooperation requires agreement on tasks. What precisely must we do to achieve our goal?

- Cooperation requires division of labor. Who is responsible for each part of each task?

- Cooperation requires achievement of sub-goals. What are our short-term goals, and how will we know when they have been accomplished?

- Cooperation is not a perfectly smooth path. What is the likelihood that we can overcome disagreements and disputes? How will we deal with conflict?

- Cooperation requires respect for others. What are the problems faced by our partners? What are their strengths? What are their weaknesses?

- Cooperation must produce results to be successful. Eventually, the efforts at cooperation must pay off. If the goals have been set unrealistically high, the efforts will be doomed to failure. If they have been set too low, the constituency will reject the effort.

The results must be communicated to all those with a stake in the effort—even those who don't know they have a stake in the effort. It is, finally, the citizens/taxpayers who must be satisfied if cooperative efforts are to produce the desired results.

Finally, to ensure the project will have the best possible chance to succeed, the following activities are suggested:

- Review the literature and research to identify programs that have been effective in dealing with similar problems.

- Visit other agencies that have projects underway designed to alleviate similar needs.

- Develop alternative programs for consideration.

## Joint Ventures With And By Cities And Counties

The main distinctions that funding from cities and counties enjoy is that this level is relatively close to the average citizen, it offers many joint venture possibilities, applicants usually face less competition and if it is a locally originated grant program, you can more easily impact the RFP guidelines and the evaluation standards.

Today, there seems to be a shift in the balance from fund distribution via block grants to distribution through categorical grants. In practical terms, this shifting means there are more local political considerations to take into account when applying for federal grant dollars. For this reason, it is a very good idea to get to know not only the funding officials in Washington but also in the state capital and regional, county and local government offices. Non-profit and community based organizations (NPOs and CBOs) should also meet periodically in round table discussions to consider common interests and possibilities of joint proposals, linkages, etc. These agencies have taken on greater roles since the "tax revolt" of the late 1970s and early 1980s made governments interested in cutting payrolls and contracting out with specialized agencies. Whether it is in regard to governmental agencies or NPOs and CBOs, the greatest amount of funding in the recent past has been for "secondary services"—health, job training, social services and housing—and largely to persons in the lower income groups. The bulk of this money has been in project or categorical grants.

# *Summary*

At this juncture you, and your significant others—direct supervisors, council, commission and, of course, consortium and/or joint venture partners, need to have a serious chat about what you will do about the "fit" between your original ideas and needs and what a given source offers. One alternative you may wish to consider is to break your "wish list" into several smaller fund requests to several different sources. In any event the outcome of this idea refinement meeting should be a plan of action, including work assignments and deadlines.

Grant proposals using joint ventures have as much or perhaps more of a need to be clear and concise since the parties involved are often not at the same physical location and at times may even be "friendly rivals" outside of this project. At the risk of repeating what has been said earlier, we offer the following. 1. Be sure to relate your methodology to your stated goals and objectives in a point-by-point format. Timelines and graphic time charts are useful if not essential. 2. In your timeline, give yourself enough time! Timelines also play a very valuable role in coordination with your colleagues and associates. 3. Be specific about products and deliverables. Your own staff and any cooperating organizations or joint venture partners, must "buy off" on the tasks, deliverables and products, and deadlines. When you do this you are on the right track, when you don't, you could be heading toward disaster. Next up is advice on how to dissect a proposal and keep track of the vital parts.

## Sample Outline of a Joint Proposal

A joint proposal to study, analyze, evaluate, and ultimately create a state agency mortgage guarantee insurance program for:
- low to moderate income first time home-buyers
- multi family rental housing for low and moderate income consumers

## Tasks

1. **Identify and describe the problems**
   *(Our Department Does This)*
   A. identify and describe the problems
      1. first time buyers
      2. rental housing owners
   B. provide a description of the effect on mortgage credit availability that mortgage guarantee insurance would provide
   C. how underwriting and pricing criteria could be adjusted
   D. alternative methods for payment of the coverage premium
   E. options to be exercised in the event of default.

2. **Analysis of proposed solutions**
   *(Your Department Does This)*
   A. handling of the ratio and amount of coverage consistent with lender risk exposure
   B. various options of restructuring the reserve requirements
   C. appropriate cancellation and claims policies for such a program

3. **Financial and Administrative aspects of the proposed solutions**
   *(Our Third Party Consultant Does This)*
   A. various methods to capitalize the insurance fund
      1. at little cost to the state

    2. at no cost to the state
- B. administrative options
  1. use existing programs
  2. new state programs
     - a. with local governments
     - b. with the dreaded private sector

## Methodology
1. **literature search**
2. **surveys of selected key informants**
   - A. individuals involved in government mortgage insurance programs
   - B. lenders
   - C. real estate licensees who work in the subject area

## Products
1. **criteria presently used by mortgage insurers**
2. **adjustments deemed necessary to implement a new program**
3. **problems foreseen in program implementation**
4. **recommendations**

## Background Of The Proposal Team
- A. demonstrated knowledge of mortgage guarantee services
- B. knowledge and practical experience relating to the development of government programs
- C. experience with developing private programs
- D. State University as a research entity
- E. Financial and organizational features

## Sample Joint Venture Letter

Memorandum

June 26, 2002

TO: Colleagues in the Department of Finance, Real Estate and Law. School of Business; Department of Economics, School of Social and Behavioral Science

FROM: _____, (title)
 Student Services Division, State University

SUBJECT: Joint Proposal from State University (SU) to the Dept. of Real Estate—"Feasibility of a State—Sponsored Mortgage Guarantee Program for Low and Moderate Income Home Buyers"

The following is an outline of a possible SU proposal that we would like you to consider. The topic is an important one for all state residents and one in which I am sure parties in your department will have an interest and expertise to offer. We would appreciate your circulating the attached outline and RFP to interested persons. We have scheduled a no-host luncheon meeting for Monday, April 29, at noon in the Chart House Restaurant to consider the feasibility of our campus submitting this grant.

The amount of funds allocated to the study is $160,000 and the work must be accomplished within 190 days, probably beginning mid May 2003.

While there is a relatively short lead time for this submission, I believe we can have a very competitive proposal if we can get an early start and collective assistance in the next week or so. If you cannot attend the Monday meeting, please give me a call at (123) 456-7890 and let me know if you and/or other parties might be interested.

Thank you.

Attachments (2)
"Feasibility of a State-Sponsored Mortgage Guarantee Program for Low and Moderate Income Home Buyers"

CHAPTER 7

# Dissecting the Request for Proposal

◆ **What is the real purpose of the RFP to the funding source and to the organization seeking funds?**

◆ **Is there anything that I should do with the RFP when it first arrives?**

◆ **After I submit my grant proposal, does the RFP still have any importance to me and our project?**

**A**s you go about this task, it has been proven useful to build some checklists and outlines as you go along. Consider creating these six checklists as you dissect the RFP and organize your grant writing ideas:

- Required elements of the proposal as taken from the RFP
- A checklist of the deadlines, addresses, contact names and numbers
- The essential "packaging" instructions, i.e., number of copies, sent where, how reproduced, forms requiring original signatures
- The narrative of the methodology section of your proposal
- A list of the key words, hot buttons or sizzle sentences that are pertinent to proposals in this topical area
- A list that reviews the officers or key staff of the funding source and indicates personal or professional contacts.

These outlines and checklists could be copied on colored paper and shared with those on your grant writing team. You might also want to put information for each project, or each funding source, into one of the many database programs offered by software manufacturers. That way you will have an electronic version of critical information that can be easily transmitted, shared, updated and downloaded for future proposals. Very likely you will need to consult these lists regularly and will want to be able to find them easily.

The balance of this chapter features some more strategic advice. This includes how to add materials not directly required by the RFP that make your organization look good, tips for developing a network of contacts and sources for assistance in writing grant proposals and the establishment and maintenance of an effective referral system.

## *Organizing to Respond to the RFP*

Writing a grant has been made much easier with the invention of computers. For those who sit outside of the realm of technical things, you can still be successful, but hopefully you will have a friend or two with word processing wizardry.

Computers become critical allies because there is almost never enough time to leisurely prepare a grant proposal. The ability of computers to ease editing, updating, revising and storing of information is critical. Simple rough notes or key words can be saved and first put into outlines, then sentences, followed by a full blown and complete proposal.

Staff biographies, name lists, demographic data and like material can be stored as a "boilerplate" and dropped in with a keystroke or the touch of a button. To ease the grant writing process, find and become familiar with a computer word processing program and locate a machine or two to use. If you can acquire, beg, or borrow a laptop or notebook computer, you can even turn brainstorming notes and field interviews into priceless prose with (almost) considerable ease.

Another important first step is to play what veteran grant writers call the "rough budget game." As the name implies, this is an exercise in which the prospective grant applicant roughly estimates the actual costs of doing the work required and examines if the "profit," overhead, and/or salary figures are sufficient incentive to A. do the work, and B. inspire the organization to sponsor the application. This is another of the "go or no go" decision points in which the romance, excitement and thrill of the grant chase is put aside in favor of a realistic, candid and conservative appraisal of what the proposed program will cost and if, in simple terms, it is worth the effort if the grant is awarded.

A logical next step is to overlay the above rough budget process with the odds of being selected as the successful applicant. If the margins are close, and the odds very long, the "no go" or decline to submit decision may well be in order.

The deadline for grant submission, as well as any internal deadlines, is important to know and understand. Is a postmark acceptable, or must the proposal actually be in-hand by a certain date? How much time is required for internal clearance? All of these items should be part of the grant writer's personal calendar and are as critical in deciding whether or not to apply as the budgeting process just described. In addition, make sure that the persons in authority who may need to sigh off on your proposal will be available on the days, or hours, when you expect to need their signature. Be respectful of the lead time they may need to read and review, and possibly change, your document. Also, have in mind alternate authority figures who can sign in their absence if a given individual in the approval stream is suddenly unavailable.

## Flexibility of Funding Sources

The notion of flexibility among funding sources has long intrigued grant writers. Some proposers become very strategic in their plans to "attack" a grant source. Even for those organizations and individuals who are less competitive, it is useful to have an idea of the level of flexibility for an agency and/or program. The Ladder of Funder Flexibility. Figure 5 divides agencies into three main categories,

Open, Constrained, and Rigid with degrees or levels within each.

The most unstructured funding source is placed on step one of the Ladder. These are funding programs with no RFP, no deadlines, and no goals statement. This type of program simply accepts inquires year around without any particular preferences. The disadvantages of this type of an agency to the grant writer is that this total lack of guidance may well result in your doing a lot of work for people who are not interested in your efforts.

The second step on the ladder is for agencies with program goals only, meaning that they decide on an annual or similar basis what broad issues they want proposals to address, i.e. homeless women, children at risk, migrant labor, and then leave the actual approach, cost, details, to the grant seeker.

In the next level, step three, referred to as "constrained", some of the "openness" of the bottom rungs disappear. A step three funding source has an RFP procedure, but is a source open to year round proposals.

Step four is for organizations that require an RFP and are open to proposals only for a specific period or periods of time, i.e. quarterly. Although these sources have specific, limited, time periods in which they consider new proposals, they are open to a wide variety of organizations. There are more funding sources at this level than any other level.

The funding sources found on step five are only open to proposals at one specific time and applicants/bidders must meet certain, specific qualifications to be eligible.

The least flexible level, labeled Rigid, is the type of agency that requires a pre-proposal letter, in a sense a query letter or mini-proposal, prior to allowing the applicant to submit a full proposal. Although step six agencies may seem to be hard nosed, this is a more humane approach than the unstructured approach since the sponsoring organization invests some of their time evaluating your ideas before you prepare a full proposal, the production of which is time consuming and costly. After screening these pre-proposals, the sponsoring organization may realign their RFP, withdraw it, or proceed to solicit proposals from invited organizations.

The top rung of the Ladder of Funder Flexibility, step seven, is for agencies and organizations that demand that potential applicants submit general qualifications, references and the like for the agencies file. This RFQ (request for qualifications) process appears elitist and discriminatory against new organizations and groups, but is designed, like Step 6, to have only the most likely-to-be-funded proposers investing their time and effort on a proposal. It also allows the funding organization to know in detail the special qualifications of organizations available in the marketplace.

More and more local governments are using the RFQ process in

## *Ladder of Funder Flexibility*
## *Type of Agency Contact*

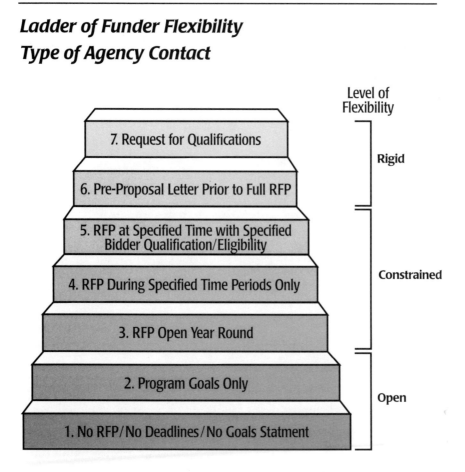

Level of Flexibility

7. Request for Qualifications

Rigid

6. Pre-Proposal Letter Prior to Full RFP

5. RFP at Specified Time with Specified Bidder Qualification/Eligibility

4. RFP During Specified Time Periods Only

Constrained

3. RFP Open Year Round

2. Program Goals Only

Open

1. No RFP/No Deadlines/No Goals Statment

*Finding Funding:*
*The Comprehensive Guide to Grant Writing*                    Figure 5

their re-granting of monies to local agencies. This process restricts the number of proposals to those with the best chance of getting funded, unearths information about new agencies or agencies who have recently changed or enlarged their scope of services and softens the blow to less-qualified grant seekers before they invest their time and effort in preparing a full proposals.

## The Elements Of A Typical RFP

While there really is no typical RFP, most of what you may encounter will have some or all of the following information. Of course, if you find some important information missing, you should certainly contact the funding source for clarification. However, wait until you have a full list of questions, as opposed to making repeated calls and thus giving the appearance of being disorganized.

- **Name of the agency**. Be sure to note all divisions, offices, etc. of the sponsoring organization since your materials may not be routed properly if your are not precise.
- **Name or title of the program or project to be funded**. Copy this information correctly and be alert for program numbers as well as words, i.e., A Title VII Project #92:036 "Study of the Whooping Crane in West Virginia."
- **Eligibility**. Who may apply? Individuals, organizations, only governments, groups meeting certain standards, etc.
- **Deadline**. The date or dates the proposal must be in. Check also to see if postmarked material is acceptable. Call if this is not clear.
- **Purpose of the proposal/narrative**. As noted later in this chapter, this may include what the sponsor feels is important in such categories as need, objective, procedures/activities, project management, budget, location, facilities, personnel, preferences and/or set asides (i.e., money pre-allocated only for special groups such as Indian tribes, small businesses, minority groups, youth, inner city projects), etc.

- **Cost and price information**. This may be expressed in a dollar amount, or left open.
- **Evaluation and other matters**. Here the sponsor may indicate on what basis a proposal will be reviewed, selected, special areas that are priorities with the sponsor, etc.

## Dissecting the RFP: A summary and some samples

Much as a scientist or medical doctor would dissect an organism to see what the key elements are, so should the grant writer dissect the rules of the road, the RFP, to be better prepared for writing a winning proposal. The following six items are key questions or points for our examination:

- Eligibility
- Dates and deadlines
- Fit with your needs
- Fit with your staffing
- Joint venture possibilities
- Appropriate dollars

It might be useful for you to write the answers to each of these questions on a separate card, or as part of your Grant Action File. It will be useful in both selling your proposal to your internal customer, your supervisors, council or commission, as well as to your joint venture partners and ultimately to the funding source. Let's now turn our attention to internal clearances.

## Obtaining Clearances

- Internal deadlines may be very early
- Determine the deadlines of your joint venture partners
- Allow time to re-connect with your own bosses
- Make sure the dollars are in the right spots and everybody agrees

The "traditional" RFP also has some interesting aspects that deserve special attention. First, the agency gives a nice philosophical point of view at the outset. Carefully read and re-read this, and try to reference these overall perspectives in your final proposal. The 12 categories seem to cover a wide spectrum, but the grant reader should be a little suspicious as to whether any agency really would give equal emphasis to such a wide range of topics. The informational meeting or bidders conference or the funding source liaison may give a clue to which topics are most likely to be funded. Finally, with the list of cities to be served, this RFP seems to invite services that will cross more than one town boundary, thus a joint venture, a small consortium proposal, or similar arrangement would appear to have high funding potential.

### Protest of Awards and Appeal of Decisions

Approach a funding source that has rejected a proposal in a friendly manner, since repeat proposals often are successful. However, your boss, council, or colleagues may want to know why the proposal was not selected, so from the perspective of "how can we make this better in the future" carefully ask for a review of a failed proposal. Ask for information on who the successful applicant was, and this in turn could be an opportunity for a sub-contract, or a subsequent alliance or joint venture.

## *Special Considerations*

You can appreciate the mix of science and art that will come into writing the proposal. At times you must be precise and "color within the lines," and at times be creative, innovative and imaginative. The challenge of balancing these duties within the often restricted time frame that one has to meet a grant deadline is significant.

There are a number of tips for when you feel that the guidelines in front of you don't fit the needs that you and your organization have. We suggest revisiting your source lists.

## *Problems are usually categorized into one of three areas:*

- The RFP is not broad enough in terms of tasks
- They are not a perfect hit in terms of funding levels (to low or too high!)
- You do not meet their preferred funding source profile in terms of staffing, service area, etc.

## *We offer the following "fixes" to the above dilemma:*

- Don't forget to use your key informants and special interest groups for advice on other places you might look.
- Contact (preferably by email) professional specialists including the staff of legislators. You can find them in the directories of the Congress, state legislature, etc.
- Revisit your key informants and keep on searching on the Internet.

Another proactive step you can take at this point is to use the Grant Makers Decision Tree (see Figure 6, on page 130) to decide if you want to go forward or not. Note the questions as you go down the tree, and the "branching" that takes place depending on whether or not you answer "yes" or "no" to each question. Sometimes a decision to not go forward, or go back to the drawing boards, is the best choice of all.

The following are samples of typical RFPs submitted in the human service area. The first is an innovative form where the proposers have more leeway to be creative. The second is more traditional, where the grant writer is directed to propose services in predetermined categories. Compare and contrast these two forms and imagine how you would respond to them. How would you organize your time and effort to meet the deadline with a quality effort? Filling out the sample proposal form at the end of this chapter will give you the opportunity to imagine how your proposal would have been rated. When you have finished that exercise you will better understand some typical RFPs and project rating systems. Knowing what agencies typically look for, what they value and to what degree they value it, should be of considerable assistance in building a successful proposal.

# Some Samples Of An RFP

In the RFP samples at the end of this chapter you can observe some of the nuances and differences found in typical RFPs. When you first get a new RFP it is usually good to make several copies and put the forms away for safe keeping. That way you can mark up and note the RFP and still have a "clean" copy for later. Now let's examine in some detail the samples included.

## The Grant Writer's Decision Tree

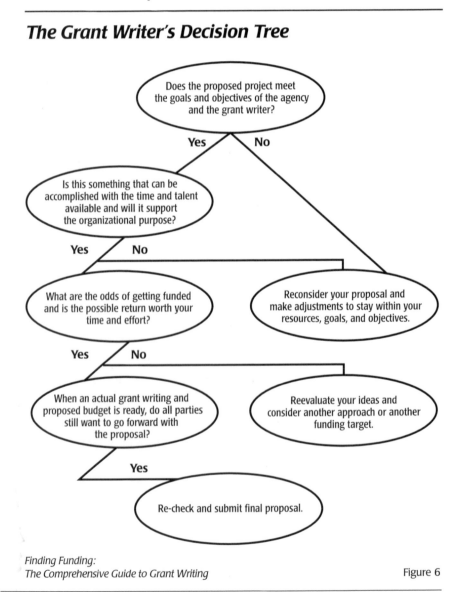

*Finding Funding:*
*The Comprehensive Guide to Grant Writing*

Figure 6

Looking first at the Child Development RFP found at the end of this chapter, you will notice in Section I-B that the funding source has already provided you with definitions of key terms. It is advisable to accept these definitions unless you feel you must challenge them for some important reason. In Section III certain specific qualifications are mentioned and again these are areas that need to be stressed, i.e., "bilingual/bicultural services..." and later in III A 2. "cooperative and collaborative networks...." In this case the funder also wants a current organization chart, which surprisingly, many grant seekers don't have at the ready. Allow time to get this together since the strain of deciding on who's where in your own organization chart may prove more challenging to the applicant agency than any collection of grant elements. Similarly to the problems of producing an organization chart where none previously existed (or was woefully out of date) is the frustration the grant writer can face when answering questions in III A 3, Funding Base. If incomplete records of past activities are all that you have, they will not be a very good reflection on the competency of your agency to apply for new funds. Again, many a grant writer in the past has had to "tidy up" old records in order to answer the questions on a new RFP.

The "traditional" RFP also has some interesting aspects that deserve special attention. First of all, the agency gives a fairly nice philosophical point of view at the outset. Carefully read and re-read this and try and reference these overall perspectives in your final proposal. The 12 categories seem to cover a wide spectrum but the grant reader should be a little suspicious as to whether any agency really would give equal emphasis to such a wide range of topics. The informational meeting or bidders conference or the funding source liaison may give a clue to which topics are most likely to be funded. And finally, with the list of cities to be served, this RFP seems to invite services which will cross more than one town boundary, thus a joint venture, a small consortium proposal, or similar arrangement would appear to have a fairly high funding potential.

Overall, to borrow a transit analogy, the RFP is a road map, with most but not all the details. There are generally more clues and guideposts than are noticed on the first inspection. There are definitely a number of "stop" and "go" signs: a list of pre-conditions, expectation, and rewards. Punishments and appeals are occasionally included depending on the attitude of the funding source. The more legalistic they are the more stringent (and usually longer) the RFP is. The key is to fully understand what is wanted by what they say, develop your list of questions and concerns about what they don't say or have not said clearly, and get answers either through the bidders conference/informational meetings or by direct contact with the program liaison. The funding source truly wants a successful applicant. They must in many cases "use it" (the grant funds) or "lose it" (not be able to give as much next year) so beyond their natural concern for bettering conditions in the area of their responsibility they have practical reasons for wanting a successful project. You want the same thing, it is just a matter of finding the common ground.

# The Review Process

The following discussion is to help you, the proposal writer, better understand the review process, the criteria for selecting proposals and some questions you should address in making clear to the reviewers your knowledge and ability to conduct the project.

Proposals are usually logged into the funding agency by their proposal number. Therefore, it is mandatory you have the correct identification number on the cover page or as otherwise directed. Funding agencies often suggest a title for the project and prefer that you use their title. In some instances the agency may ask that you put no identifying information on the cover page so that reviewers select proposals strictly on merit. Read and reread the instructions and if in doubt make an inquiry as to proper format.

Reviewers are then selected and assembled in one place to evaluate proposals. They are given a criteria point system such as the one below on which to judge each proposal. They will be looking for a strong emphasis on the feasibility of conducting the project and the commitment of your agency to carry out the work. Although you should attempt to be concise in the writing of the proposal itself, appropriate supporting documentation is essential. After a thorough review of proposals, agency staff contacts the winning applicants, and the tentative award letter is sent.

## Proposal Review Criteria

The following review criteria were taken from an RFP and are presented here as an example of what funding agencies look for in a proposal. The numbers at the right side of the initial heading are the percentages that each section count in the review process. These "points" are used by the reviewers as a baseline for each section. The discussion that we have included in each section is presented in an actual review form as questions might ask by the reviewers as they study and rate the proposal. This list finishes with a discussion of "negotiation" which is often (but not always) an important part of the selection and award process.

# Sample of a Proposal Review and Rating Point System

## Sample Review Form

**1. Need**                                   *Maximum points — 5*

Present your concise and direct overall awareness and understanding of the need and how this proposal will bring improvement or solution.

In addition to the specific criteria for evaluation of the proposal, the reviewers will consider how you are addressing the problem, your capacity to conduct the project, the feasibility of your procedure and the broader impact as a contribution to the improvement being sought.

**2. Objectives**                           *Maximum points — 10*

State the objectives which must be attained to complete

the project. Objectives should be stated in measurable terms.

Describe how you will bring about the outcomes you desire. The objectives should clearly relate to the need (problem). The activities should clearly relate to the objectives. The cost (budget) should clearly relate to each activity and objective. The cost to attain each objective must be indicated.

### 3. Procedures/Activities          *Maximum points* — **15**

Describe the procedures and/or activities that will be utilized to accomplish each of the project objectives. Each activity must be accompanied by a budget factor.

Describe the sequence of activities utilizing a time line with narration. In order to help communicate the key features of the approach you are taking to accomplish your objectives, give consideration to the following: What specific actions will be made possible by the project- Who will be the change agents undertaking these actions- Why did you select this approach to achieve your objectives (have you tried it on a more modest scale, or do you know of experimentation with it)- What reasons can you give to believe your approach to the need would work, regardless of the fact that it has never been tried- What easily recognizable "products" can you produce-

### 4. Project Management          *Maximum points* — **30**

Provide a detailed management plan for the operation of the project.

Indicate evidence of the commitment of project staff, describing their responsibilities and the amount of time they will be devoting to project activities. Provide a description of their prior experience related to the subject area of this project and a resume for each of the principal project staff. A description of the duties, responsibilities and experience of each subcontractor and a resume for each of the principal staff must be submitted. Prospective contractors must include a list of similar consulting contracts undertaken and successfully concluded.

Under the section "Project Management" you must describe prior experience and the capabilities of the project director and staff. The reviewers will be making a judgment as to whether the project is realistically capable of showing performance in terms of the people and funds allocated to the task. At this point it is vitally important to remember some classic marketing advice, the essence of which is that too often sellers do not understand buyers. The concept is critical if the grant writer is to "get into the mind" of the grant giver.

Knowing then what the "buyer" wants, the proposal should provide evidence of commitment to the success of the project. Indicate a track record of success in this type of activity. Has your institution or firm allocated any of its own resources to the project- Have the potential beneficiaries been involved in the planning. Does the success of the project depend on agencies or institutions other than your own and have they made a commitment to the conduct of the project- Have those who will implement the project been involved in the planning- If not, and the key personnel are to be chosen later, be sure to include a complete job description and the duties of such personnel.

**5. Location/Facilities**                         *Maximum points — **10***

Identify the headquarters, site(s), and location(s) of the project activities and show evidence they are available when needed.

Describe how and why locations/facilities for project activities were selected.

**6. Budget**                                      *Maximum points — **15***

Provide a detailed budget, including an explanation of how the funds of this project will be expended. Include specific rates and amounts.

Show the proposed cost of each activity (See Activities).

Provide a summary of the budget using the form shown on Exhibit E.

At this point usually if it is government funding the federal or state Department of General Services must approve contracts, and is now placing an emphasis on the cost effectiveness of projects funded through the programs. Although cost has always been a significant factor in reviewing proposals, this new emphasis is being stressed because of recent legislation and requirements to attain the greatest value for the tax dollar. Private funding have guidelines too but generally are less stringent.

**7. Evaluation**                    *Maximum points — * **15**

Describe the in-house or external formative and summative evaluation methods to be used with this project and the methods to be used in treating evaluation data. Identify both immediate and long-range outcomes and the relation of those to the need statement.

In the "Evaluation Section," describe how you intend to determine whether your project has accomplished its objectives. You should be able to identify some threshold indicators of success for immediate objectives. Indicators of success should be responsive to the objectives, since evaluation is measuring outcomes against pre-stated goals and objectives.

## Notification of Award

Notification of proposed awards and denials of awards are usually mailed to all competitors on the same day a notice of the proposed awards has been posted. Funding agencies will usually notify by telephone those proposers whose projects have been selected. Successful bidders must agree to all terms and conditions of any resultant grant with the sponsoring agency.

If you make the final cut, the funding source may also request additional and more detailed information of your organization or from all of the "finalists." In case of very large grants, finalist organizations may be required to make a presentation to the agency staff. Following all presentations, the agency will select and execute an agreement with the organization whose proposals most closely respond to the program's goals and objectives.

If, in the judgement of the agency, submissions made at any stage of the process are unacceptable, they usually reserve the right to reject any and all submissions and to re-advertise the opportunity. If you find yourself on the grant giving side of the process, you would be well advised to have some solid proposal rating sheets ready to inform inquiring applicants of their relative strengths and weaknesses in the hope that they will improve their proposals in future years.

## Negotiation of the Grant

Negotiation of the grant is often (but not always) an important part of the selection and award process. While a proposed Grantee will be selected because of the quality of the proposal submitted in relation to other proposals received, it does not necessarily mean that the grant will end up being written exactly as proposed. Often proposals contain requests not in keeping with the agency's policies, or objectives may be included which are not appropriate within the mandate of the enabling legislation. These types of problems, as well as the need to introduce the proposed grantee to the specific policies and procedures that will be employed during the monitoring of the grant, often mandate the need for a face-to-face meeting between the proposed grantee and funding agency staff.

Following announcement of the proposed award, the funding agency program officer will contact the proposed grantee. This person may be called the agency grant consultant, or liaison. The program officer will identify areas of change necessary (if any) to execute the grant offer. A site and time will then be arranged for grant negotiation if necessary. Often, grant negotiation (the fiscal part) is done by conference telephone call. The grant manager has responsibility for including appropriate personnel in the negotiation process. The agency may also specify extra duties for the grantee such as periodic project reports.

Upon completion of the negotiation, a mutually agreed scope of work, budget and any special provisions necessary will be completed. The grantee will have been apprised of all policies and procedures of the funding agency that affect the grant. The agency staff will then complete the appropriate documents and guide the grant toward execution.

## Common Causes for Rejection

The following are the most common causes of rejection or denial of a grant award:

- Submission of an incomplete proposal (failure to provide required documents).
- Failure to use or altering required forms or formats.
- Non-responsive to RFP—not responding to specific RFP goals and objectives.
- Proposing organization is technically ineligible.

## Protest of Awards and Appeal of Decisions

It is not advised to approach a funding source that has rejected a proposal in less than a friendly manner since repeat proposals often are successful. However, your boss, council, or colleagues may want to know why the proposal was not selected, so from the perspective of "how can we make this better in the future" carefully ask for a review of a failed proposal. Sometimes you may also ask and receive information on who the successful applicant was, and this in turn could be an opportunity for a sub-contract or a subsequent alliance or joint venture.

When an agency wishes to protest or appeal a tentative award decision, they must usually file a written protest. The protest must usually be received by the granting agency within two weeks of the posting of tentative awards, and must include a full and complete written statement specifying grounds for the protest. Protests are usually limited to procedural grounds such as the two following:

- The funding agency failed to apply correctly the standards for evaluating the proposals as specified in the request for proposal. Consult the project liaison for timelines and procedures

- The funding agency is proposing to award the grant to a bidder other than the bidder given the highest score by the agency evaluation committee, however don't get your hopes too high because they usually have rules that allow this.

Note that each funding agency will specify its own grounds for protest. It is often a good idea to review the "problem" other applicants have experienced as well as the success stories.

This form of follow-up, conducted in a friendly non-adversarial manner, displays interest and offers insights that can yield dividends in subsequent proposals.

## A Final Note

As a first step in gaining some of the knowledge and techniques needed to respond to Requests for Proposals (RFPs), Requests for Bids (RFB's), Requests for Qualifications (RFQs) and similar program announcements, this chapter features a section on the review process that most proposals go through. Study the sample RFPs included in this chapter and answer the study questions that follow. This will assist you in identifying the critical parts of an RFP and help you learn how to dissect key elements so that you can identify all required RFP parts and understand their purpose. A point-by-point discussion of what is needed to respond to the RFP's various elements as seen by proposal reviewers is also included.

# Sample RFPs

The following are three sample RFPs on Child Development, Housing, and Education. You will note that although they have some common elements, each RFP requires slightly different information.

## Child Development RFP Sample

The material that follows was taken directly from an RFP that was issued from the Office of Child Abuse Prevention, a state agency.

## I.  Introduction

    A.  Purpose

The Office of Child Abuse Prevention (OCAP) within the Department of Social Services (DSS) is calling for proposals to fund innovative child abuse and neglect prevention and intervention programs in accordance with the Welfare and Institutions Code. The total funding available is $169,000 for FY XX-XX (January 1, 20XX through June 30, 20XX) with a projected $336,000 for FY XX-XX. One project will be selected for each of the three geographic areas to provide the following:

- Innovative support services to Asian families at risk of abuse and neglect or involved with CPS. Project design must include effective techniques to secure participation by culturally and linguistically diverse families.

    B.  Definition

        1.  Innovative:

An innovative project design is one in which there are new or changed services or service mixes. This RFP is seeking unique approaches to: outreach, use of resources, techniques in securing participation and/or meeting the needs of culturally and linguistically diverse or geographically dispersed families.

        2.  Asian Families:

The target population for this RFP is the Asian family. For the purpose of this proposal, "Asian" shall be defined broadly to include the various people who have immigrated to California from the cluster of 32 countries in the Pacific Rim: including China, Japan, Korea, Philippines, Samoa, Tonga, Malaysia and Indochina [Vietnam, Cambodia, Thailand]. Although specific programs will vary according to community need, the primary function of innovative projects for Asian families is to provide access to services for a population traditionally reluctant to seek help because of language and culture differences.

## II. Scope of Proposal

A. Goals of Innovative Projects for Asian Families:

- To reduce the incidence of child abuse in California's Asian population.
- To provide "innovative child-centered approaches that indicate promise of quality cost-effective services to prevent child abuse and neglect." [Ch. 1398, AB 1733 Papan]
- To emphasize positive cultural values.
- To support voluntary family involvement with service programs when families are in crisis.

B. Description of Activities

- Projects selected for funding will provide a specific service or a range of service to suit their particular community and target population. Although innovative program design will be the basis for selection, a range of services may be applicable for this population. Attached is a list of program activities currently funded. This list provides examples only; other services are allowable.
- Data Collection: Each project shall keep records and conduct an internal evaluation. Each project shall also be evaluated independently by an evaluation grantee selected by OCAP. Information will be collected as requested by OCAP and the organization conducting the independent evaluation. This information will be provided to OCAP and the independent evaluator for monitoring, evaluation and research purposes. Willingness to cooperate in this evaluation process will be a condition of grant awards. The organization chosen to conduct the external evaluation will be required to protect the confidentiality of information.
- Reports: Projects will be required to provide OCAP with quarterly progress reports and a final summary report within 45 days of the grant termination date.
- Criteria for Continued Funding After the First Six Months: To qualify for continued funding during FY XX-XX, each agency or organization must meet the following goals:

(a) Submission at time of grant renewal of a detailed budget and scope of work for FY XX-XX.

(b) Submission at time of grant renewal of a letter of support from the local county department concerning dependent children as described in W&IC Section 300, to wit, the welfare and/or probation department, indicating continued support and cooperation with the funded agency.

(c) Overall successful performance of the terms of the grant, to be determined by DSS-OCAP.

## III. Instructions for Proposal Content

A.  Agency Background                                   **25 points Total**

This section should be no more than ten [10] double-spaced typewritten pages.

1.  Agency/Program Activities                         **5 points**

This section should be no more than two (2) double-spaced typewritten pages. Give a brief description of your current activities, services and program including the following:

- Identification and discussion of past and current child abuse and neglect prevention and intervention activities. Discuss any barriers or obstacles to success encountered and what your organization learned from the situation.

- Agency's capabilities for providing services to minority [specifically Asian] populations. Include your agency's capabilities for providing bilingual/bicultural services and give specific examples of previous coordinated efforts with minority service agencies and community organizations.

2.  Organization Structure                            **5 points**

This section should be no more than two [2] double-spaced typewritten pages. Give a brief description of your organization, including the following:

- When, how and why organization was stated:

- Statement of purpose, goals and philosophy;
- Cooperative and collaborative networks with other like organizations;
- Copy of organization chart;

3. Funding Base: **5 points**

This section should be no more than two [2] double-spaced typewritten pages.

- Provide a list of funding sources and amounts for the past three [3] years of operation. Identify by program title, funding source, amount of grant, indicate if ongoing [spread sheet format is preferred].
- Identify any special contribution capabilities of the bidder such as the ability to assume any costs for such items as equipment, facilities, supplies and services of volunteers. Describe how these funds will be used to support and/or enhance funding requested in your proposal. CAPIT has a mandatory minimum 10 percent in-kind "match."
- If your agency is private nonprofit, provide information demonstrating past fiscal responsibility. Bidders are encouraged to submit a completed copy of a current financial report, preferably completed by a Certified Public Accountant. Information about any failures or refusals to complete a contract or grant must be provided.

4. Current Personnel **5 points**

This section should be no more than two [2] typewritten double-spaced pages. Give a brief description of personnel used in the provision of child abuse and neglect prevention and intervention activities, including the following:

- Identify current staff and recruitment method.
- Identify how current staff use culturally/linguistically sensitive treatment modalities to the population served.

5. Meeting the Needs of Asian Families **5 points**

Describe past Agency/Program Activities related to the

needs of the target population—Asian Families. This section should be no more than two [2] double-spaced typewritten pages.

- Describe your community and how your current program met the need for services.
- Identify how your program interfaces and networks with other programs within the community.

B. Program Narrative (Total 40 points)

This section should be no more than ten (10) double-spaced typewritten pages.

1. Population to be served                                    **10 points**

   Give a description of the following:

   - Identification of geographic and cultural diversity of the Asian population in your community.
   - Identification of population and proposed number to be served. Be specific in terms of age groups, ethnicity, language and culture, and areas where services are to be provided.

2. Program purpose and description                  **10 points**

   Give a description of the following:

   - Proposed program, in order to meet the needs of Asian families and children who are at high risk of child abuse or neglect.
   - How the program will provide services addressing the cultural and linguistic needs of the population.

3. Innovativeness                                             **10 points**

   Discuss the ways in which you regard your project design as innovative [e.g., in design of services, service mixes, efficient use of existing or inexpensive resources, selection of target population and techniques to secure participation by high-risk parents, meeting the needs of culturally and linguistically diverse or geographically dispersed families, etc.

4. Personnel to be used                                    **10 points**

   Give a description of the following:

- Staff to be added to your organization and volunteers used in order to implement proposed program. Provide job descriptions and minimum qualifications for those staff positions directly involved in child abuse and neglect prevention and intervention activities.
- How staffing reflects the cultural and geographic nature of the community, including multi-cultural/bilingual staff.
- If subcontractors will be used, include descriptions of their staff and services they will provide. The grantee will be held responsible for the performance of any subcontractor(s) utilized.

C. Scope of Work                                    **Total 20 points**

Prepare a scope of work for a period of six months: January—June 20XX. Also prepare a 12-month projected scope of work for the next FY [XX-XX]. Use the attached form to prepare the scope of work. The form may be duplicated, but not altered. Copy and attach as many pages as you need to present your scope of work. This section should be of such quality that it "stands alone," giving the reader a clear idea of what you are doing to assess your activities. The scope of work should provide the following:

- Identification of specific goals and specific objectives related to the goals. They should be realistic, time-based and measurable.
- Goal: A goal is a broad general statement of what you plan to accomplish with your program. This may be one goal for the program or separate goals for identifiable and distinguishable areas of your program.
- Objective: An objective is a single sentence that states what you are going to do. Objectives are the bound, measurable statements that lead to accomplishing the goal.
- Implementation Activities: Specific activities that you will do to accomplish your stated objectives. Most objectives require several steps. Program details are included here.

- Time Lines: Each time line should indicate when you will start and finish each activity for the objective. For most activities, stating the entire grant period as the time line for the activity is inappropriate. Time lines give the time sequence that activities follow.

## Self Review Questions For The "Child Development" RFP

- As a guide to checking your ability to dissect an RFP why not try these questions on yourself and see how you might answer them if this were a real grant writing
- What do you know about the agency making the request for proposals? What would you like to know that you do not find in the RFP?
- How large, in dollars, do you think your hypothetical proposal under this competition should be? What could you do to find out more about the optimum grant size?
- Briefly describe the target population. If your community or service area does not have all the target population, how would you handle it?
- What is the general nature of the type of service or activity the sponsors will fund? How do you show that you can do that? Where in the proposal will you have the chance to make your case for the innovative content of your proposal?
- What should you be prepared to tell about your organization, yourself and your associates-?
- Are there any special rules for the budget of this project? What comments could you make about funding in general and the expectations about the continuity of effort?

## Housing RFP Sample

### Introduction And Program Requirement

The Orange County Housing Authority (OCHA) is the largest provider of rental assistance to lower-income families in your state.

In spite of its effort, thousands of low-income families remain on the authority's waiting list for assistance. Median rents are among the 10 highest in the country. A rental vacancy rate of under 3% makes affordable rental housing very scarce. Therefore, the need to develop new resources to address the rental housing needs of low-income families is considered to be one of the highest priorities of the Orange County Housing Authority (OCHA).

OCHA Operating Reserve Committee will accept proposals from public and non-profit private agencies or organizations to provide innovative housing services for low-income families.

OCHA is specifically interested in projects that can demonstrate a need for a new service, that can revolve their funding or make pay-back arrangements, and that would have a good opportunity to attract outside funding to allow the project to continue operating.

Projects must primarily address the needs of very low-income families (those making 50%-and-below the Department of Housing and Urban Development median income as adjusted for family size).

### Examples of categories that will be considered are as follows:
- Counseling, referral and advisory services for purchasers
- Rental maintenance or repair of housing for low-income persons
- Shared Housing
- Cooperative Housing
- Education or Training Programs
- Self-Help Housing
- Revolving Fund Programs
- Rehabilitation Programs
- Programs Affecting Safety
- Public Information
- Research or Special Studies
- Housing Service Projects (example: homeless, handicapped, etc.)

### Funding may be in the form of the following:
- Initial grant for loan for start-up cost/demonstration project.
- Loan for expansion of established project. Terms to be negotiated.

### Service provided must be in the following jurisdictions:

| | | |
|---|---|---|
| Buena Park | La Habra | San Juan Capistrano |
| Costa Mesa | La Palma | Seal Beach |
| Cypress | Los Alamitos | Stanton |
| Fountain Valley | Newport Beach | Tustin |
| Fullerton | Orange | Westminster |
| Huntington Beach | Placentia | Villa Park |
| Irvine | San Clemente | Yorba Linda |
| Laguna Beach | Unincorporated Areas | |

OCHA will conduct an informational meeting on this proposal at 2043 N. Broadway, Santa Ana, at 9:00 a.m. on _____. Please contact Alice Hammond, (714) 555-3005, if you plan to attend.

## Self Review Questions for the Housing Services Projects RFP

As a guide to checking your ability to dissect an RFP why not try these questions on yourself and see how you might answer them if this were a real grant writing assignment:

- Briefly describe the target population. If your proposal does not address all the community service areas, how should it be handled? How would your strategy change from the Asian Family proposal just discussed?
- What ideas do you have about the committee that will make decisions on the proposals? How would you prepare for a meeting with this committee?
- Develop a short concept statement or work plan for three of the "categories" listed in the RFP. Develop a hypothetical organization for yourself and discuss an agency or agencies you might joint venture with in a proposal.
- If you were not successful in receiving funding this year, what strategy or tactic would you consider to improve your chances for getting funding next year?

A final note on evaluation is offered here in a slightly different form. In this sample a scale is used rather than the point system described earlier. Read through this "scale" evaluation system and compare it with the "point" system.

## Education RFP Sample

**Overview:**

Your State Department of Education is sponsoring Technology Literacy Challenge Grant (TLCG), a program designed to stimulate effective applications of education technologies in communities across the state. The challenges to be addressed include:

- Uses of information technology to improve learning in our classrooms, homes and workplaces,
- The need for teacher training and support services,
- Development or modification of software that involves students in engaging activities to meet high academic standards, and
- Creation of strong partnerships to link our schools with new learning opportunities at home, in the community, and at work.

When you have dissected the RFP and gleaned the above essential information, you need to prepare an analysis for your management group, collaborators and joint venture partners. What follows is a brief example of what this could look like:

**Analysis:**

All school districts may apply. The funds available are federal grant monies, passed through to states to be disbursed to school districts that apply for funding. Last year, awards ranged from $82,000 to $4,088,914 (Big City Unified). We expect the average grant size to be awarded in the range of $200,000. Last year, there were 185 grants awarded.

Two criteria are proposed to be used to select applications for funding: significance and feasibility. Essentially what they are saying is "Prove to me your project is both important and can be done."

Other considerations for government funding in this area: schools or districts that are technology poor (compared to national standards), economically poor (as measured by free school lunch programs) and have a component for disabled users (as defined by the Americans With Disabilities Act).

It may be most efficient to have colleagues pursuing these data while you wrestle with other parts of the proposal, such as refining a needs assessment, project methodology, evaluation, etc.

## A Sample Proposal Evaluation Form:

### PUBLIC ARTS AGENCY

Proposal#_____        Application deadline:_____

1. **HUMANITIES CONTENT**: Are the disciplines of the humanities central to this project and their contributions clear? Are humanities scholars involved in planning, implementing and evaluating project?
   (inadequate) 0  1  2  3  4 (excellent)        **Score:**_____

2. **VALUE FOR AUDIENCE**: Does the proposal describe its importance to the out-of-school adult public and the need for the project in light of other work done in the field? Are the project's format and outreach plans appropriate for attracting a diverse audience?
   (inadequate) 0  1  2  3  4 (excellent)        **Score:**_____

3. **STAFF AND CONSULTANTS**: Do members of the project staff have the appropriate qualifications and experience? Have members of the target audience helped plan the project?
   (inadequate) 0  1  2  3  4 (excellent)        **Score:**_____

4. **PLAN OF WORK**: Are the objectives and plan of work sharply defined, clearly stated, and capable of realization?
   (inadequate) 0  1  2  3  4 (excellent)        **Score:**_____

5. **BALANCE**: Do project activities include participants from a range of different disciplines and perspectives on the topic? To what extent is dialogue encouraged between participants and audience?

    (inadequate) 0  1  2  3  4 (excellent)          **Score:**_____

6. **BUDGET**: Is the budget appropriate to the scope and anticipated results of the project? Is no more than 25% of the total request allocated for administrative staff salaries?

    (inadequate) 0  1  2  3  4 (excellent)          **Score:**_____

7. **EVALUATION**: Are the project's plans for evaluation specific, appropriate to its format and likely to be realized?

    (inadequate) 0  1  2  3  4 (excellent)          **Score:**_____

8. **COUNCIL PRIORITIES**: To what degree does the proposal address such Council priorities as:

    a) reaching an underserved audience?

    b) reaching an underserved area of the state, such as a rural area?

    c) reaching underserved sponsors, such as community colleges?

    d) re-representing successful projects in other times and places?

    (inadequate) 0  1  2  3  4 (excellent)          **Score:**_____

---

RECOMMENDATION:                    _____ Reject _____ Re-submit
          _____ Fund With Conditions _____ Fund Without Conditions

Comments: (include possible conditions) _____
_____
_____
_____
_____

# CHAPTER 8

# Writing the Grant Proposal

◆ **What are the basic elements of a grant proposal?**

◆ **Is there an easy way to organize data to aid in the grant writing process?**

◆ **Are there any simple tips on grant writing that I should know?**

All funding sources, including federal, state and local government and especially foundations, like to fund good projects prepared by good people with good plans for pursuing good ideas. Notice we said "good": greatness is not required. Your grant proposal must not promise to find a cure for the common cold or outline a plan to stamp out ignorance by the turn of the century in order for you to get it funded; but your proposal must outline a plan that will do something good, and you must demonstrate that you have the means and motives to use funds in what funding source sees as a proper manner.

While that is what obtaining external support is usually all about, such general guidance does not provide much operational assistance as you actually write your grant proposal. This chapter will discuss the basic elements of a successful proposal. We'll explain why it is important to understand the funding sources to which your request will go and what they will be looking for in your proposal. Later, we'll describe an alternative to asking for cash, the Program-Related Investment. After that, this chapter will also describe an outstanding tool to help you organize your grant writing tasks, the Grant Action Files, and since time is always at a premium we will present a list of "Fifty Time-Saving Tips for Grant Writers."

Finally, we'll discuss ways to evaluate your proposal. It is important that you test your new proposal on others, including those outside your organization, before submitting it. Expect to rethink and rewrite your proposal and then to rewrite it again once more before sending it off to your prospective funding source.

# Basic Grant and Proposal Elements

Briefly, your proposal should contain most of the features and address many of the questions listed below:

## Clear Summary of What will be Accomplished

Make an objective assessment of the importance of the problem addressed. Set forth the major features of the proposed plan clearly and logically. Use a minimum of professional jargon and avoid broad, sweeping generalizations (such as those scattered throughout this book).

## Compelling and Believable Plan

Create a sense of urgency, a sense that this work must be done now and by your group. Convince the funding source that your group is the one to do it; this is especially important if this is a competitive issue. Address other groups as well: Are other groups meeting this need? If not, why not? Might other groups be able to meet this need if funded? And if other groups are performing a similar function, or parts of your proposed function, clarify how your plan differs and why that difference is important.

## Description of the People Involved

Give brief explanations of positions and their corresponding duties, the biographies, short resumes or curricula vitae for each key individual proposed and a defense of the qualifications of these people in view of the job to be done.

## Realistic Financing Scheme

Create a realistic budget for the duration of the project. Many foundations prefer a limited time horizon for their funding, usually two to three years, and may even set an outside limit such as five years. Government funding is usually one year at a time, but it is useful to suggest the total project duration in your proposal. Whatever the timeframe is, be sure your budget fits it. List any projected income by source. List all projected expenditures broken down in logical categories such as salaries, benefits, rent, travel, telephone, supplies, equipment and so on. And if you have a plan for achieving eventual self-support, or for developing funding sources other than those solicited here, note that in this plan.

## Assure the Funding Source You'll Use Appropriate Organizational Arrangements

Often, funds are administered by an outside fiscal agent; be sure that is specified in your proposal if that is your plan. Also mention that you will receive appropriate guidance from a responsible board of trustees, directors or advisers and provide a list of proposed board members and their duties or responsibilities.

The details of what your proposal must include are often buried in the details of the RFP. For easy reference, however, we've created a set of easy-to-follow proposal checklists for your use in planning and evaluating your proposal. These checklists cover the preface of your proposal and your executive summary; an introduction of your agency and the key personnel; a needs assessment, where you lay out the need to be met; a goals-and-objectives checklist, describing what your project seeks to achieve; and a methodology checklist, where you lay out the activities your project will undertake to achieve the goals. These checklists and other important template materials are included on the Grantwriters Diskette.

## *Know Your Funding Source*

Funding sources are as varied as the projects and usually all of them have specific preferences and restrictions. For example, many funding sources will not underwrite construction projects. Some shy away from general support, preferring instead to support specific projects. Some foundations prefer to serve within a limited geographic area; this is also particularly true for grants made by state and municipal governments. Whatever the restriction, most funding sources focus on their unique mission and programmatic goals.

Usually, government and foundation grants are made to organizations and to institutions, rather than to individuals. While grants to individuals are permitted by tax law, they are rare and require special conditions approved by the Internal Revenue Service.

Government grants are frequently made for pre-determined amounts, making them virtually fixed-price contracts for which there is little value in "under-bidding." Some foundations have evolved highly specific notions about the size of grants they feel appropriate to them, a range that they may indicate in advance, or which can be easily determined by reviewing a list of grants from the last several years. Keep these funding limits in mind when preparing grant proposals, as falling outside of these parameters could affect the success of your proposal.

Foundations in particular try to stay alert to new and better ways of making constructive social contributions; grant-making and program-related investments—an alternate source of funds discussed below) are both suitable approaches to this goal, and there may be others. Should foundations, for example, channel some of their administrative and operational spending into socially productive endeavors? This might, for example, entail the choice of a woman or minority-owned printer to prepare the foundation's annual report so as to spur entrepreneurship to these specific targeted groups. It might also entail a limited, special-experiential education or job-apprentice program for unemployed, at-risk inner-city youth.

Because foundations are looking for more creative uses for their resources, if your project really merits seed-money foundation support, push your plan—even if it deviates substantially from the general guidelines outlined in this chapter. Push the envelope! Think outside the box! Devise new approaches when the old ones no longer appear effective.

In short, this section can be summed up in one sentence: Get to know and understand the reach and interests of the funding source from which you seek assistance.

## What the Funding Source Looks for in a Proposal

What criteria do funding sources use in assessing proposals? They vary, of course, but include many of the following considerations.

- The competence of the organization making the proposal. Does the organization have the expertise and experience to do the work? What has been the organization's history and performance in past projects, if any? Is the project staff up to the task? Often a funding source will ask for references and will assess both the quality of the references and of reference sources themselves. They will also solicit the opinions of outside proposal reviewers, either professionals or specialized consultants, and will often ask the opinion of past and present members of the organization's staff.

- The feasibility and realism of the proposal. Is the need truly current? Is this the time for this endeavor? Is the plan proposed adequate to the problem addressed? Is the sponsoring agency or institution clearly enthusiastic about the substance or the proposal? Are the proposed facilities and staffing sufficient for the job?

- The importance and utility of the venture to the community, or to society at large. Is there a demonstrable need for this project? Whom will your project benefit, and how? Is it based on strong ethical and moral premises? Will there be a measurable improvement if the venture is successful? Will harm be done if it fails?

- The originality and creativity of the proposed venture. Is the project presently part of another program, or duplicate or overlap other present or past programs? Is it new and innovative? Alternatively, does it help conserve beneficial programs that might otherwise atrophy or be lost? Could the project be better carried out elsewhere, or by other persons or organizations?

- The appropriateness of the project to the funding sources' policy and program focus. Is the program consonant with the current program objectives of the funding source? If so, does it address an area that should receive priority in consideration of proposals?

- The prospects for leverage and pattern-making effects. Will the project draw in other financial support (if needed)? Will it produce significant changes within a wide circle? Will the results be transferable to other projects, and to other localities? Pilot projects often "sell" because the funding source can envision their original investment being multiplied at no additional cost.

- The need for support. Are funds available in any existing budget? Are other public or private sources more appropriate (other units of government or foundations more active in the field, other private institutions or individuals)?

- The soundness of the budget. Is it adequate for the job to be accomplished, but not so generous as to be wasteful? Is it evident that the project director (or principal support staff) is familiar with the administrative intricacies of conducting the proposed project —and that all contingencies have been carefully identified and planned for?

- The persistence, dedication and commitment of the proposers. Have proposers persevered in efforts to secure needed funds? Have they devoted sufficient time to planning and launching the venture? Is this project one of their primary interests or a major professional preoccupation?

- The existence of objective evaluation methodology. Will the project staff maintain adequate records to demonstrate success of the project? If the project lends itself to statistical evaluation, has provision been made for recording and analyzing relevant data? Where necessary, has appropriate evaluation advice been sought?

# Selling Your Idea to the Funding Source: The Bridge Over Troubled Waters

Part of a grant writer's job is to sell the feasibility of your idea or project to the funding source. The following model uses the concept of a bridge over troubled waters to simplify the [process for both the grant seeker (and his or her organization) and the grant giver. Taking the long view of the bridge we realize that the "troubles" or problems/needs/etc. can be of any one or several types, health, education, welfare, infrastructure, etc. By starting on the left you can see

## Bridge Over Troubled Water

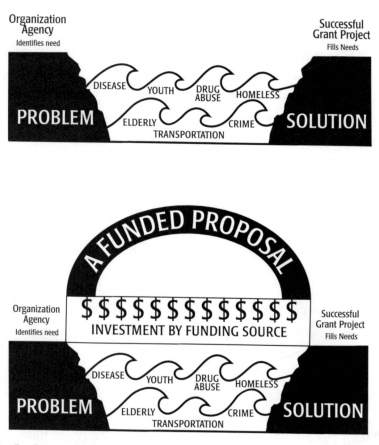

Finding Funding:
The Comprehensive Guide to Grant Writing

Figure 7

that the grant writer should first be able to state the problem, persuasively and clearly. Next you must be able to state (and sell) the solution. The planks of the bridge, represented by the dollar signs, are an attempt to convince he funding source that you know and clearly understand the problem, can see the solution, and need only a fixed or finite investment in their money to connect the problem with the solution. Whether or not you adopt this model, you will be well served to have a similar, and hopefully simple before and after concept to help sell your proposal.

# *Grant Action Files*

Many who seek grants find the process complex, difficult to deal with and ultimately frustrating. They become overwhelmed with the enormity of putting a whole proposal together and frequently either delay starting the application process until too late to do an adequate job or avoid applying at all. This situation is exacerbated because grantseekers do not receive announcements with sufficient time remaining to assemble application materials and accompanying instructions, conduct the essential research and write the proposal. Too often, getting the proposal together becomes a race against the clock instead of a quality effort.

The Grant Action File is an aid to self-discipline that enables the grant writer to regularly collect (in small pieces) elements that will later be needed to write an effective grant proposal. Having these small elements ready to work on at any time, well before all the data or grant matter is ready, will allow you to write your grant proposal from the "inside-out."

Many grant writers choose the easiest parts to write first, both to get them out of the way and to "get the juices flowing;" then they tackle more difficult sections. This way of viewing the task of preparing and applying for grants is taken from How to Get Control of Your Time and Your Life by Allen Lakein. A philosophical favorite of busy people in general and grant writers in particular, Lakein describes a mouse confronted with a large piece of cheese. It does not attempt to eat it, or to move it intact. He says that the mouse either gnaws holes in the cheese or takes it away in pieces—in other words, a little at a time. The same applies to grant seeking: approach each part and work on a bite-sized portion until you have finished. Then nibble the next piece.

A most successful grant consultant of the 1980s, David G. Bauer, advanced these thoughts with his concept of a "Proposal Development Workbook" (PDW). By using this approach and avoiding the feeling of being overwhelmed, Bauer estimates that the PDW can save 50 percent of the time required for proposal preparation. Bauer likens each section of a proposal to a piece or a hole in the Lakein's cheese. In his PDW, each significant step in the grant-seeking process is represented by a tab or section in the three-ring binder that makes up the PDW. Bauer and his associates recommend a section for each required part of the proposal.

## *Elements of a Grant Action File*

1. Executive Summary
2. Background of the Grant Seeker
3. The Needs Assessment
4. Project Goals and Objectives
5. Methods and Procedures
6. The Budget
7. Front and End Pieces, Appendices and Forms
8. Evaluation

*Finding Funding:*
*The Comprehensive Guide to Grant Writing*                    Figure 8

Grant Action Files are an advanced technology to add boilerplates from your collection of printed materials, news clippings, statistical reports, demographic data pertinent to your proposal, samples of similar grant applications, proposal guidelines, names, addresses and telephone numbers of key informants/contacts, boilerplate paragraphs and so on. Inexpensive, color-coded computer diskettes complement each section of the notebook.

Since you may be working on more than one project at a time, it is a good idea to keep each project in its own Grant Action File notebook. If you are in a computer-equipped office, even one using outmoded equipment and/or software, take advantage of the computer's power to help you organize material. Create a separate folder on your hard drive or server for each project, not to duplicate but to complement the contents of your Grant Action File notebook. Back up these computer files onto tape, another hard drive, your server or computer, and keep the back-ups current.

Even if you have the latest computers, it is always prudent to back up digital material onto inexpensive diskettes. Use a separate diskette for each project, its color matching that of the cover on your Grant Action Files; for example, a green diskette and green file folders may be used for your transit grant, a yellow diskette and file folders for your housing grant and so on.

Many publishers (including Bond Street, the publisher of this book) sell sets of grant category tabs for use in your Grant Action File notebook. You may also wish to consult a good stationery store and develop your own custom set of binders, color-coordinated files and diskettes.

## Proposal Management Using Grant Action Files

The following sections contain lists of items that proposal writers place in Grant Action Files. These items will vary with the project and the agency or foundation to whom the proposal will be sent, but they include virtually all the items that reviewers and agency personnel look for in proposals submitted for funding consideration. In the Appendix you will find an interesting, and humorous, mock case-study exercise and sample letter proposal.

## Grant Action File Part One: The Executive Summary

Writing an executive summary before creating any other sections seems to defy logic, but experience nevertheless shows that most

RFPs indicate that they expect the first section of a grant proposal to be a summary of what follows. In addition, your internal customers—your Technical Advisory Council, Board of Directors, commission, manager, or whomever—must be convinced to support your effort; writing the summary allows you the opportunity to use language more colorfully and persuasively than elsewhere in the proposal. This kind of writing displays the true art of grantsmanship, the critical difference between successful proposals and also-rans.

The executive summary describes each facet of your project: the who, what, where, why, how and how-much of your project and how they relate to each other. An executive summary differs from an introduction in that the latter usually serves to establish the credibility of an organization through the introduction of testimonials, by citing the individuals who comprise their Board of Directors and with historical and current project information while the former provides an opportunity for the applicant to reinforce their organization's credibility by describing the people involved and citing a record of accomplishment and achievement. It is the first thing that the grantor reads. When several proposals compete for limited funding opportunities, this section is often the only part read by first-round proposal evaluators.

Finally, writing the executive summary forces you to refine your vision and focus on essentials. In preparing the executive summary, gather materials that simply and forcefully make your case. By the time you finish the first draft of your grant proposal, you should know a great deal more about your subject than when you wrote the summary, and therefore you will probably choose to update, rewrite and polish this critical first section at that time.

**A clear, concise executive summary will often include the following:**

- Identification of the applicant and a phrase or two about the applicant's credibility.
- The reason for the grant request: the issue, problem or need to be met.
- A brief statement of the objectives to be achieved through this funding.

- The kinds of activities to be conducted to accomplish these objectives.
- The total cost of the project, any funds already committed, and the amount asked for in this proposal.

*Here are some helpful tips for preparing the executive summary:*

- Include appropriate organizational history information (if not required to be in another section) to establish credibility and longevity.
- Enumerate current and past activities, focusing on accomplishments and measurable impact to show your productivity.
- Describe your clientele: who are they, how large a group are they and why their needs are important. Specify what qualities make them special (either unique or universal).
- Use quotes or letters of support from experts, influential people, or other organizations. Habitat for Humanity, for example, surely includes a letter or quote from former President Jimmy Carter in its grant applications. Affiliations, whether personal or professional, are important.
- Include positive independent evaluations, if possible.

## Grant Action File Part Two: Background of the Grantseeker

This section is vital to professionally yet pridefully present the positive points of the proposer. It includes the following information:

- When, how and why the organization was started.
- A statement of purpose, goals and philosophy of the organization.
- Significant events in the history of your organization.
- Prior and current activities engaged in by your organization, including other funded projects.
- Accomplishments and impact of activities from prior funded projects. Use of statistics and other records is particularly powerful and effective.
- Size and characteristics of your constituency or clientele, especially those who will be served by the project described in the proposal.
- Assistance asked of you and given to other organizations.

- Referring agencies (if you provide direct services).
- Your funding sources and any positive comments on your work they have made.
- The results of internal or external evaluations of your programs.
- Quotes from letters of support from clients, other agencies, experts in the field, or public figures.
- Important publications authored or published by your organization.

## Grant Action File Part Three: The Needs Assessment

The "needs assessment" or "problem statement" is most often the critical part of your project or grant plan: it represents the reason behind your proposal and must bring into sharp focus those conditions in the lives of your clients or constituents that you wish to change. This brief narrative looks at that particular situation, relates it to similar situations that exist in other communities, and shows the broader implications of your program.

### The needs assessment should:
- Be clearly related to the purposes and goals of your organization
- Include at least one stated objective for each problem statement
- Be supported by evidence drawn from your experience, from statistics derived from authoritative sources and/or from the testimony of persons and credible organizations known to be knowledgeable about the situation
- Be of reasonable dimensions: i.e., something that can realistically be remedied over the course of a grant
- Be stated in terms of clients or constituents, rather than the needs or problems of your organization. Statistics are preferred, but if they are not available, at least provide anecdotal data or narrative.

## Grant Action File Part Four: Project Goals and Objectives

After the important needs have been identified and their priorities established, the next step is to determine project goals and objectives. Goals are the most important anticipated accomplishments of your project, or what needs it will attempt to alleviate. Stating a program's broad, general goals should give direction and focus to the behavioral objectives and activities developed for your project to reach its intended accomplishments.

Goals are imprecise, general and long-range: no specific behaviors or criteria are given. An example might be, "to reduce youth unemployment during summertime;" another might be, "to provide affordable housing to all residents of the City of Xanadu." Note that in neither goal is there mention of how this is to be accomplished.

While goals are useful, most funding bodies also require a more precise outcome: these are often called "performance" or "outcome" objectives. By either name, objectives measure outcomes against your stated goals. They are meant to give specific focus to the proposed program. Objectives also contain no reference to methodology, but they do require some unit of measurement so that they may be quantified and evaluated: How many of your objectives did you accomplish? How close did you come to achieving your objective? Such questions will be asked in your next funding cycle.

Objectives often begin with the action phrases like "to increase," "to decrease" or "to reduce." For example, an objective may be "to reduce, over the next summer, summertime unemployment among high-school-age youth by 20% as compared to the average youth summer unemployment rate of the last five years." This statement may be quantified in many ways: you might calculate youth summertime unemployment rates and find the average over the last five years, determine what 20 percent of that figure is and set that as a reduction goal or state that this reduction might be seen when youth-unemployment figures become available after next summer.

Performance objectives generally focus on specifying a desired behavioral change and on how that change will be measured. A clear statement of objectives increases the probability of a successful project. The key task is to determine how your goals and objectives will eventually be measured: For example, you might define who will do it, such as a designated internal/participant observer, external independent consultant or funding source staff. You might also define when these measurements will be made, such as monthly, quarterly or annually. Finally, you might ask what the time required or necessary prerequisite will be to bring about the desired change.

Here are two examples of how a performance objective may be stated, both textually and in a table. The statement, "By the end of the first project year, 40% of the eligible recipients will have been interviewed by project staff in their present living quarters and their housing needs determined as indicated in HUD Standard 86-47 to a 90 percent level or higher" could be represented in a table as follows:

| | |
|---|---|
| Who: | Project Staff |
| Behavior: | Identify and interview eligible recipients |
| Conditions: | In present living quarters |
| Method of Measurement: | Compare with HUD Standard 86-47 |
| Time: | Within one year |
| Level: | 40 % of eligible participants at 90% level or higher |

Your set of objectives, when accomplished, should provide evidence that the goals of the project have been reached, and that the needs of the learners have been met.

### Here are some tips for writing goals and objectives:
* Keep it simple.
* Relate objectives directly to your problem statement.
* Define who is affected, how they will be affected (in measurable if not numeric terms), and exactly when these objectives will be met.
* Do not include methodology if your statement of objectives contains statements which sound like, "...by taking at-risk kids from the streets and employing these youths to paint our dilapidated schools..." then you have strayed into methodology.

## Grant Action File Part Five: Methods And Procedures
The methods of your proposal reveal your creative solution or unique approach to the problem faced in your project as you describe

the steps to be taken to achieve the desired results. The basic requirements of the methods and procedures section are clarity and justification. Your methods should be readily understandable, and they should be accompanied by an explanation of the rationale underlying your choice of them, as well as who will be doing what. In other words, why do you think your idea will be successful? Usually this justification consists of a description of the grant applicant's past work, and/or the presentation of other evidence in support of your thesis that your solution will fix the problem.

The "methods" or activities are the detailed description of what you propose to do to accomplish or meet the objectives that you stated in the previous section. If project objectives are to be met, you will need to know: (1) what you will have to do; (2) who (the staff members) will be needed to do it; (3) how long they will work; and (4) the materials that will be needed to accomplish the work. These are all a function of what you set out to accomplish, so the best way to proceed is to develop methods to meet the objectives. Rather than inflating your budget for this project, add several methods that would help ensure the meeting of each objective. When the final award is negotiated, you will gain much credibility with the funding source by eliminating some of these methods instead of lowering the price for the same amount of work.

### The methods and procedures section usually includes such elements as:

- A description of program activities in detail: how do they insure fulfillment of objectives?
- A description of the sequence, flow and interrelationship of activities.
- A description of planned staffing of the program: who is responsible for what?
- A clear description of the client population and method of determining client selection.
- A description of the scope of activities that can be accomplished within the stated time frame and with the resources of your agency.
- A description of facilities and materials to be used in the project.

- A typical weekly schedule followed in the project.
- A description of trips to be taken or visitations to be made.
- A list of conferences, meetings, and dissemination activities.
- A specification of work to be carried out.
- A description of the sequence of activities for a typical individual or group participating in the project.

In order to reach the goals and objectives of your program, certain activities will have to be planned and carried out. The activities section of a proposal should specify what the participants, consultants, administrators and other personnel will be doing in order to attain the specified goals and objectives. These activities are sometimes referred to as process objectives.

Determining program activities involves deciding what processes are most appropriate for participants to reach the objectives. It also involves deciding what activities project staff must carry out to insure that the project meets the ends that it set out to achieve. Often a funding source will offer a grant based on an important or particularly expert member of the project team, and they will expect to see that person in the project work schedule to a degree consistent with their salary.

## Grant Action File Part Six: The Budget

Perhaps the thinnest of all your Grant Action Files is the budget file. The reason for this is that for some reason most grant writers prefer to delegate the preparation of the budget to some specialist elsewhere in the organization or at least put it off until the last moment. So what goes into this part of your Grant Action Files? Several items should be relatively standard material:

- The RFP guidelines for the budget including information as to whether the budget is included with the "technical" or narrative portion of the proposal or is submitted "separately."
- A copy of the history of previous grant support your organization has recently received-amounts, dates and funding sources.
- The basic salary schedule and job descriptions of the type of staff that will be used in the project.

- Your overhead or indirect cost rate (as a percentage of project costs) and what services, space, equipment and so on are included in that rate.

- Budget notes for items that might need explanation, either to please your internal budget folks or to illuminate your funding source. These budget notes should be reserved for items that are more clearly understood with additional detail.

- Your rough notes on travel costs, mileage rates and number of out-of-town trips, including per-diem and lodging costs.

When you have these materials, you can then more easily build the costs for the various elements of the budget (see Chapter 10 for a full explanation.) It is very much like planning a family vacation: calculate roughly the miles driven, nights on the road, expenses for materials, presents, snacks, services, speeding tickets or whatever else is appropriate. Simply plan. And while we encourage you to remember the New-Age management adage, "Perfect planning makes perfect," for the purpose of this work don't let your inner critic beat you up. Broad estimates will slowly but surely be refined and evolve into a logical spending plan meeting the needs of both the funding source and the fund recipient.

## Grant Action File Part Seven: Front Pieces, End Pieces, Appendices and Required Forms

As you build your proposal by adding "flesh to the skeleton" of your outline, it is sometimes easy to overlook the elements that are a part of this file: front pieces, end pieces, appendices and required forms.

The most commonly required front piece is the Executive Summary, which is addressed at length in Part One of your Grant Action File. This relatively short item—usually one to two pages, at most—serves a number of useful purposes. It is filed and used by the funding source to report to their own board (and to other current and future applicants) the projects they have funded. A second and equally important audience will be information provided to those associated with the applicant, including boards, councils, commissions and consortium partners. Often a draft of this front piece is used to gain pre-approval from the potential joint venture partners and/or to ease the approval or "signing off" process necessary for permission to actually submit the final application. While the summary obviously cannot be completed until the whole work plan is known, an early, first or second draft version is useful. It is frequently circulated to the project team and partners to determine what obstacles or objections to internal approval may exist while there is still time to correct them. Rushing for internal clearance at the last minute often signals to your own project team that the whole proposal has been hurriedly assembled.

*Rushing for internal clearance at the last minute often signals to your own project team that the whole proposal has been hurriedly assembled.*

Looking at the end pieces, the most common ones are a summary, notes for future funding and project deliverables. The benefit of using the Grant Action File method is that as you think of things you simply create them, or copy or clip them, and put them in the file. When it is time to prepare these, the grant writer doesn't have to search far and wide or test their memory for an item, a phrase, source or sample that has not been touched for some time.

An appendix may be another vital element of a grant proposal. The appendix is a good place to put longer resumes or curricula vitae, annotated bibliographies, samples of forms or surveys and the like.

Some funding sources control the appendix as closely as they do the narrative or main body of the proposal. A good tip is to make a check list of what can be included in the appendix while reviewing the RFP; this will tell you what can and cannot be included in the appendix.

Very often your funding source will make multiple copies of your submission; this is particularly true for government funders. If you suspect that the funding source will be making multiple copies of your submission, consider making all appendix items available on a one-sided 8-1/2 by 11-inch standard sheet. High quality photocopies often work well for this purpose, particularly if you want to use your elaborate four color tri-folded organization brochure. Very seldom will you be allowed to include video cassettes in your appendix, but that is a legitimate question you could pose to the contact person for your funding source.

It is a good idea to number the pages of the appendix, such as A-1 through A-40, for example; in that way you can add this useful detail to the Table of Contents and ease the work of the reviewers when they look for certain required material.

Required forms are still another category of materials that likely will have to accompany your final submission. The RFP will guide you as to how many originally signed copes are necessary, and how many copies in total. Some standard forms may be used at the front of the proposal, perhaps as a cover sheet and some with the budget, but many may be included in an appendix. Most government forms and many foundation forms are down-loadable from the Internet but if they are not, be prepared to find a friend with a typewriter. Your checklist is critical in keeping track of these details.

## Grant Action File Part Eight: Evaluation

This section of the Grant Action File may or may not actually be used in writing the grant proposal; it will help you prepare your grant for evaluation by the funding source.

Most evaluation systems measure outcomes against pre-stated goals and objectives. This is alternately referred to as "product evaluation," "outcome evaluation," "program evaluation," "impact evaluation" or "summary evaluation." Product evaluation most often uses procedures that determine the extent to which the program has achieved its stated objectives and the extent to which the accomplishment of objectives can be attributed to the program.

Another component of the evaluation process reviews the actual conduct of the program; this is called "process evaluation." Process evaluation most often uses procedures that determine if the program has been conducted in a manner consistent with the plan and the relationship of program activities to the effectiveness of the program.

*Several reasons why an evaluation plan is important:*

- Designing a product or outcome evaluation forces you to examine the clarity of your objectives, the ease with which they can be measured and the possibility of their being achieved. For this reason, you need to consider the concept of program evaluation at the beginning of and throughout the program planning process.
- Process evaluation may allow you to achieve economies in the conduct of your programs, as you examine the costs and benefits of its different aspects.
- The funding source's acceptance of your evaluation plan reduces the chance of its conducting its own evaluation of your program in ways for which you are not prepared.
- A deficient evaluation plan will dramatically narrow the chances for funding for your project, because foundations and government agencies may give away money but they expect results that make sense and can be explained to board members.

*A number of ways funding sources use evaluation plans:*

- Evaluation provides administrators with data on which to base program decisions.
- Evaluation provides the staff with data to reinforce their efforts or to recommend new directions in which to move.
- Evaluation can be used by policy makers as a tool in directing the agency into productive channels.
- Evaluation, when it shows evidence of the strengths of your programs, can provide motivation to clients and potential clients of the organization.
- Evidence of the evaluation of prior efforts reassures current and future funding sources of the diligence and sincerity of the applicant.
- Evaluative data is a powerful instrument for an agency's public relations program.
- Evaluation can help others in your field to anticipate problems in implementing similar programs and provide yardsticks against which they may measure their success.

If there are people within your organization who are or have been involved with evaluation, contact them early in the grant-writing process. And there are several templates in the Grantwriters Diskette you can use to create your own evaluation plan.

## Putting the Project Plan Into a Timetable

Now that you have built an inclusive and useful Grant Action File, this is a good time to begin consideration of a realistic calendar of events or timetable to provide an actual time perspective for your project and to help coordinate personnel and resources.

*The timetable should include the following information:*
- Activities or tasks that are to take place;
- Personnel involved in each activity, including who is responsible for its completion;
- Products or deliverables from each task;
- Percentage of project completed on a task-by-task basis;
- Inclusive dates for each task or activity's duration.

You may choose to provide the information in the form of a flow chart, Gantt chart, PERT chart or any method which most clearly presents the above information. Alternative plans that rest on contingencies or differential plans for various group leaders should be noted wherever appropriate.

Two samples of these information summaries follow in the next serveral pages. First, a simple Task Timetable and then a Project Management Overview. Please note that we have shown only the first four tasks of a thirty task project.

*A simple task timetable is shown to the right:*

## Fifty Time-Saving Tips for Grant Writers

No doubt you feel overwhelmed by all the things you have to do to write your grant proposal. To lighten your load, here is a list of tips compiled from the work of experienced grant writers. Some are

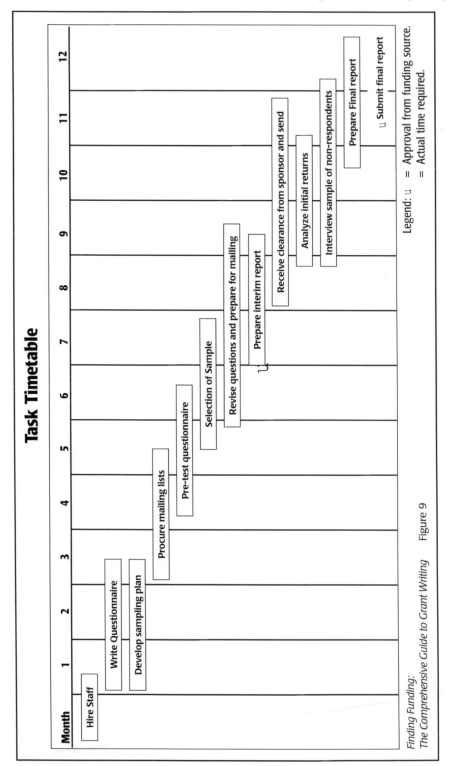

## Task Timetable

| Month | 1 | 2 | 3 | 4 | 5 | 6 | 7 | 8 | 9 | 10 | 11 | 12 |
|-------|---|---|---|---|---|---|---|---|---|----|----|----|

Hire Staff

Write Questionnaire

Develop sampling plan

Procure mailing lists

Pre-test questionnaire

Selection of Sample

Revise questions and prepare for mailing

Prepare interim report

Receive clearance from sponsor and send

Analyze initial returns

Interview sample of non-respondents

Prepare Final report

ʊ Submit final report

Legend: ʊ = Approval from funding source.
= Actual time required.

*Finding Funding:*
*The Comprehensive Guide to Grant Writing*   Figure 9

shortcuts while others ease the chores of organizing, writing, joint venturing, coordinating and such. Browse these tips now, but be ready to come back to them when needs arise—and they will!

1.  **Make a "To Do" list each day**. Put the items in priority order, and work on the most important items first. Try to complete each high priority item before moving on to the next.

2.  **Set aside uninterrupted "prime time" to grant-related tasks**. Eighty percent of the important tasks will get done in 20% of the time, so be sure to put at least 20 percent of your time aside to work on the most important things. Prime time should be uninterrupted time and set at hours that you work best: if you are a "morning person," work in the mornings; if afternoons are quietest and give you the least interruptions, work afternoons.

3.  **Clear your desk completely before working on a project**. This will encourage you to focus on the task at hand thus avoiding starting on an easier, low priority item.

4.  **Keep track of your time in 15-minute segments** for a day or two to see where your time goes, then decide if what you are doing is important and what you might delegate.

5.  **Set deadlines for yourself and your collaborators.**

6.  Work at home as much as possible: you'll have fewer interruptions, and get work done while you would ordinarily be commuting.

7.  **Always consider the benefit you'll get out of a time investment.** Get the best ROI, "return on investment."

8.  **Use a calendar** to remind you of things you'll have to do in the future, both for friend-raising and fund-raising.

9.  **Observe the "Principle of Enlightened Mediocrity:"** that is, realize that perfection takes too much time. Do it well enough to get the results you want and no better.

10. **Think of yourself as an hourly rather than salaried employee.** Ask yourself, "Did I accomplish (fill in a figure) $_____ worth in the last hour?"

◆ ◆ ◆

11. **If you're not sure what to do with a piece of paper, toss it.**

12. **Make minor decisions quickly.** Save time for the important things, like project design and proposal writing.

13. **Use "boilerplate" to speed grant writing assignments.** Boilerplate is standard, repeatable copy you can use over and over in different proposals.

14. **Delegate whenever you can.**

15. **Have volunteers digest books** and long reports for you.

16. **Say "No" more often.**

17. **Break large tasks into smaller ones**, then attack each small task until the job is done.

18. **Work on a project task until it's done.** This saves you time re-acquainting yourself with that item when you return to it.

19. **Ask yourself, "If my life depended on getting this done quickly**, what would I do?" Then ask, "Why don't I do it that way?"

20. **Have things to do in spare moments** (on the bus or train, waiting in line, waiting for your computer to download), such as project-related reading and planning.

◆ ◆ ◆

21. **Relax, exercise and schedule free time.** Overwork will make you less efficient in the long run. Stay fresh but work in controlled bursts of energy and creativity. Don't forget to refresh your social contacts with your joint venture partners, it's not nice to just work your partners with no play along the way.

22. **Think positive.** Don't spend time thinking on past rejections; instead, think of mistakes as a learning process and progress towards getting funded, and benefit from them.

23. **Reward yourself for jobs well done** instead of punishing yourself for mistakes.

24. **Write only when necessary.** Dictate or phone your messages unless there's a need to put them in writing.

25. **Learn speedwriting or shorthand.** Or consider the $1,000 solution: a laptop computer.

26. **Set personal goals**, and ask yourself how your daily work is bringing you closer to those goals.

27. **Minimize interruptions whenever possible.**

28.  **Plan before acting**. The time you spend planning will help you avoid time wasted correcting predictable mistakes.

29.  **Get expert input**. Don't "reinvent the wheel." Ask yourself, "Where can I get suggestions to make me more efficient?"

30.  **Crystallize, summarize, and record decisions** and agreements you make with others. Save time by not having to reconstruct past meetings.

◆ ◆ ◆

31.  **Save low priority items in one place**. Then set aside an afternoon to do them all.

32.  **Set aside time that is not interrupted by the phone**. If you do not have a secretary, either switch your phone off, use an answering service or purchase an answering machine (good ones are under $100). In each case, leave a message with an emergency number. The emergency number can be a colleague or an unlisted number into your office used only in emergencies.

33.  **Prioritize your tasks** into "A's" ("my life depends on doing it"), "B's" ("I'd like to do it today") and "C's" ("It should be done sometime"), and do the "A's" first. Ask yourself what would happen if you didn't do some task at all; if the answer is "Nothing significant," don't do it, or make it a "C."

34.  Use forms, including macros, to **speed repeated tasks.**

35.  **Have volunteers, interns, even clients** perform grant-related work.

36.  **Put data you refer to often in proposal writing into your Grant Action Files**. Put a copy of dated rough drafts and a copy of the original RFP into tabbed, three-ring binders for easy retrieval.

37.  **Prioritize your best grant prospects** in terms of both ideas and sources.

38.  **Use brainstorming to quickly generate project ideas**.

39.  **Use consultants**.

40.  **Use commercial research services** and read newsletters to cut down on research time.

◆ ◆ ◆

41.  **Keep files of successful and unsuccessful proposals**, your own and those of like organizations.

42. **Get endorsement letters in advance or early on in the process**. E-mails and faxes are nice, but an endorsement on original letterhead is a powerful persuader.

43. **Hire a part-time or free-lance editor** or use a grant writing firm.

44. **Set aside scheduled time to talk with the boss**. This helps minimize time-wasting meetings and phone interruption. Do the same for the people you supervise.

45. **Always decide what decisions you want made at meetings**, not just the topics for discussion. Have an agenda.

46. **Answer incoming correspondence (especially e-mail) immediately**, even if you only say that you will furnish more information later. Choose carefully the style of response (formal letter, memorandum, personal note). Always keep a copy on a tickler (calendar) or e-mail file until the subject at hand is resolved.

47. **Hold five-minute "priorities" meetings** with secretaries, office staff and other key colleagues about 20 minutes after work begins each day to agree on high-priority results desired that day.

48. Purchase, beg, borrow, barter or otherwise **secure access to fax machines, scanners and a reliable telephone system**. A cell phone with voicemail is very nice.

49. **Develop a Project Management Overview** (sample follows) to help in building the proposal and managing the grant.

50. **Share the praise, share the credit—and share the work**.

## Evaluators

Setting up an evaluation is quite straightforward: you need to determine who will do the evaluation, how it will be done and to what standards. Within these simple areas, however, is much planning. Should we use an inside or outside evaluator—or both? How much should be budgeted for evaluations? What standards should be set? How often should they be done? In this section we dissect the evaluation process and give you answers.

# Sample of a Project Management Overview

## "Official Title of Your Project"

**Grant Application:**    Your Organization

**Description of Objective:**  Organize Project Team and Liaison with Funding

**Project Title:**    Distance Delivered Vocational Education via New Technology to California Rural Communities

**Source:**    U.S. Department of Agriculture: Fund for Rural America Program

| Task No. | Task Description | Product or Results | Responsible Persons | Time Period | Percent of Project Completed |
|---|---|---|---|---|---|
| 1 | Organize project team and liaison with funding source | Plans and schedules | Project Director | January 2003 | 2% |
| 2 | Overall project orientation for team leaders and initial public information activities | Orient project team and technical site coordinators. Brief overview, Update overall plan | Rod Johnson Paul Brett Sue Nguyen | February 2003 | 5% |
| 3 | Training of technical site coordinators | Real hands-on experience with two-way tele-communication and other related technologies | Tim Pitchford Dennis Arnold Marv Kaplan | March 2003 | 10% |
| 4 | Marketing program | Letting the rural citizens know about the educational opportunities that are available. | Barb Mendez Art Cabey | Mid February to April 1, 2003 | 5% |

*Finding Funding:*
*The Comprehensive Guide to Grant Writing*

Figure 10

## Who Will do the Evaluation?

You should consider asking someone outside of your organization—a university professor or an impartial expert/practitioner in the area, for example—to evaluate your program will often give you confidence in your system of evaluation. These evaluators usually receive a fee so as to ensure their perceived impartiality and to assure that enough time will be taken with the evaluation process. After all, how much time will a busy professional take in inspecting a project if he or she is not being compensated? Paying evaluators is a standard expense; don't forget to put these costs in your budget.

Alternatively, an evaluator from inside your organization may be used. Is anyone on staff qualified to perform the evaluation? Their credentials should be mentioned in this section and be included in appendices. And that person should be separately compensated.

## How Will the Evaluation be Done?

Your evaluation should be linked directly to your objectives. If you have nine "process" objectives (steps in your program) and one overall objective, be sure that you have evaluation protocols for each step. If you cannot find a way to evaluate a step, return to your objective and clarify it.

You can use any rational method of evaluation. For example, if your program is to evaluate the use of computers to enhance the writing skills of elementary-school students, you might pre-test third-grade students in your school and pre-test third grade students who will not be involved in the program; then, after the program has been implemented, you should test both groups again to see if there was improvement in writing skills in the target group. This kind of quasi-scientific, empirical data is most recommended.

Alternatively, you may make a blind evaluation: test all students equally, both those involved in the program and those which were not, both before the program begins and after it has been implemented; then, after you have rated all students as having made "dramatic improvement," "some improvement," or "no improvement": note which students were from which group. Project administrators would hope that classes with computers made significantly greater improvement than the class that did not.

Whatever type of evaluation plan you use, it is best to talk with experts to determine how you might empirically measure the accomplishments of your objectives. These experts could also suggest, or even become, candidates for outside evaluators.

## What is required?

The key to a successful evaluation plan is to know what is expected by the funding source; then you can tailor your plan to match their expectations. If your funding source requires monthly reports of five to 10 pages, plan and budget to deliver those reports on time. Also, it is a good idea to learn who will be reading these reports. Government funders may be less likely to accept anecdotal data; corporate funders, on the other hand, may not care as much about the scientific underpinnings of what you do, as how the program is affecting clients on solving problems.

Is cost-effectiveness a value of the funding source? If so, be sure your evaluation system includes cost-benefit and cost-effectiveness analysis. Don't let this be a surprise two weeks before your report is due! Even if the funder doesn't require a certain level of "return on investment" if the data makes you look good, be sure to include this information in your periodic reports.

## Evaluation Plan

As with most parts of the project process, the best way to begin is with a plan. The evaluation timeline can be laid out in many ways. The following is a simple evaluation plan that lists the evaluation to be completed, the methodology to be used and the time frame in which the evaluation is to be completed. This is simple and straightforward, but can be tailored to fit your program as needed.

| Time Frame | Evaluation Activity | Method |
| --- | --- | --- |
| September | Survey staff competency | Questionnaire, pre-test |
| September | Determine baseline competence of clients | Questionnaire, pre-test |
| December | Review program process of both staff and clients | Questionnaire, post-test |
| December | Evaluate level of instruction | Interview staff, clients |
| May | Annual review of program process with both staff and clients | Questionnaire, post-test |
| May | Evaluate level of instruction | Interview staff, clients |
| June | Evaluate project objectives | Questionnaire, interviews with staff and clients. |
| July | Summative evaluation | External evaluation |

## An Alternative to Cash: the "Program-Related Investment"

The foregoing set of considerations and questions apply primarily to grant requests, but may also relate to proposals for program-related investments, or "PRI's." These are loans, guarantees, stock purchases and similar devices by which foundations support organizations, often profit-making organizations at that, which further the foundation's program priorities but do not involve the granting of cash.

Program-related investments for many community-based and non-profit organization grant programs are sanctioned by the 1969 Tax Reform Act which provides, in part, that "...investments, the primary purpose of which is to accomplish one or more of the purposes described in section 170(c)(2)(B) and no significant purpose of which is the production of income or the appreciation of property, shall not be considered as investments which jeopardize the carrying out of exempt purposes." Section 170(c)(2)(B) is that portion of the Internal Revenue Code that broadly describes charitable, educational and similar worthy purposes, contributions for which are usually tax deductible.

A PRI is not made for ordinary investment purposes but to serve some tax-exempt purpose chosen by the foundation. It is analogous to a grant and may be made for any purpose for which a grant might be made; so far, however, relatively few foundations have actually committed resources to PRI's. If your project can't qualify for a foundation grant, you might try selling the notion of a program-related investment. Here are a few "selling points":

A PRI may be more efficient than a grant in improving the social return on a foundation's total resources. This is because investments are expected to return part or all of the principal invested, and sometimes even additional earnings on the funds, while grants rarely return anything.

PRI's may be particularly appropriate to foundations with a special mission to innovate, forge new instruments and support demonstration projects with high leverage. They can be seen as effective vehicles for foundations to supply risk capital to underdeveloped sectors of the nation.

PRI's may be useful where grant funds are not available or insufficient. For example, some experts find there is a critical need for foundation money in fields such as ethnic minority and women's entrepreneurship where venture capital remains scarce but PRI dollars may be of great benefit.

# Summary

## Getting Ready to Write: A Summary of Advice

The following summarizes much of what we have just discussed. As you are writing the first draft of your proposal keep these points in mind. The first category is making the problem clear and persuasive. To do this follow these guidelines:

- Let non involved persons read your statement

- Scan the RFP for hot words and terms
- Go back to your original brainstorming notes
- Ask do we do this at all then
- What's the most important reason
- Don't forget to look at other successful proposals
- Always cite your sources
- Don't overwhelm the reader with too many good words-keep it simple, forceful, readable and a little bit urgent

The next area you should tackle, and do it sooner in the process as opposed to later, is obtaining clearances. **Some points to ponder:**
- Get Internal clearances very early
- Be sure to check with joint venture partners
- Re-connect internally with your own bosses if the joint venture partners change their roles in any significant manner
- Make sure the dollars are in the right spots and everybody agrees-you bosses, your partners, and yourself!

Sometimes you might be asked to make a re-proposal presentation to your own organization and representatives of your joint venture partners and even, at times, someone form the funding source. Advice here is short and simple.
- Plan your presentation
- Know your audience
- Control the presentation environment
- Less is better than more
- Anticipate the "lumps in the oatmeal"

Finally, here is some advice on the world of joint and cooperative ventures. The single biggest hurdle that both sides most overcome or adapt to is fiscal control and information flow.

**Some key points in this area are:**
- Do they share long range plans (maybe even private secret stuff)
- Do both sides sincerely want to cooperate

- Do partners have significantly differing long term goals
- Are they in competition in other areas
- Is there a significant conflict in legal rules & regulations that each must follow
- Do both sides have a mutual (and balanced) feeling about the importance of the overall success of the mission

### *And some final bits of wisdom for new and old grant writers:*

- organize your ideas
- prioritize
- collect data—qualitative and quantitative
- develop a work plan
- consider joint ventures
- find a funding source

### *Time your organization*

- organize your time
- keep good records
- don't be a loner
- set and make your deadline
- get it out the door!!

# CHAPTER 9

# An Alternative: The Letter Proposal

◆ *My funding source won't accept unsolicited proposals. What can I do to interest them?*

◆ *What are the elements of this "pre-proposal letter"?*

◆ *Do you ever send your idea along to a prospective funding source without mentioning the funding amount you are seeking?*

In the preceding chapter you learned how to write the long, often-complex document called a funding or grant proposal. In this chapter you will apply your new analytical and qualitative skills to a much smaller document that may serve the same purpose. You will note that some of the material in this chapter is replicated elsewhere in the book. That is because we feel sure that while some readers will take the linear approach and progress sequentially from chapter one, many, especially those with grant-writing experience, prefer to sample the book smorgasbord style, skipping from chapter to chapter to nibble what they please. We also recognize that others, especially newcomers to grant writing, will prefer to start with the shorter document, moving on to the full proposal after their writing muscles are toned and ready. In either case, bearing in mind that the letter proposal is always very brief, you should tailor your approach to your funding source's worldview. Thus, if a grantor is known to be very picky about evaluation, beef up that section, even at the expense of shortening others.

## Letter Proposals

Many funders, overwhelmed by the increasing number of long proposals they receive, ask applicants to send in "letter proposals." Also known as a short proposal or query letter, it may be used as an informal means to convince a funding source to invite you to submit a full proposal, or to find out, with minimum effort, that the grantor is or is not interested in your project. If the funding source allows it, this brief document may serve as a formal proposal itself. A letter proposal is a great way to "shop" your idea to a funding source with a much quicker turnaround response. (If you are confronting the deadline for a full-scale proposal, however, it would be prudent to forego the letter version and comply with the RFP.)

Your letter proposal should be no more than two or three pages, emphasizing the bridge you see between the most important elements of your proposal and the interests of the funding source you are submitting it to. Most authorities feel that it is appropriate to have as many as three letters circulating simultaneously. Here are the essential elements of letter proposals:

- Open with a strong topic sentence and forcefully indicate the expected products and benefits of your proposal and how they mesh with the stated or implied purposes of the fund source.
- Without overwhelming the reader, remind the fund source that your organization has the track record or potential to do the job.
- Remind the fund source of previous contacts or previous contracts you have had, or at least why you are similar to an organization that they have funded in the past. End your letter by suggesting what action you would like next, i.e., an appointment to discuss your project further, a referral to a sister agency, or a healthy, possibly face-to-face, critique.

To be even more specific consider the following checklist for letter proposal writers, which gives you a proven format for an effective letter proposal. Feel free, however, to change the order and content to suit your special situation. Just make sure that you retain a logical flow between each paragraph of the letter and the one that follows it.

## A Letter Proposal Checklist:

o **Addressee** — either the person who requested your proposal, or the funding source's official "contact person." Always address it to the funding source, not to a home or unrelated business address.

o **Introduction** — state your reason for writing. Examples: "We write at the suggestion of..." or "We write to describe a project that we think you will be particularly interested in..." Then give a one page description of what your project does.

o **Focusing** — tell the funding executive why you have applied to their organization or agency in particular. Example: "We note with great satisfaction your continued support of the visual arts in the St. Louis area..."

o **The Need** — in one or two sentences, state the societal need your project addresses. Use one well?chosen statistic to document the need as you see it. Example: "More than 500 people die of cancer each year in Kellysville."

o **Your Solution** — In three or four sentences, outline your proposed project. Present it as a solution to the need you've just described. Then state one or two specific, measurable, objectives of the program.

o **Client Benefit** — Rather than going into detail about what you do, describe the direct benefits to clients from your project.

o **Unique Features** — Point out the ways that you are different from and better than others in your field or geographical area.

o **Budget** — state a one figure budget for your project. If possible, state it as a per client figure. Example: "This budget represents a cost of $4.57 per client served." (See **The Budget** for other good examples)

o **Your request** — An excellent approach is "Because of your interest in _____, we feel that you will share our enthusiasm about this project. We are requesting a grant of $ _____ to..." Follow your request with a mention of any other funding source that has given you support.

o **Closing** — end the letter with a request for follow up: a meeting to discuss proposal further, the submission of a longer full-scale proposal, etc. Keep the initiative; say you will call them at a specified time.

o **Signature** — one or two ranking organization officials should sign the letter. Generally, but not always, the Board of Directors or its representative also will sign.

## Guidelines on Letter Proposals:

Generally, a letter proposal should not exceed two or three single-spaced pages. Its purpose is to convey a great deal of information quickly to a funding executive.

Spend as little time as necessary describing what you do. Try to emphasize the client and community benefits of your work. (i.e., the results of what you do).

Tailor your letter to the expressed interests of the funding source. Emphasize those things your research tells you will motivate this funding agency to give.

If you are submitting your proposal through a "contact," mention it briefly at the opening of your letter, but don't go into detail. Any indication you are trying to use a connection to get funded may alienate other agency decision makers.

## Review your draft letter proposal through the eyes of a funding agency

Although it may be only a single page, your proposal must describe the following, with each accorded equal weight:

### The need for the project, as determined by:

- The magnitude, severity and/or urgency of the problem your project will address;
- The scale of need for services or activities provided by your project.

Describe the problem or opportunity you wish to address in both its local setting, and in a national or international context. You may focus on a single topic, or you may address more than one topic in a single project. **As you tell this story, describe:**

- How central is the problem to your institution's vitality or effectiveness?
- Does the same problem affect other institutions around the country?
- Have attempts to remedy the situation been made by you or by others in the past, and with what results?
- What are the likely local and national consequences of successful completion of your project?
- Will other institutions or organizations benefit or learn from your experience in ways that would enable them to improve their programs and services?

### The significance of the project, as determined by:

- The potential contribution of your project to increased knowledge or understanding of problems, issues, or effective strategies;
- The extent to which your project involves the development or demonstration of promising new strategies that build on, or are alternatives to, existing strategies;
- The importance or magnitude of the results or outcomes likely to be attained by your project;
- The potential to replicate your project in a variety of settings.
- The community "good will" that could be a by-product of funding.
- Funding sources will appreciate any evidence that you can include to illustrate how your project differs from and improves upon previous efforts.
- Describe your project's potential contribution to increasing knowledge and the likely utility of the products (such as informa-

tion, materials, processes, or techniques) that will result from it. It is your responsibility to create a context within which reviewers can assess your project's importance.

- Demonstrate how, directly or indirectly, the principal beneficiaries of your project will maybe be served. For example, an academic faculty development proposal should articulate the relationship between what teachers will experience and what their students will learn.

- Fund sources seek to make the most of limited funds by supporting projects that can become models for others. Your proposal should include a discussion of the project's potential to be replicated and/or implemented elsewhere. Before any project becomes a model, however, its proponents must prove that it has achieved its aims. Therefore, an evaluation plan that focuses on precisely how well the project succeeds in meeting its goals is an essential component.

- Bear in mind that if your project activities are heavily dependent on external funding, it may be difficult for others to adapt them on their own, and this may reduce your project's potential impact.

### *The quality of the project's design, as determined by:*

- The extent to which it is appropriate to, and will successfully address, the needs of the target population or other identified needs.

- The extent to which the goals, objectives, and outcomes to be achieved by the proposed project are clearly specified and measurable.

- Your strategic design must address the central causes of the problem you are addressing, based on your own research and experience, and on previous experiments by others. Scatter-shot approaches to vaguely defined problems are poor prospects for funding.

### *The quality of your project's evaluation, as determined by:*

- The extent to which the evaluation will provide guidance about effective strategies suitable for replication or testing in other settings.

- The extent to which your design for implementing and evaluating will provide information about the effectiveness of your approach or strategies.
- The extent to which evaluation methods are thorough, feasible and appropriate to goals, objectives and outcomes; and
- The extent to which evaluation methods employ objective performance measures clearly related to your project's intended outcomes, and are likely to produce quantitative and qualitative data.
- Evaluation is an important part of your plan, and your proposal should describe how you intend to document activities and results. Save details of your evaluation design for the final proposal, but state here your evaluation objectives.

### The quality of the management plan, as determined by:

- The plan's adequacy to achieve objectives on time and within budget;
- Clearly defined responsibilities, timelines and milestones for accomplishing project tasks.

### The quality of project personnel, as determined by:

- The qualifications, training and experience of key project personnel;
- The extent to which the applicant encourages applications for employment from persons who are members of groups that have traditionally been underrepresented based on race, color, national origin, gender, age, or disability. (Many private-sector funding sources do not care much about these issues, but if your personnel demonstrate diversity, mention it.)
- Qualifications of key personnel, including the project director, consultants or subcontractors, should be briefly stated, focusing on experiences relevant to your project's application.

### Adequacy of resources for the proposed project, as determined by:

- The extent to which the budget is adequate to support the proposed project;

- The extent to which costs are reasonable in relation to your project's objectives, design and potential significance;
- The demonstrated commitment of each partner in the proposed project to its implementation and success;
- Adequacy of support, including facilities, equipment, supplies and other resources from the applicant organization;

Potential for continued support of the project after funding ends, including demonstrated commitment by appropriate entities to such support.

It should be clear that you carefully allocated appropriate resources and personnel for tasks and activities described in your proposal. Even at the preliminary proposal stage, you should prepare an estimated budget carefully: requesting insufficient funds jeopardizes the project's success, and over-estimating costs is equally hazardous. Before doing this initial budget, however, determine if the funding sources will purchase facilities or support equipment purchases. If not, these costs must be borne by your institution and the budget should reflect this.

Proposals should include plans to disseminate findings to inform others and allow them to make use of your experience. Your information dissemination plan should show that your proposed means of dissemination are appropriate for your project and if they improve upon methods used elsewhere. Your narrative should be a clear description of who will do what, when, where, why, and with what anticipated results. Goals and objectives should be clearly identified and measurable. Evaluation is critical, and personnel and funding issues must be addressed, along with dissemination of results.

## *Writing Shorter Means Writing Better*

When you have only a few pages to deliver the main points of your argument, every word must accomplish a purpose. This is true of all writing. In practice, however, most documents and grants could be trimmed by 10 or 15 percent and lose nothing of value. Therefore, many of the tips and techniques discussed in this chapter will be equally useful in writing complex and detailed proposals.

---

## Writing Tips:

- **Don't be afraid to start over.** Often your first few sentences or paragraphs are flawed or skewed. It is usually better to start over than to force what follows into an awkward style.

- **Each paragraph is to a writer as a block of marble is to a sculptor.** Sculptors have a vision of the statue hiding within a hunk of stone, and remove and discard everything that is not part of this vision. In other words, sculptors choose what to leave out. They begin by chiseling away the big parts, then work with progressively finer and more precise tools until, at the end, they are polishing with sandpaper. Your task is the same. Writers, however, create their own "marble." If you make a mistake while sculpting, it is easy to replace words, phrases or sentences that were erroneously removed.

- **Write with nouns and verbs.**
  Construct each sentence as though the adjective warehouse has burned down and the Siblinghood of Unaffiliated Adjective and Adverb Guilds are in the midst of a job action and will supply only a fraction of the material you usually use.

- **Eliminate unnecessary words from sentences.**
  Read each sentence aloud and ask yourself if there is any word that could be removed without changing the sentence's meaning. Question the value of each word, and if it is marginal, cut it. A rose is a beautiful, thorn-stemmed, fragrant blossom, but probably not if you expect to get your grant funded.

- **Use dime words instead of $10 utterances.**
  Don't order bouillabaisse if chowder will do. A scintilla is not a bit better.

- **Use the right word.**
  A community is not always a neighborhood. A college is a school,

but not every school is a college. If Gouda sells your tale better than imported cheese, use it.

- **Eliminate unnecessary sentences from every paragraph.**
  Each sentence must move your story forward. If not, take it out or move its idea to another sentence.

- **Recast sentences to eliminate words and gain clarity.**
  Consider that moving or changing the subject of a sentence could make reading or understanding easier. Ask yourself if you could approach a thought from a different direction.

- **Read drafts to a colleague.**
  Better yet, read them to an adolescent.
  According to legend, Napoleon employed a simple corporal whose only task was to review each message before it was sent to subordinate headquarters. If the corporal didn't understand the missive or found it ambiguous, it was rewritten. If a child can understand what you have written, adults will get it.

- **Eliminate widows and orphans.**
  When you think that a paragraph is tight as can be, check its last line. Is it a single word, or a fraction of one? Go through each sentence and remove words until the last line is at least half the length of the others.

- **Edit on paper.**
  While computers are useful for creating, revising and editing, things look different on paper. Print out your work to edit final drafts.

- **Let it cool before serving**
  When you think that you are finished, wait at least two days—a week is better—then review your work. You will always find something that needs changing.

- *Repeat The Two Steps Above*

It is amazing how many small but critical errors are discovered by reading the work after it has slipped from the writer's short-term memory.

# Sample Basic Pre-Proposal Letter To A Foundation

June 5, 2002

Dr. Jules Lesner
Executive Director
c/o Foundations of the Wealthy Family
1250 Shaded Boulevard, 2nd Floor
Any Town, USA 98765

Dear Dr. Lesner,

I am pleased to followup our phone conversation with a pre-proposal for the Wealthy Family Foundation/University Home Economics Department Laboratory Expansion program which will open our facility to disadvantaged and underrepresented children from the local community. This partnership would allow the Wealthy Foundation and State University to achieve their goals of building human resources through programs to involve parents in their children's educational achievements and offer opportunities to those children who otherwise would not be able to participate.

The local community is as diverse as it is large. Poverty and lack of education are common in an area with the region's most acclaimed university. Children are often the hidden losers as a result of a stagnated economy and language barriers. The Home Economics Department of State University can educate these children during a crucial stage of their development, but also work with their parents to ensure that primary school is a time of progress and not stagnation.

Your foundation can be part of this effort to give children the headstart that can lead to academic success. Poverty should not be a barrier to early childhood education, and this partnership can launch a community effort that fosters this type of innovation for our children and our future.

Thank you in advance for your consideration of our idea. If you or your colleagues have questions about this unique opportunity, please feel free to contact me. The Home Economics Department looks forward to working with the Wealthy Family Foundation.

Sincerely,
J.T. Smith
Chair

## Sample of basic proposal letter to a foundation – short version

Dear (funding source),

The (state the problem in one sentence.)

One possible solution (or service, etc.) is (state the solution).

To bridge the gap between this problem and this solution we are seeking a funding source to (generally describe the size and scope of the funds or gift required– i.e. build a library, pay for flu shots, assist in travel, provide cash, technical assistance, etc.)

We hope that you share this interest with us and can meet (or speak, or write to) us to discuss mutual interests in the very near future. Thank you.

Sincerely,

# *Editing and Revising Complex or Lengthy Pages*

Below are paragraphs from actual pre-proposal letters. The first iteration is the original, the second is an edited version, the third represents how this thought might be distilled for a letter proposal.

### Original Letter – Sample One

#### *Building a statewide network...*

For the past 12 years, the Local Center for Environmental Causes has supported the development of local action groups. These approaches to policy reform purposely try to educate elected officials with the goal of new local rules and regulations to protect the environment and organize public education courses. Building these networks and enrolling a common group of citizens has proven to be a powerful factor in increasing issue engagement and responsible development of endangered resources.

What we seek to do next is build a strong network of environmental action expertise throughout our state. Many promising community programs have been discussed or initiated in other states as well, and their proponents have relied on us for needed advice.

We are seeking external support for a national dissemination project focused on strengthening and sustaining these incipient programs. The center is working closely with 21 area organizations to assess, and evaluate their community environmental education programs. The experience and knowledge gained by these institutions will be featured in a national conference in the final year of the grant project.

## First Edit

### *Building a statewide network...*

The Local Center for Environmental Causes has supported the development of local action groups for the past 12 years. These groups seek to educate elected officials to encourage new local rules and regulations that protect the environment and organize public education courses. These networks are proven and powerful factors in increasing issue engagement and responsible development of endangered resources.

Many promising community programs have been discussed or initiated in other states as well, and their proponents have relied on us for advice. We now seek external support to build a statewide network of environmental action expertise.

This national dissemination project will focus on strengthening and sustaining incipient programs. The center is working closely with 21 area organizations to assess and evaluate their community environmental education programs. The experience and knowledge gained by these institutions will be featured in a national conference in the final year of the grant project.

## Final Edit

### Building a statewide network...

The Local Center for Environmental Causes has supported the development of local action groups since 1987. These groups educate elected officials to encourage new rules and regulations for environmental protection and education, and have proven their value in protecting endangered resources. Because similar networks in other states rely on us for advice, we now seek support for a national dissemination project to strengthen and sustain incipient programs. The center now assesses and evaluates 21 community environmental education programs; their data and insights will be shared nationally.

## Original – Sample Two

### Creating Cyber Classrooms Via New Technology

Not everyone in our state will enter the information age when they need to, and the teachers of our district want to do something to level the playing field for all of our children.

The focus of our proposed project TOP HAT is "To Organize Programs for Hispanics and Technology." The key elements of this project center on providing opportunities for school teachers in our region to learn how to use the information technology equipment in their classrooms and apply it to produce new learning conditions and outcomes for the largely Hispanic student population of that area. Discipline-specific teacher teams could jointly plan technology applications and cooperative instructional strategies for various content areas, with the assistance of the project's full-time, on-site instructional technology specialist, during a daily 90-minute planning period. We offer a unique setting for the project, in a secondary school (grades 7-12) where aspiring teachers are used as teacher's aids, and this will maximize the project's impact by involving not only current teachers but a cohort of future teachers as well.

## First Edit

### *Creating Cyber Classrooms Via New Technology*

Disadvantaged children often fail to enter the information age; teachers in our district want to level the playing field and enable access for all children.

The key elements of our proposed statewide project, "To Organize Programs for Hispanics and Technology (TOP HAT) center on providing opportunities for school teachers to learn how to use information technology equipment and apply it to produce new learning conditions and outcomes for the largely Hispanic student population of our area. Assisted by TOP HAT's full-time, on-site instructional technology specialist, discipline-specific teacher teams could jointly plan technology applications and instructional strategies during a daily 90-minute planning period. Our unique project setting, in a school (grades 7-12) with many student teachers, will maximize the project's impact by involving not only current teachers but a cohort of future teachers as well.

## Final Edit

### *Creating Cyber Classrooms Via New Technology*

Many disadvantaged children fail to enter the information age; teachers in our district want to enable access for all children. Our proposed statewide project, "To Organize Programs for Hispanics and Technology (TOP HAT) will provide opportunities for teachers to develop information technology skills to produce new learning conditions and outcomes for our largely Hispanic student population. Assisted by an instructional technology specialist, discipline-specific teacher teams could jointly plan technology applications and instructional strategies. Our setting, in a school whose faculty includes student teachers, will maximize the project's impact by involving two generations of educators.

## Original – Sample Three

### *Improved Immigrant Education...*

As your grant announcement so clearly states, there are increasing numbers of under-prepared native-born, immigrant and international language minority students entering workforce. One powerful ally that we have in working with this condition is a recent joint venture we have formed with our Local State University. Through our staff and that of the University, faculty will receive assistance in dealing with the instructional demands of this burgeoning student population who will or are entering our workforce. Project LEAP AHEAD is a three-year development effort to train faculty at State University, other nearby campuses, and institutions nationwide to integrate language and content instruction in courses across the disciplines and thereby improve the academic literacy of language minority students. This project builds on the original Project AHEAD, a successful government supported project in which selected general education courses known to be linguistically and conceptually challenging were enhanced with a language development focus.

## First Edit

### *Improved Immigrant Education...*

As your grant announcement states, there are increasing numbers of under-prepared, native-born, immigrant and international language minority students entering our workforce. A joint venture with our Local State University will prove itself powerfully effective in alleviating these language and cultural deficiencies. University faculty will receive assistance in dealing with the instructional demands required to prepare their student population to enter the workforce. Project LEAP AHEAD is a three-year cross-disciplinary development effort to train faculty at State University, other nearby campuses and institutions nationwide to integrate language and content instruction, and thereby improve the academic literacy of language minority students. This project builds on the original Project AHEAD, a successful government-supported project in which linguistically and conceptually challenging education courses were enhanced with a language development focus.

## Final Edit

### *Improved Immigrant Education...*

Increasing numbers of under-prepared and English challenged students are entering our workforce. A joint venture with our Local State University will alleviate language and cultural deficiencies to better prepare students for the workplace.

Project LEAP AHEAD is a three-year cross-disciplinary development program to train faculty at State University and institutions nationwide to integrate language and content instruction, and thereby improve academic literacy in English-deficient minority students. This builds on Project AHEAD, a successful project in which linguistically and conceptually challenging education courses were enhanced with a language development focus.

## *Summary*

Whether preparing a short letter proposal or the longer, traditional proposal, your writing must match the task at hand. Additionally, using clear and concise language without subjective annotations or hyperbole will go far with your prospect funding source. Remember, fund grantors are human too, and they want to be assured that your program is the "best" match for their grant funds. This means that you will need to speak the language of the grant funder (use words from the RFP, or Request For Proposal) to help set the tone and build a good first and lasting impression with your funding source. In the next chapter, you will learn the fundamentals to prepare a detailed and effective budget to attach to your proposal. Remember, the funding source is focused on selecting the program that "best" fits their funding guidelines and underscores their program interests and ideals. Your job is to present that "best" fit in your proposal for funding.

# CHAPTER 10

# The Budget

◆ **What is the most important part of the project budget?**

◆ **What can I do if one part of my budget has too much money and another part too little?**

◆ **I have heard about indirect costs, overhead, and administrative costs— what are they and are they different?**

This chapter takes the reader step by step through the process of preparing the grant budget from a forecasted, cash and non-cash needs basis to completing the budget. Your budget will include project line item cost details, so it's important to apply the feedback you gained during the grant proposal pre-writing stage into your budget preparation. Remember that many types of grant funding formulas depend on the grant. With in-kind or soft match funding, certain definitions and terms apply to this type of funding such as indirect project costs or overhead. These are identified and explained here. Suggestions for easy project bookkeeping are also made, as well as how to successfully negotiate with funding sources on budget matters, including into your contract funding enhancements and time extensions at ZERO expense. Finally, two budget formats are presented in detail: the traditional line item budget and the more innovative unit cost budget.

# Budgeting Overview

Preparing a proposed project budget includes planning what materials, facilities, personnel, evaluation and contracted services will be necessary for carrying out the project as described. Contributions of personnel, hardware and facilities by the proposing agency may have already been noted in the proposal. Reasonable estimates should be included for items and services to be purchased with special project funds. It may be helpful to include estimates of how much money is needed for equipment, in-service and materials to start up the project and how much will be needed for personnel and materials to maintain it. The time you spend developing your proposed budget will help you better administer the project once you are funded (see related information contained in Chapter 11 "Project Administration").

*The time you spend developing your proposed budget will help you better administer the project once you are funded.*

As for the proposals themselves, funding sources have different requirements on the type of budget information requested, with foundations typically having less extensive requirements than federal agencies. The following budget design will satisfy most funding sources, allowing you to design your own budget for widest audience potential and, with minor changes that the sources tell you about in the RFP (refer to Chapter 7 "Dissecting the RFP"), can be adapted to fit most federal agency requirements. This recommended budget contains two components: Personnel and Non personnel. In most grant programs (excluding capital building projects and equipment purchases), approximately 80 percent of the budget falls into the three components of the Personnel section. For producing the final budget and including this in your proposal, please refer to the formatted templates contained on the Grantwriters Diskette.

## Governments and Nonprofits Underwrite Socially Useful Projects

Now more than ever, you will notice in your home town that you must pay to use public tennis courts, that the cost of visiting state and federal parks has risen, that more and more parking meters have appeared on side streets, that fines for parking and traffic violations have risen dramatically. The reason: Many municipalities now engage in pay-per-use fund raising strategies to keep taxes low. In some states, property tax reform has forced government to find new ways of funding its projects. Rarely, however, do pay-per-use programs cover the entire cost of a program. Governments, which are nonprofit organizations, try to raise money by the means available to them, and then spend it. When it comes to providing funds for programs, public and private funding sources realize that their money will be spent. The return on their dollar is a most important barometer of the successful implementation of the program they are funding.

## Ask For What You Need

As you begin budgeting, realize that success in the public sector is measured ultimately by your program's positive effect on solving or ameliorating the problem experienced by the client population. So don't shortchange yourself. Be sure to include a funding plan for every aspect of your project. For example, if you are seeking funding for a "free needle" plan for addicts in your city (with the goal of reducing hepatitis and AIDS in the community) and you intend to enclose instructions with the needles, don't forget to include paper and copying cost in your budget. You may need to hire a linguist to translate the message into five different languages. Put it all in the budget. Funding sources are suspect of programs that seem "too good to be true." Greater positive impacts on the addict community are more important than an extra few hundred dollars in the budget for reproduction and translation. Therefore: Budget for all expenses, and ask the funding source to cover those costs.

## Budgets are Tied to All Other Sections of the Grant

As planning tools, budgets are inextricably linked to Goals, Objectives, Needs, Methods, Staffing, Directing and other strategic steps toward getting things done in an organized manner. Each of these steps must be considered while creating the budget, and the budget, in turn, will clarify your methodology and objectives.

Start your budget with the timeline developed in the methodology section, and begin by affixing numbers to it. Do we need a full-time receptionist, or is the afternoon the only time clients come in? Does your organization have a bulk-rate mailing permit, or will it have to get one to mail surveys throughout the town? If Downtown Chevrolet donates the vans, who will pay for their gasoline and maintenance?

The budget process forces the grant writer to make the same sort of evaluations that the funding source will do. Is it worth spending $100 million to cure a disease that affects 100 people worldwide? It may be. If I am raising money to redistribute to the homeless, how can I be sure the money will be spent on food and shelter, rather than on vices? Grant writers must first convince themselves that their program is worthwhile. They must look at the budget and evaluate whether their OBJECTIVES are still sound and meet the NEED of the client population, whether the funds should be spent on the METHODOLOGY selected in the grant proposal, or if there is another, better way of achieving these GOALS.

Writing budgets was delayed until the tenth chapter because grant writers often find numbers daunting. We have been training ourselves in the craft of clear, concise and logical writing to compose compelling stories that convey need, or establish credibility. Writing the budget now forces us to re-examine our draft proposal in real-world numbers, and to make sure it all adds up to success. Don't be afraid to throw the numbers around. Remember: Always state needs in terms of your client population.

## The Secrets Of Sub-Contracting

Having already made the case for joint and cooperative ventures, and exposed the power of synergy that comes with more than one organization working on an idea it's time to share "The Secrets of Subcontracting."

A subcontract may be required if a portion of the work to be performed under an agreement is to be provided by an agency or organization other than your own. The need for a subcontract should be addressed during preparation of a proposal to a sponsor. Your supervisors likely will require the proposed subcontractor to provide written approval of its participation in the work proposed under the proposal and the costs they will charge.

Soliciting bids or providing a sole source justification for the subcontract requires special procedures. There are two main ways to find a sub contractor, from an unknown source or from a known source (as a sole source). In either case it is wise to have some or all of the following information.

- List of potential bidders (including name, address, phone number).
- Pre-proposal conferences. List the time, date, and place of any planned meetings with potential bidders to discuss RFQ requirements prior to the submission of the RFQ.
- Sample transmittal letter.
- Statement of work.
- Performance milestones or schedule of work to be performed.
- Inspection and acceptance conditions.
- Evaluation criteria.

## If you are using the "Sole Source" method some special advice follows

If the services required are unique or one-of-a kind, and only one subcontractor exists to provide those services, the Project Director may submit a Sole Source Justification. In order to obtain a subcontract via a Sole Source Justification, the Project Director should obtain at least one bid solicitation and provide full justification, including reasonableness of cost, to support the selection of a subcontractor. Otherwise, it may be necessary to bid out the subcontract, which will require preparation of a Request for Qualifications (RFQ) as above noted.

# *Budgeting: Bottom Up!*

Traditional budgeting is top-down: Management determines how much funding is allotted to each department and where it will be spent. For nonprofit organizations especially, bottom-up budgeting is essential so that an accurate program budget may be established. Bottom-up budgeting is the process of involving your staff, and the people who actually perform the duties involved in your methodology, in the budget process. This means consulting the counselors in your home for battered wives, talking to the volunteer who typesets and copies your newsletter and soliciting the opinions of the receptionist who greets your client population as they enter the door.

The battered-woman's counselor may find that those whom she counsels need more clothes than the one outfit currently provided by the program, that having two or more outfits would go far toward boosting their self-confidence and assimilation into social settings. The volunteer typesetter may have a lead on a cheap new laser printer or an attractive alternative to photocopying large numbers of documents. The receptionist may alert you that no parking is available during busy times at your facility. Managers need to know these things in order to budget for these expenses and find some funding to increase the quality of service. Funding sources will give additional funds to help a program improve and experience more long-lasting results. And the best way to find out is to ask those who know best.

## Put Budget Flesh On Project Bones

As we noted in the overview to this chapter sound project budgets include a clear list of materials, facilities, personnel, and contracted services. You need to identify all the matches, hard match of cash, and soft match of such items as contributed personnel, hardware and facilities. Again use reasonable estimates for items and services to be purchased with special project funds. It is helpful to include estimates of dollars needed for equipment and materials to start the project and how much will be needed for personnel and materials to maintain it.

You will find that funding source requirements for budgets differ, with foundation requirements less extensive than federal agencies. The following budget design will satisfy most funding sources that allow you to design your own budget and, with minor changes that the sources will tell you about, can be adapted to fit most federal agency requirements. This recommended budget contains two components: Personnel and Non personnel. You can expect that in most grant programs, (excluding capital building projects and equipment purchases) approximately 80 percent of the budget falls into the three components of the Personnel section.

Note, however, that many proposals fail or are sent back for additional detail when the proposer overlooks a minute detail or peculiar request. It is a safe practice to never assume anything, and be prepared to justify each budget decision made. Careful planning will be of great value when you are striving for funds, and also when you are preparing to conclude your grant and have your close-out audit or financial report. The following examples are typical, but not necessarily all that you will need to submit to your funding source.

# *Personnel*

## Wages & Salaries

This is the part of your proposal that almost everybody in the funding source's review procedure will read. Keep in mind that good people get periodic pay raises, that consultants charge much more than salaried employees—usually, whatever the market will bear— and that most jobs include at least some fringe benefits, even if it is only the employer's contribution to the employee's Social Security trust fund. And take note of donated time at its market value.

*We suggest using this type of a format:*
- Name and title of each person working on the project
- percent of time charged to this project
- Salary on an hourly, daily, weekly or monthly basis

Donated = Total)

How does this appear in a completed budget? If you are employing an Executive Director or Project Director at a salary of $3,000 a
month (a very modest wage), working full-time (100%) for the entire
grant period (12 months) and you are asking the funding source to
provide that salary, it looks like this:

|  | Requested | Donated | Total |
|---|---|---|---|
| Executive Director @ $3,000 per mo. (100 percent time) | $36,000 | -0- | $36,000 |

You may list all staff this same way. If any of your staff are being
paid out of another source of funds (for example, a staff person
assigned to your project by another agency) then you total their salary
and put it in the "donated" column. This column might also be called
"non-federal" share in the case of federal programs, or also "matching" or "in-kind" contribution. Like this:

|  | Requested | Donated | Total |
|---|---|---|---|
| (2) Counselors at $1,700 per mo. (50 percent time) x 6 mo. | -0- | $10,200 | $10,200 |

This means that you will have two half-time counselors on your
staff for six months and their salaries are being paid by somebody
other than the funding source you are applying to. You still put their
full-time salary in the budget ($1,700 per month), take half of it (they
are only working 50 percent time), multiply the $850 by the six months
they will be working on this project (yielding $5,100), and multiply by
2 (the number of people employed in this capacity). This gives you a
total of $10,200 of donated counselor services in this project.

What does the $3,000 per month figure for the salary of the
Executive Director mean? It may represent his or her actual salary for
each month of the year. However, particularly in a new program, it

- Amount donated or offered as "in-kind" contribution
- Total compensation for this person (Requested +

may not. Most organizations develop a five-step salary schedule for each job in the organization. The salary range for an Executive Director might look like this:

| Step A | Step B | Step C | Step D | Step E |
|--------|--------|--------|--------|--------|
| $2200/mo. | $2400/mo. | $2600/mo. | $3000/mo. | $3200/mo. |

If you have developed this kind of salary schedule for each position, then you can place in the monthly salary column of your budget the middle step of the salary range for each position, place an asterisk next to each quoted salary and a note at the bottom of the salary section telling the reader that all salaries are listed at the middle step of the salary range for that position. Then you can attach your salary schedule to the budget. This method allows for a good deal of flexibility in fixing salaries for individuals who are hired.

For example, you may have somebody in mind for the Executive Director's job who is presently earning $1,600 per month, and who would be delighted to come to work for you at the first step of the salary range for Executive Director ($1,800 per month). On the other hand, there may be an outstanding candidate for the job who is presently earning $2,000 per month, and who wouldn't come to work for you for less than $2,100 per month. Using the salary range in this manner allows you to employ either person, at the appropriate salary, with the assumption being that all person's salaries will average out toward the middle of the salary range.

How do you determine what the salary range for an Executive Director for your agency or project ought to be? The federal government requires that all of your salaries be comparable to the prevailing practices in similar agencies in your community. (These examples are purposely kept low to facilitate ease of understanding.) To justify the salaries you build into your budget, you should obtain information from other local agencies regarding the salaries of persons with job descriptions, qualifications and responsibilities similar to those of the jobs in your agency. You might go to the local city and/or county government, the school district, the United Way, etc. By comparing the jobs in your agency with the jobs at other local agencies, you plan a salary for each position, and you keep the "comparability data" on hand, should you be asked by the funding source to justify your staff salaries.

## Fringe Benefits

In this section of the budget you list all the fringe benefits your employees will be receiving and the dollar cost of these benefits. Some fringe benefits are mandatory—but these vary from state to state, so you will have to determine what they are for your agency in your state. Mandatory fringe benefits may include State Disability Insurance, unemployment compensation, retirement contributions, etc. Most nonprofit agencies when they are started, may vote not to participate in Social Security. These fringe benefits are all based on the hypothetical rate of 5.85 percent of the first $10,000 of each person's salary. Therefore, an entry for FICA on your budget might look like this:

|  | Requested | Donated | Total |
|---|---|---|---|
| FICA at 5.85% x $87,000 | $5,090 | -0- | $5,090 |

**Note:** *$87,000 is the total of all salaries, up to $10,800 for any one person.*

Some fringe benefits may be paid not on a percentage of salary, but with an absolute dollar amount for each employee. For example:

|  | Requested | Donated | Total |
|---|---|---|---|
| Health Insurance $50/mo.<br>x 8 employees x 12 mo. | $4,800 | -0- | $4,800 |

How do you determine what fringe benefits to provide to employees in your agency? What about workers compensation and similar charges? Be sure to allow funds for all mandated benefits. If you already operate a variety of programs, your answer is simple. Employees in a new project receive the same fringe benefits as those you already employ in some other activity. The federal government in most part requires this parity. If you are starting a new agency, or haven't formulated a fringe benefit policy yet, then you go through the same process as you did when establishing your salary schedule — you provide in fringe benefits what is comparable to the prevailing practice in similar agencies in your community.

## Consultants & Contract Services

This is the third and final part of the personnel section of your budget. In this section you include paid and unpaid consultants, volunteers and services for which you contract. For example, your project may not be large enough to warrant hiring a full-time bookkeeper, and you may want to use a bookkeeping service to keep your books. An entry in your budget will look like this:

|  | Requested | Donated | Total |
|---|---|---|---|
| Bookkeeping Service at $75 per mo. x 12 mo. | $900 | -0- | $900 |

You should be running your two totals columns—requested and donated—through your entire proposal, so you have a choice of where you put the cost for this service. If you are going to pay for it, it goes in the "requested" column as seen above or in the donated column as seen below if the service is offered without charge by a friend, associate, board member, etc.

|  | Requested | Donated | Total |
|---|---|---|---|
| Bookkeeping Service at $75 per mo. x 12 mos. | -0- | $900 | $900 |

It is often important to develop as much donated services and equipment as possible. No funding source likes to feel it is being asked to carry the entire burden of a project. If the project really means something to you and to your community, then you should have been able to develop a substantial "matching" contribution in your budget. Other kinds of contract services that might be included would be for auditing, public relations, technical assistance, etc.

In this section you can include all of your volunteer assistance. How do you value a volunteer's time for budgetary purposes? Federal agencies maintain lists of various types of jobs and assign a value to each hour of volunteer time for each position. For example, the time of a professional social worker may be valued at $7.50 per hour, and would look like the following in your budget:

|  | Requested | Donated | Total |
|---|---|---|---|
| Volunteer Social Worker @ $7.50 per hr. x 4 hrs per week x 40 wks | -0- | $1,200 | $1,200 |

The figure which you receive from a federal agency volunteer valuation list may be less than the actual current hourly salary of the volunteer. In that case, you may use the actual hourly salary, but be prepared to substantiate that figure. Or, the volunteer may have previously worked as a paid consultant for $10, $15 or $20 per hour. You can use that figure if you can document it.

With all of your volunteers you are required to deliver the promised volunteer services, just as if the funding source was actually paying their salary, and you will be asked to document the work performed by volunteers and keep records of their volunteer time which may be audited in the case of a federal grant. The "In-kind contribution form" on the Grantwriters diskette is helpful in documenting volunteer activity.

# Non-Personnel

## Space Costs

In this section list all of the facilities you will be using, both those on which you pay rent and those that are donated. Rent you pay, or the valuation of donated facilities, must be comparable to prevailing rents in the geographic area in which you are located. In addition to the actual rent, you should also include the cost of utilities, mainte-nance services and renovations, if they are absolutely essential to your program.

## Rental, Lease or Purchase of Equipment

Here you list all of the equipment, donated or to be purchased, that will be used in the proposed program. This includes office equip-ment, typewriters, computers, copying machines, audio visual equip-ment, etc. Let discretion be your guide in this section. Try to obtain as much donated equipment as you can. It not only lowers the cost of the program, but it shows the funding source that other people are involved in trying to make the program happen and that their support will be there when the grant dollars are gone.

## Consumable Supplies and Meeting Room Rental

This budget category refers to supplies such as paper clips, paper, pens, pencils, etc. and often your meeting rooms. A reasonable figure to use is $150 per year for each of your staff for their desktop con-sumable supplies. If you have any unusual needs for supplies, add them as well. In addition, you may be planning on making a work-room available for collating, mass mailings or meetings of communi-ty persons, then put in a separate figure for that. For example:

| | Requested | Donated | Total |
|---|---|---|---|
| 18 staff x $150 per year | -0- | $2700 | $2700 |
| Supplies for community workroom x $30 per meeting x 12 meetings | -0- | $360 | $360 |

## Travel

Divide the travel section of your budget into local and out-of-town travel. Avoid large lump sums that require interpretation or will raise questions at the funding source. Try for actual costs that reflect cur-rent research and are credible. Remember, on local mileage all of your staff won't be driving on the job, and not all drive the same amount.

## Sample Line Item Budget

| Budget Item | Detail of Request | Total Request |
|---|---|---|
| Personnel | | |
| Project Coordinator | 75 % time @$4,000/mo | |
| | x 4 mo June-Oct | $12,000 |
| Office assistants (3) | $7.50/hr x 900 hours | $6,750 |
| Principal investigators (12) | $2,000 each as consultants | $24,000 |
| Clerical assistant | $6.25/hr x 700 hours | $4,375 |
| Three outside consultants (3) | $4,000 flat fee each | $12,000 |
| Senior consultant | $375/day x 40 days | $15,000 |
| Fringe Benefits (@ 6 percent) | Includes FICA, WC, etc. | $4,448 |
| **Travel** | | |
| Local staff travel | 3760 miles @ 0.26/mi | $ 978 |
| Out of town travel | $7,500 | $ 7,500 |
| **Communications** | | |
| Printing | Includes final reports | $3,364. |
| Postage | Includes survey returns | $1,850 |
| Telecommunications | | $1,175 |
| **Supplies** | | |
| Desktop consumables | For office and computer | $900. |
| **Overhead** | | |
| | @6% (Approved rate of | |
| | 40-34%t waived as in-kind) | $5,660. |
| **Total Requested** | | $100,000 |

*Finding Funding:*
*The Comprehensive Guide to Grant Writing*

Figure 11

| | Requested | Donated | Total |
|---|---|---|---|
| **Out of town travel** | | | |
| (1) Community Organizer to NAVE training program in Chicago, June 8-13, $447 round-trip airfare; 4 days per diem @ $116 | $911 | -0- | $911 |
| **Local travel** | | | |
| Exec. Director at 100 mi. per x 12 mos. x.265 per miles | $318 | -0- | $318 |
| (2) Community Organizer @ 500 miles/mo. x 12 mos. X .265 mile | $1,590 | -0- | $1,590 |
| **Total Amount of Request** | $2819 | -0- | $2819 |

Out-of-town travel is a very vulnerable section of your budget. Plan and justify it as completely as you can.

## Telephones

Remember installation costs! This part of the budget should reflect the number of instruments you will need times the expected monthly cost per instrument. Justify or explain in advance any extensive out-of-town calling that you will have to do.

## Other Costs

This catch-all category may include items like:
- Postage
- Fire, theft and liability insurance
- Dues in professional associations paid by the agency

## Subscriptions

Publications and promotions, the cost of which may be broken into

- Printing
- Typesetting
- Video production
- Addressing, if done by a service
- Mailing (separate and distinct from office postage above)
- Advertising and promotion
- Any other items that don't logically fit elsewhere.

## One Page Budget Summary

From the above, you can see in detail how budgets are created. Obviously, this amount of detail can weigh down a proposal, and may even cause problems if the funding source has limited the total proposal package to a set number of pages. Accordingly, it is important to be able to summarize your budget in no more than one page, even if there is more budget detail elsewhere in the material submitted. The preceding one-page budget summary was created using the tables feature of Microsoft Word, selecting the appropriate number of columns and rows, using headlines, bold face and flush right for numbers as would be useful. A copy of this form is included in the document diskette.

## Notes On The Proposed Budget

### Fringe Benefit

In this section of the budget we have listed minimum and basic fringe benefits expected as mandatory despite the status of project employees as either faculty and students or outside consultants. These fringe benefits may include State Disability Insurance, unemployment compensation, etc.

### Space Costs

The applicant will contribute as in-kind the use of offices, labs and other facilities to include the cost of utilities, maintenance services and renovations, if they are absolutely essential to this project.

## Other In-Kind Items

As above, the in kind includes office equipment, typewriters, computers, copying machines, audio-visual equipment, etc. In addition, the applicant will also provide consumable supplies and meeting room rental. With an approved indirect rate of 40 percent, the applicant's acceptance of 6 percent represents a cash match of $22,911 to this project.

## Products and Deliverables

The product of this study will be a report answering each of the questions, with appropriate attachments and details, according to the timeline as approved.

## A Model Of Unit Cost Budgeting

- The RFP Requirements
- The following unit cost budget is taken from an actual human services grant.
- Note to Applicants
- The service area for this project includes the entire metropolitan area with a target population as described below. Proposals must identify the clients served in terms of the target populations. A description of how the agency will recruit or obtain referrals from other groups must be included in the proposal. (Attachments not included with this example.)
- All information must be provided to the clients in a culturally, linguistically and developmentally appropriate manner. Strategies and methodologies must be sensitive to the communities, educational needs and correlate with the ways in which the communities receive and process information.

## Available Funding

A total of $1.9 million is available for 12 months for eligible proponents targeting adolescents, substance abusers, single parents, males, grandmothers and/or homeless families. It is anticipated that 15-20 proponents will be awarded contracts ranging from $25,000 to

$100,000, depending on proposed activities. There will be no awards over $200,000.

## Service Objectives and Service Fees

The attachment lists all objectives that will be considered for reimbursement. Each objective listed also contains the maximum costs that will be reimbursed and the mandatory evaluation forms that will be used for primary documentation.

Since contracting with community agencies to provide prenatal outreach and case management is a new service, the county may be willing to work individually with agencies and renegotiate unit costs. This will not occur before agencies have at least 2-3 months of experience with implementing objectives. At the time of negotiation, the agency must have detailed documentation to substantiate unit cost changes. Documentation must include fiscal and programmatic data supporting reasons which coverage of a particular target group and/ or geographic area requires greater reimbursement.

## Scope of Work

The Scope of Work SOW) shall include one or more goals and at least one or more objectives for each goal. In addition, implementation activities and evaluation statements must be included for each objective.

## Goal(s):

The goal of this project is: Promote and coordinate a single local effort that improves prenatal outreach and addresses unmet needs.

## Objectives:

A statement on what measurable service will be delivered. Service (e.g. 100—150 people seen in outreach) that will be achieved for each objective.

## Implementation:

Describe your agency's design for meeting each objective. List specific steps that will be taken to deliver the service stated in the objective. For example: Hire staff, obtain equipment, engage in activities to identify and recruit potential clients, promote services to appropriate clinic, etc.

## Timelines:

Every activity listed needs a timeline—a beginning and ending date for the activity listed.

## Methods of Evaluation Objectives and Documentation:

- **Evaluation:** Each objective shall have a corresponding evaluation statement that describes the outcome of the service delivered. What was observed? What was the final result? Did the service provided make a difference? This information will be gathered via mandatory evaluation forms. Identify the forms to be used. Additional evaluation steps that should be in your plan include recording attendance with sign-in sheets, pre and post-tests, etc.
- **Documentation:** The paperwork that is referenced in the "implementation activities" and maintained on file with the contractor for review purposes such as case records, plans, logs, analyses and summaries of data, etc. All case management services must be documented on Form 14.

# *Unit Cost Budgeting*

## Sample of an Applicant Response to Unit Cost Budgeting

### *Outreach And Case Management Objectives*

### Outreach Objectives

- Conduct one-on-one counseling sessions to provide assessment and intensive, individualized education to individuals at the following site(s) away from our agency's routine services:
  **Unit cost:$ 28.45/person**

- Conduct one-on-one outreach to program participants and individuals at the clinics run by our agency:
  **Unit cost:**       **$19.48/person**

- Conduct small events (< 50 people) in churches, community centers, housing projects, and other local agencies to foster awareness of the Outreach & Case Management Project.
  **Unit cost:**       **$434.00/event**

- Conduct medium-sized events (50-100 people) in churches, community centers, housing projects and other local agencies to foster awareness of the Outreach and Case Management Project.
  **Unit cost:**       **$667.30/event**

- Conduct-large events (>100 people) in churches, community centers, housing projects and other local agencies to foster awareness of the Outreach and Case Management Project.
  **Unit cost:**       **$1,176.30/event**

- Conduct outreach via the following media venues:
  Purchasing ad space: $140/ad
  TV/radio interview: $210/interview
  **Press release:**    **$140/coverage**

- Present prevention messages to teen-age individuals via teen theater performances to small (<=30) audiences. Fifty percent of the program participants will score at least 75 percent on the program post test and demonstrate a positive attitude toward non-smoking choices.
  **Unit cost:**       **$458.60/performance**

- Present prevention messages to teen-age individuals via teen theater performances to large (>30) audiences. Fifty percent of the program participants will score at least 75% on the program post-test and demonstrate a positive attitude toward non-smoking choices.
  **Unit cost:**       **$540.40/performance**

- Conduct single session seminars, focus groups, or other group meetings with health professionals with the intent of 1) educating about the program and the need to refer high risk individuals and/or 2) to discuss needs of the target groups and effective means for outreach and enrollment in case management services.

  **Unit cost:**          **$107.70/session**

## Outreach and Referral Objectives

- Conduct small group (<30 people) educational counseling/support sessions covering topics such as pre-conceptual issues, pregnancy-related topics, high-risk behaviors, nutrition and parenting skills to adolescents, substance abusers, single parents, males, grandmothers and/or homeless families. Provide appropriate referrals to at least 25% of participants.

  **Unit cost:**          **$358.35/session**

- Conduct large group (>30 people) educational counseling /support sessions covering topics such as pre-conception issues, pregnancy-related topics, high-risk behaviors, nutrition and parenting skills to adolescents, substance abusers, single parents, males, grandmothers and/or homeless families. Provide appropriate referrals to at least 25% of participants.

  **Unit cost:**          **$253.46/session**

## Case Management Objective

- Provide case management to women. At least 60% of pregnant women enrolled in case management services will be followed to full-term.

  **Unit cost:**          **$68.60/woman/month** (using nurses)
  **Unit cost:**           **$54.92/woman/month**
                          (using Master's level social worker)
  **Unit cost:**          **$49.97/woman/month**
                          (using Bachelor's level social worker)

  *(These unit costs include incentives, assistance with travel and child care and other services/items provided to women under case management.)*

# Unit Cost Budget:
# Outreach and Case Management

**I   Service Objectives***

| Objective | Category Number | Proposed Units | Unit Cost | Reimbursement |
|---|---|---|---|---|
| Outreach | 1 | 1,000 | $28.45 | $28,450 person |
| Outreach | 2 | 24 | $253.46 | $6,083 session |
| Case Management | 1 | 100/9 mos | $68.60 | $61,740 case/mo. |
| Total for Service Reimbursement | | | | $96,273 |

**II   Program Development****      $10,000

**III  Administrative Costs**      $21,255
(20 percent of services and start-up fees)

**IV  Indirect Costs (10%)****      $12,753

            **Grand Total**      **$140,281**

\*    Use higher end of range described in Scope of Work
\*\*   Start-up reimbursement for up to $5,000/month limited to maximum two months
\*\*\* Budget justification must document costs included in the indirect rate with justification for percentage used

## A Note about Indirect Costs
Some programs, particularly those conducted within a large insti-

tution such as a college or university, also include an indirect cost figure. Indirect costs are paid to the host institution in return for its tendering certain services to the project. The host may manage the bookkeeping and payroll, assume some responsibility for overseeing the project, take care of maintenance and utilities costs, etc. The first time an institution conducts a federally funded program it projects what these indirect costs will be. Subsequently, there is an audit by the federal government, and an indirect cost figure is fixed which will hold for the institution for all subsequent federal grants until the next audit. The range of these indirect costs typically runs from 20 to 65 percent or more.

# How to Calculate In-Direct or Overhead Costs

## Add On Method

There are two primary ways to calculate your indirect cost. The first is the simple add on indirect cost method, in which you merely total all the charges for salaries, equipment, travel, supplies, services and the like, and "add on" the overhead at your approved rate. This occurs much like the manner in which sales tax is added to your bill at the end of a trip to the shopping center.

### Computationally it might look like this:

| | |
|---|---|
| Salaries | $56,990 |
| Supplies | 960 |
| Travel | 2,819 |
| Communications | 1,000 |
| | |
| **SUB-TOTAL** | 61,769 |
| Overhead @ 40% | 24,708 |
| | |
| **PROJECT TOTAL** | $86,477 |

## Fixed Price Method

The second method is the fixed price including in-direct cost method. This method is used when the grant source has a fixed amount to award and the applicant must fit both their overhead and project costs to the exact amount of the funds available, or slightly less than the funds listed if there is a strategic purpose to "under-bidding."

Taking the $100,000 available from our mythical funding source, what would be your first guess at how much must be set aside for overhead and how much is available for all other project costs? One is tempted to say $40,000 for overhead and $60,000 for the project. That would be a $11,000+ mistake; you short-changed yourself and your project team. The formula is simple: merely assume that X (1) = your project costs, then add on .4X (40 percent) to get the value of 1.4X. $ 100,000 divided by 1.4 X equals the amount of your actual project costs. Look at this example:

**X = PROJECT COSTS +.4X (OVERHEAD) = 1.4 X $100,000**

| | | |
|---|---|---|
| Total Funds Available | (1.4X) | $100,000 |
| Overhead @ 40percent | (.4X) | 28,571 |
| All other project costs | (X) | 71,429 |

If your overhead rate is more or less, simply remember that project costs always should be represented as X, then add the fraction that represents your overhead or indirect costs (25 percent, 32, 60 percent, whatever it is) and then solve for X.

## Budget Narratives:

Some funders will ask for budget narratives to clarify terms and/or line items.

*Some examples:*

- **Receptionist:** This half-time position serves as the first line of communication between clients and our organization. Specific responsibilities include answering all incoming calls, greeting clients and sponsors at the entrance and light filing.

- **Travel:** Director will attend two national conventions at currently undisclosed cities. Roundtrip plane fare within the continental United States has been estimated at $1,800 per trip. Director and Associate Director will also attend monthly regional meetings in Santa Monica, California. Administrators will carpool, and round trip mileage is estimated at 45 miles, times $0.32 per mile.

## Budget Summaries

This is a "big picture" look at the budget of the program. It is broken down into personnel costs and non-personnel costs, and thus covers all costs. More often, however, your funding source will require a line item budget, where these expenses are more fully explained.

## Line Item Budget

Computer technology facilitates budget building by providing professional platforms to present your material. Often, budget forms are available in PDF form for download, printing and filling out. Some more sophisticated Adobe Acrobat users offer the form in a format that may be filled out in Acrobat, leaving blank fields for your numbers, categories and titles.

Notice also how this particular funding entity divides costs into set-up costs and operating costs. Other funders may split costs into personnel and non-personnel costs. However the data is requested, follow their instructions. Get answers to questions by calling them or via e-mail. When provided with a form, it is essential that your budget match the format provided.

## Project Revenues

Typically, funding sources want to see the other sources of revenue for the project. This is to ensure the project's success, and to see what other organizations are involved in it.

Potential funders will be impressed if you have secured a major funder to support your project. For example, if the Ahmanson, Ford, or Rockefeller Foundations thinks you're OK, as evidenced by significant pledged financial support, then you should appear "pre-qualified" to other funding sources that you are soliciting. A careful review of your previous funding support from all sources is both effective and critical in the establishment of your track record as a responsible program operator.

Some funders require a multi-year budget. In this case, you must be prepared to provide this information. You must indicate which revenues are committed, and which are anticipated. Finally, be prepared to indicate both the hard match (cash), and the soft match (in-kind).

## *Summary*

The budget is never the easiest part of a proposal, but it is vitally important to ensure that the funding source will look favorably upon your proposal because they are assured of your competence to do what you propose. You may choose the traditional line-item budget, or the more innovative unit cost budget. In either case, be clear. When in doubt, explain or detail, and always be accurate. Double check your numbers! A misspelled word can be overlooked, but an error in the budget can lead to your proposal's disqualification. Budgets are the skeletal frame by which funding sources gauge the strength and reliability of your program. Keep in mind, however, that while a budget must be as specific and as accurate as possible, it is an estimate, an informed guess about the cost of events and programs yet to happen. During the budget-making process, be prepared to make program changes based on information or new insights that your budget reveals. Few people enjoy making a budget: It may seem dehumanizing because planning ahead eliminates certain choices of action. Nevertheless, there will be no funding without an acceptable budget, so start early and keep at it. You may wind up with a more expensive program than you first imagined, and therefore you may have to go back and make changes to your program and proposal. But in budgeting as in all writing, practice makes perfect

Beyond all the facts and figures that you have just read about budgeting, the following two simple ideas may be the most important

—and literally worth their weight in gold, at least as they relate to mental health. The mental health of the grant writer.

## Budget Secret Number One:

There is a chance that your project will not be finish by its anticipated completion date. That might happen because of something your organization has done, or failed to do. It might be because of something the funding source did. It might be through no one's fault at all: An off-season hurricane, a 100-year flood, a fire, an earthquake. But if your completion date arrives and you have made no provisions otherwise, expenses will continue to come in after your funding clock has run out. Therefore, always ask for the right to do line-item transfers within your budget. This means that after permission or notification (there is a large difference) by the funding source, you may move amounts of money from where it is not needed to where it is needed. This should not occur often, or too early in the process, but the right to make it happen can be critical in completion of your assignments. Usually this affects small amounts of money in the last quarter, but the principle is very important.

## Budget Secret Number Two:

When you first build a budget, you cannot forecast every expenditure. Many a principal investigator, project director or like administrator has faced a spending deadline with work yet to be completed. Therefore, at or near the end of the contract, ask for the right, for a "No Cost Extension in Time." Always allow for at least another 90 days. This simple request is almost always granted if the contractor has been a responsible performer up to that point. Some funding sources even feel that they are getting "extra" work for the same original grant. In any case, when you see the need arise, remember the value of this action and hopefully your careful and hard work on your budget from proposal through implementation will be rewarded in bringing your work to a satisfactory conclusion for all parties. If it is too late to change a proposal budget when you read this, and your grant is funded, remember: Forgiveness is usually easier to obtain than permission.

## Budget Checklist

- Consider both your internal and external audiences
- Don't forget to obtain early internal clearance
- Use budget notes to appease and explain
- Clearly delineate costs to be met by the funding source and those provided by the applicant or other parties
- Offer budgetary detail to relate to the proposal narrative
- Give detailed support for all major expenditures
- Estimate and project costs that will be incurred at the time of the program, if different from the proposal writing
- Explain all amounts of miscellaneous or contingency funds, in kind or soft match, and similar items
- Include all items asked of the funding sources and all paid for by other sources.
- Include all volunteers
- Give appropriate details on fringe benefits, separate from salaries
- Detail expenses for all consultants
- Separately detail all non-personnel costs
- Explain indirect costs where appropriate
- Ask for enough money to perform the tasks described in the narrative
- Check your math. Check it again.

## Model Grant Budget

| LINE ITEM | DONATED | REQUESTED | TOTAL |
|---|---|---|---|
| Executive Director | $20,000 | $10,000 | $30,000 |
| Project Coordinator(s) | | | |
| 2($25,000 per person) | | $50,000 | $50,000 |
| Fiscal Officer | | $30,000 | $30,000 |
| Accountant (10 days @ $300.) | | $3,000 | $3,000 |
| Communications | | $3,400 | $3,400 |

| LINE ITEM | DONATED | REQUESTED | TOTAL |
|---|---|---|---|
| Travel | | $2,225 | $2,225 |
| Desk Top Consumables | $1,000 | $1,000 | $2,000 |
| Outside Services | | | |
| (printing, data analysis) | $2,000 | $4,500 | $6,500 |
| SUB-TOTAL | $16,000 | $121,125 | $137,125 |
| Indirect Costs | | | |
| (overhead) | $41,138 | $13,712 | $54,850 |
| **TOTAL** | $57,138 | $134,837 | $191,975 |

**NOTE:** *This agency will reduce its normal indirect charges, approved rate of 40%, to 10% as an additional in-kind and donated contribution to the project. Other donated and in-kind efforts are expressed as pertinent to each budget category.*

## Sample Task-By-Task Timeline for a 16-Week Study

| PROJECT TASK | JULY | AUG. | SEPT. | OCT. |
|---|---|---|---|---|
| Develop Questions | XX | | | |
| Collect Initial Data | XX | XXX | | |
| Analyze Data | | X | X | |
| Revise, Critique and | | | | |
| Collect More Data | | | XX | |
| First Draft is Prepared | | | X | |
| Critique and Revision | | | XX | |
| Present Final Report | | | | XX |
| **LEGEND: X = ONE WEEK** | | | | |

## A Fiscal Manager's Rationale For Indirect Costs And Special Reports

Direct Costs—Direct costs are those that can be identified specifically with a particular research project, an instructional activity or any other institutional activity; or which can be directly assigned to such activities with relative ease and a high degree of accuracy.

Indirect costs or Facilities and Administrative Costs-F & A costs are those that have been incurred from common or joint objectives and therefore cannot be identified specifically with a particular project. Such costs may include: general administration expenses, sponsored programs administration expenses, operation and maintenance expenses, library expenses and departmental administration expenses.

Facilities and Administrative Costs are defined by the U.S. Office of Management as those that are incurred for common or joint objectives and therefore cannot be identified readily and specifically with a particular sponsored project, an instructional activity, or any other institutional activity.

## Budget and Activity Reports

Regular monthly computer generated reports are issued on every account. Monthly reports provide financial data on a current month and project-to-date basis. The financial data consists of budget, actual expenditures and encumbrances. Encumbrances represent purchase orders not yet paid.

## External Reports

Your Finance Office also prepares and submits financial and other reports as required to external sponsors of contracts and grants. These reports are generally financial in nature and most of them concern the request of funds to cover expenditures incurred. In addition, most sponsors require other final reports such as property, invention, or final technical reports.

# CHAPTER 11

# Finishing Touches and Project Administration

♦ *How can I get my grant reviewed before sending it?*

♦ *How should my grant be sent—UPS, FedEx, US mail or What?*

♦ *How can I get governmental officials to help me get my grant funded?*

**F**inishing touches may come at a time when the grantwriter is weary but they are important for the success of your proposal and useful in the administration of your newly funded project. We'll discuss the process of reviewing your grant proposal, both personally and by others, and include a look at how your grant will be reviewed by the funding source. A key element is the project timeline which is not only a guide during the writing of the proposal but also is the basic element in your management plan. While timelines are not always required in your grant proposal, they serve two functions, organizing yourself and your staff and impressing the funding source with your sense of organization and your commitment to delivering project products on a known schedule.

Any agency, whether preparing grant requests or not, needs a strong support team. This team is made up of employees, volunteers, interns and friends outside the organization. When preparing a grant, and even after the grant has been submitted for approval, this team can be a key part of the process, and we'll discuss that in this chapter.

We'll also discuss politicking or lobbying, directly and indirectly, the funding source. This activity needs to be undertaken with a gentle, even delicate hand, so as not to offend the funding source or apply pressure to parties that do not like pressure. Some additional guidance in this area is included in a list of 10 tips on how to approach such sources.

Finally, we'll cover a few details that will arise when your grant is funded. While these are actually beyond the scope of grant writing, keeping these things in mind during the grant writing process will make them easier to accomplish when the grant is funded.

While this material is presented rather late in the book, you may wish to apply some of this knowledge early in your grant writing process. Lining up the support team, holding pre-review sessions and approaching special funding sources can't be left for the end of the process but must be part of your activity plan from the beginning.

# Reviewing Your Proposal: Getting a Second Opinion (Even From Yourself)

The actual writing process of a grant is a considerable task. Often the exhausted grant writer is only too ready to slap a stamp on an envelope and send the grant off. However, a careful process of reviews, both personal, internal and external, can make the difference between a contract and a rejection letter.

The first level of review is your own. Review the grant carefully. Have you covered all the issues in the RFP, if there was one, or adequately explained your needs? Have you adequately described how the project will be executed? Have you included everything requested in the RFP, such as timelines? Is the budget realistic and easy to understand?

Often the hardest part of a self-review is divorcing yourself from the work enough to objectively review your grant. You need to focus on the grant from the point-of-view of an outsider who is probably not as familiar with your program, needs and capabilities as you are. For this reason, it is great to follow up your personal reviews with evaluations of your grant from both within and outside your organization.

Your first line of review is your colleagues, the support team you gathered to assist in the grant (and which we'll discuss more below). They often have as much at stake in the success of the grant as does the grant writer: they have probably invested hours into collecting data, making interviews, or other details. They also can be the best critics, pointing out areas that could be strengthened or corrected. In this effort, the lead grant writer still needs a support group to not only complete the proposal but to eventually complete the work that is funded. All the parties, leaders or followers have a stake in the process and will enjoy the success. Simply said, people tend to support what they help create.

> *Your first line of review is your colleagues, the support team you gathered to assist in the grant.*

There is a trap in this internal review process, however. If everyone on your team is on the same wavelength (or at least a similar one) with you, the grant writer, they may be vulnerable to overlooking weaknesses in your proposal caused by "group think." Equally hazardous to your funding health, they may come down with a severe case of "The Boss Is Always Right"—especially if the Boss is the grant writer. Finally, comments like, "If I mention a change now, I'll have to do it myself" or, "I'll make an enemy in the typing pool" can have the effect of masking errors in a grant.

The first problem is both the hardest to overcome (because it often has to do with the group dynamic of the organization, the management style of the boss or where the grant writer sits in the hierarchy of the organization) but also in some ways the easiest, for it is a known problem in organizations. One of the best slogans any organization can adopt is, "It's amazing how well things go when nobody cares who gets the credit." This is also true in grant writing: if the goal is seen as the successful acceptance of the grant and not in the author, it is amazing how well a grant can be written.

The second problem was much more prevalent in the days of typewriters and carbon paper; in this era of word processing and computers, however, changes are easy to make. Adding, deleting or changing sentences or entire paragraphs can be done with a few strokes of a key or swishes of a mouse.

Finally, there is great value in an outside opinion—and getting one is often as simple as asking for one. Use the same list of contacts you used in drafting the proposal. Simply ask them, "Could I send you a copy of my proposal and a red pen and ask for your comments?" Not everyone will say yes, but even state and federal agencies, given enough lead time, will agree to conduct a pre-submission review. If they are in the review process, they may suggest someone else to whom your grant may be sent for review. Or you might ask an organization that has successfully received funding from the grantor, or one in a similar field of specialty as the topic of the proposal. It is important is to let someone completely removed from the grant writing process take a good, hard, unbiased look at the content of your work and get it back to you in time to meet the deadline.

## Developing or Refining Your Realistic Timeline Keyed to Tasks

Unless you have one of those rare RFP's that insist only that you fill out a form, you will undoubtedly have an opportunity and need to develop a realistic timeline keyed to the tasks in your proposal. This combination of a task statement with a time line makes life easier for both the grant writer and the grant reviewer.

The first step is to define your project methodology in terms of tasks. Sometimes you can break the project into discrete tasks; other times you need only note natural breaks or sequences in project activities. Such techniques as flowcharting or PERT charts can be helpful here; project-management programs are available that make this both easy to do for the grant writer and easy to understand for the reviewer. One such sample of a time line is found in the Grantwriters Diskette that accompanies this book.

The second step is to develop hypothetical best- and worst-case scenarios as to the length each task would take. Your choice of between best-case and worst-case depends on whether you take an optimistic approach to your project or a pessimistic one. Whichever approach you take, you will arrive at a number of hours, days, weeks, or months each task will consume; then, arrange each task from start to finish, with particular attention to those tasks that must be completed before starting another one and those that can be done concurrently with others. Don't forget to include downtime, meeting time, evaluation sessions and even time for holidays and vacations. Again, the project-management programs mentioned above can be invaluable here; but a simple technique involves using strips of paper to represent each task, with the strip scaled to length representative of the time required for each task (one inch equals one hour or one week, for example); these strips of paper can then be laid out so that you can visually "see" how the project will progress.

Finally, re-read the narrative of your proposal and make sure that it is synchronous with the time line you've developed. You may find you've created a time line that is longer than the time available to complete the project: either reduce the times for tasks or reorganize tasks so that they fit in the time allotted—and be prepared to live with it—or request more time in the grant. Such a review may also come after the grant has been awarded, as the actual grant award date is changed or tasks are added or subtracted. Some proposers always use actual dates, while others prefer a more generic format identifying time blocks as "Week One" or "Month One." Whichever one works best for you and your project, be ready to be flexible.

## *Printing And Mailing The Proposal*

Another favorite expression is that nobody supports an idea—no matter how good it is—if they have never heard of it. The finishing touch of printing and mailing is important because funding sources often have very strict rules on the format that they accept, font size, binding etc. and, of course, the date by which proposals must be received. When you first dissected the RFP (see chapter 7) you should have made a check list of all printing and mailing rules and deadlines. There are no small points when preparing and sending your grant proposal: Attention to detail might well be the difference between a successful grant application, a rejection letter, or believe or not, having your proposal returned unread!

One of the most common reasons for rejection of a grant proposal is tardiness in submission. Given the general human tendency to procrastinate, many grant proposals are submitted on the day they are due (and often late in the day) or even a day or two late. This is not acceptable. So what steps can you take to help yourself and your proposal?

*One of the most common reasons for rejection of a grant proposal is tardiness in submission.*

A first step is to decide how you will print your final draft. Are hand illustrations okay or will you need professionally prepared artwork? Will you need special binding, color printing, enlargements or reductions of pages or charts? Can you use them or are you restricted? Do you have a letter-quality laser or color printer available? What about signatures from internal and external authorities, budget authorities, the so-called "clearance forms?" Do you need more than one set of original signatures? Where in the proposal do they appear. Will the local VIP's sign a cover sheet with only a draft of the proposal? And who's out of town that you need, and who signs for them?

Your final output should be first class and planning well ahead for these last-minute activities will ensure that you reach that goal. You should have the printers up and working, sufficient supplies on hand, and even a contingency plan to get signatures or appendix items at the last minute. Of course, you may want to have the final copies printed by one of your local instant or quick printing companies.

You will also have to decide how your proposal will be delivered to the funding source. Unless the grantor is located in your town, dropping off the proposal yourself may not be an option. United Parcel Service (UPS) is fast and cheap, and can easily be tracked once the proposal is sent, but they do not usually deliver on weekends. Federal Express and similar overnight services cost more and are equally traceable, and can make deliveries on weekends. This is important if your proposal is due on a Monday and you find yourself making final changes on Saturday morning.

The U.S. Postal Service offers several methods of delivery, including Priority Mail (two to three days), Express Mail (overnight) and services that notify you when your grant has been delivered; they can also be traced, as can UPS and FedEx packages, via telephone or on the Internet.

In an absolute pinch, sometimes airline package services are the savior for the late, late Thursday-night proposal due by noon Friday in a distant city. After that, you may have to hire a very expensive courier service. If your neck is on the line, or if you are bidding to build an atom smasher, it could well be worth it.

There are limitations to these services as to weights, areas served and the like. Check your local area for such details as deadlines, costs, drop-off points, pick-up services and so on.

As you roar toward the deadline, hopefully your planning of people, printing and delivery will result in an on-time delivery and an absence (or minimum amount) of heartburn. Remember that as the lead person, the responsibility for all the pieces very likely rests with you. Other people may be like the blind men who touched the elephant, each "seeing" it differently. Check the whole animal out, look at pagination, look at timelines, re-check and re-balance the budget, check for correct spelling and re-read the RFP one last time to be certain that you have included all the required material as well as necessary forms and attachments. Finally, as unpleasant as it might be to consider, sometimes parties in the offices of the funding source have a preferred fund recipient in mind. Mistakes at this end of the submittal process could give them the ammunition to disallow your proposal.

## It's In The Mail And Now We Begin The Persuasive Process

If they do nothing else, team sports show us the value of team-work. While the actual writing of a grant is often a lonely task, much can be done by a support team in the preparation of the grant. The following section details elements of a support team and how they can help get your project funded.

## Boards and Advisory Committees

The most important starting point for establishing a new grant project or organization is the development of its board or advisory committee. Sometimes these boards are important to contribute technical advice and project guidance; these are sometimes called "technical advisory committees (TAC)" and should have on them "the best and the brightest" people you can find. If your project requires wide-spread political support, your board might include county chair-men of both the Democratic and Republican parties. Unless they are in the funding stream or competitors, elected county and state offi-cials are also good candidates, as could be the mayor or city coun-cilpersons of your hometown. Leaders of major local community groups like the Rotary, the Kiwanis Club or the local Chamber of Commerce would be a valuable ally. Citizen groups, school adminis-trators, clients and/or parents can even be good members of your board, both for their insight in identifying needs in your grant and in getting the grant accepted. In every case be careful that your support team has the chemistry to work together and a size that is appropri-ate—big enough to impress folks, small enough to get business done.

## Media

A news reporter or columnist (print or electronic) may seem an unlikely member of such a group, but in fact news people are very important to the success of many proposals, education projects in particular. It is useful to meet with the general managers of news out-lets to explain the project and point out its importance. The intention of the meeting is, of course, to suggest that a reporter be instructed to cover the program as part of their regular assignment. A reporter on the board can provide you with many important contacts but even a declined invitation may yield future results.

## VIPs and Significant Others

Many projects have prominent people on their boards but do not use them effectively. It may be necessary to take the time to meet individually with each person you are going to ask to be a member of the board. In the meeting, have two agendas: the first one is to convince the person of the project's worth and the value of their being on the board; the second is to convince them that your organization could be helpful to them, either now or in the future.

Meeting personally accomplishes several things. It provides an entree for future personal meetings and gives the individuals some ego satisfaction, as you deemed them important enough to request a formal appointment. Furthermore, most people will not find it a bother if you later came to them for advice; in fact, it strengthens your position with them when you need their personal intervention in a matter. Never be bashful about asking for help; you'd be amazed how a simple "Please" will yield success.

Once a project becomes successful, the board of advisors may grow into a governing body that consists of representatives of the state university, state colleges, major community action projects, corporate executives, politicians, school administrators, etc. A policy of meeting with board members individually, usually for lunch, will greatly enhance an organization's channels for success. Frequently more business is accomplished over lunch than in a traditional office meeting. Finally, one should note that if the grant recipient is an existing governmental agency, the advisory committee will likely disband immediately when the project is completed or when dissemination activities are finished.

One of the most important functions of board members is to provide the staff with contacts. An influential member of your board can probably help you contact at least 10 other important persons who can influence the acceptance of your proposal.

In addition to the members of boards attached to your organization, you will occasionally have access to individuals and groups that for the purpose of this proposal will step up and support you. These certainly must include your joint venture partners, but also can be similar organizations that are not competing for these funds, elected or high appointed officials familiar with your cause and past performance, and other prominent persons who are not in the review process. It is unethical to ask for support from persons actually involved in making the fund or no-fund decisions.

One final note: be sure that your board or TAC has a balance with all your joint venture partners and consortium collaborators. It is best if all the concerned players have a place at the table, if only to prevent them from becoming at best a silent observer and at worst an opponent of your efforts.

# *Using Volunteers Within the Project Team*

In this day of reduced staff and increased workload, volunteers and unpaid student interns have become key members of the staff of many groups. They can also be extremely useful in the grant writing process. Volunteers and interns may work on a one-time, special-need basis or in an every-day leadership or staff job; there are significant differences, however, between enlisting the help of volunteers and interns once in a while and maximizing their involvement on an ongoing basis. This section contains a discussion of the basic elements of making volunteerism an integral part of an organization's overall services in general and specifically how they can assist in the grant writing process.

Before considering the elements of volunteer program organizations, however, some time may be well spent in considering the human resources involved. The volunteers, agency or organization staff, and the recipients of the services are all people—and they have basic rights and responsibilities relating to the work being done. Volunteers will work tirelessly as partners in your projects—but each must understand their responsibilities, observe agreed-upon lines of authority and communication, respect each other's perspectives, give honest feedback and have the opportunity to say "no" or request changes. From understanding and respect will come appreciation, flexibility, creativity and effectiveness.

Several basic elements of organization are particularly important in the planning for and management of volunteers. They are discussed in the following section

## Preparation and Planning

Prior to initiating any volunteer program, those responsible for establishing the program should have a thorough knowledge of the agency's needs and priorities in order to define objectives for volunteer services and volunteer opportunities and requirements. Administrative support should be secured and staff should be involved in generating ideas and identifying appropriate volunteer tasks.

A coordinator for the program should be designated and provided with an adequate budget allocation. Generally, the duties of the coordinator are to oversee recruitment, screening, placement, orientation, training, recognition and evaluation. Direct supervision, however, is not usually a part of the coordinator's responsibility. A clear delegation of authority for the coordinator and their staff should be set out well in advance to avoid any problems in the future.

The effect of new people on all aspects of the agency should be taken into account. Acceptance of volunteers by paid staff who will be co-workers and supervisors is particularly important. Whenever possible (and within the constraints of budget limitations), the paid staff must be made aware that the volunteer program will not constitute a threat to their jobs. Ideally, this should be in the form of a memo or other written policy statement and should be reinforced in practice.

Suitable program assignments should be identified for volunteers and specific job descriptions should be prepared for each job. Job descriptions should be written to include job responsibilities, necessary qualifications, time required per week or month, name and phone number of supervisor and training time requirements. Even though grant money is often viewed as "extra" or not in the mainstream, all personnel, staff and volunteers must, uphold high standards.

Many national, state and local resource organizations that can give you information on volunteer assistance programs. A centralized collection of resource publications is also helpful.

## Recruitment and Placement

The specific programs for which volunteers are being sought should be identified. Publicity should vary according to the number of volunteers needed but should be planned well in advance of actual need. To solicit more people than the agency could possibly use would be counter-productive. Also, it is generally a good idea to start the program small so that it will remain manageable.

But be sure to consider everyone—all shapes, sizes, ages and incomes—for their potential as volunteers. Soliciting volunteers can involve newspaper articles, public service announcements, speaking engagements, direct mailings to groups or individuals, placement offices, a Volunteer Fair and so on. Satisfied volunteers often became an agency's best recruiters.

Thorough preparation should be made for the volunteer interview. Interviewers should prepare questions in advance and familiarize themselves with techniques for learning the needs and interests of the applicant without allowing the interview to become too lengthy. The interviewer should be able to refer the applicant to other volunteer sources if they do not fit into the program or simply to decline the services of unsuitable applicants.

Volunteers should be given assistance in choosing an activity suitable to their goals and needs and compatible with their skills and interests. Motives such as the desire to work as part of a team, reestablish old skills, develop new interests or test career possibilities are just as valid as the motives of sharing oneself or advancing a favorite cause. The accomplishment of a meaningful agency or organization task must be the overriding objective in volunteer placement.

The organization or agency should secure a meaningful time commitment specifically in terms of length of service and regular work schedule. If the duration of the grant project is known, be sure volunteers are informed.

## Orientation

A volunteer is a representative of the agency or organization and it is important that the volunteer represent it properly. It is a basic right of a volunteer to be oriented. Orientation is the responsibility of the volunteer coordinator and includes:

- Information about the agency and its structure;
- Information on the general purpose, objectives and philosophy of the agency;
- A clear explanation of the volunteer's obligation to the agency, their supervisor, etc.;
- Information as to how the specific program assignment relates to the overall function of the agency; and
- Mechanical information such as assigned work space, location of supplies, restrooms, use of telephones, etc.

An orientation manual covering the agency and the volunteer program could be prepared to be issued to the volunteer.

Using staff members in orientation can increase the team feeling and can help create favorable staff attitudes toward volunteers. Testimony from seasoned volunteers may also help in team-building among the new recruits.

## Training and Supervision

The supervisor of the specific program area is responsible for the training and supervision of the volunteer, either directly or through staff assignment. The amount and type of training depends upon the skill required to perform the specific assignment and the skill and expertise the volunteer brings to the program. In many cases, skills training can be given to staff and volunteers at the same time.

The supervisor must take special care in making the volunteer feel welcome and part of the team. The best overall strategy for managing a volunteer program, however, is to treat your volunteers as much like paid staff. Volunteers should receive as much attention, support, direction and recognition as your paid staff; and, like the paid staff, they should be given real responsibility and accountability.

***Ongoing direct supervision is important in order to:***

- Assure the full utilization of the volunteers' skills and energy to the advantage of the agency;
- Allow the volunteer to grow and develop through their activities;
- Maximize the benefit and satisfaction to the volunteers from their work experience; and
- Provide a forum for discussing problems and giving appraisal, evaluation and appreciation.

There may be times when it becomes necessary for the agency to terminate a volunteer. It is vital that this be done with minimal criticism to the volunteer: the supervisory and evaluation process may provide a means of helping the volunteer see why they should leave. If possible, alternative voluntary positions should be offered to the volunteer.

One way to avoid issues when terminating a volunteer is to specify the duration of the job when it is offered to the volunteer. If possible, the original job assignment should include the date when the assignment will end.

Agencies need to be especially careful if they are placing volunteers under the supervision of part-time staff, or under those less experienced in supervision. Training of staff to be supervisors is often as important as training volunteers.

## Recognition

The reasons why individuals volunteer vary widely. The greatest rewards are the personal satisfaction derived from the work experience and the appreciation expressed and implied by the staff and program participants who benefit from the services volunteered. Often the best way to express appreciation is through a formal recognition process.

Specific recognition can vary according to the imagination of the agency: certificates, mention in agency publications, community bulletin boards, special events such as luncheons, banquets, picnics, breakfasts, commemorative gifts, T-shirts, free tickets or passes to sporting and/or cultural events, paid trips (in whole or part) to conventions, conferences and workshops as a representative of the organization, and public praise at organizational ceremonies or community events. The forms of recognition are endless; each agency undoubtedly has some special means of showing its appreciation to volunteers. A simple gesture, such as a smile or a handshake, is still one of the most appreciated.

Don't forget staff recognition. When your staff does a good job working with volunteers, reward them with an appropriate form of recognition.

*Increasingly, volunteers are becoming an essential component of a grant program*

## Program Evaluation

Like any other agency program, the volunteer program needs care and periodic examination. Program objectives, training materials and methods as well as accomplishments should be examined with critical judgment based on the best data possible. Most importantly, the staff should frequently evaluate its goals, the goals for the volunteer program and its methods for attaining these goals.

Increasingly, volunteers are becoming an essential component of a grant program, stretching project dollars and increasing community involvement. Use volunteers wisely and their benefit will live on beyond the funded project.

## Record Keeping

A system for personnel records is essential for the entire grant program, but especially if you use volunteers. In the case of volunteers, the records kept should include the number of hours spent in volunteer service, an evaluation of volunteer career "growth" and any problems encountered by the volunteer. The organization should develop a system suited to its own needs and personnel requirements; the system should be as simple as possible and must be understood and used by all volunteers and staff.

Record keeping is normally a function of the volunteer coordinator, and good documentation of accomplishments can help to justify support funding for the volunteer program.

Provision should be made to accommodate volunteers who are receiving academic credit for their work. Records can also be helpful when the volunteer requests a work experience reference from the agency.

# Using Special Contacts to Lobby for You

A final point in the fund-seeking process is the prospecting for and mining special contacts. Whether they are your Senator or Member of Congress, state officials or even local benefactors, the care and feeding of special sources, contacts and VIPs are a vital part of the grantseeking process.

## Contacting Federal Officials

One of the best ways of making contacts with federal funding sources is by working through the Washington liaison offices that many states and some cities have established there. They can do much of the ground work and gain entree to many important people. Getting a state or local office to work for a nonprofit organization often depends on one's contacts in the state.

While one can schedule meetings with federal officials without contacts, it is often difficult to get a good hearing. A Member of Congress may listen politely to your presentation and express interest, but whether or not anything happens often depends on your credibility; that credibility can be established by your contacts.

External funding is the lifeblood of projects: without it, they simply cannot survive. Remember, though, that there is only a limited amount of funds for which many worthy projects complete. In this struggle for survival, you need a lot of help in getting your project recognized and making its successes known. Every project is unique, and not all strategies and practices are appropriate for your project. A concerted effort to establish contacts and to build community support through public relations can be of great benefit. This effort is arduous, time consuming and often frustrating, but it will dramatically increase your chances of funding. Here are rules to follow when meeting funding source contacts.

## Tips For Making Contacts And Meeting Influential People

- Make sure that have some information about the person with whom you are meeting.
- Never go with a prepared text in your head; you must listen with extreme care to the person you are meeting in order to decide in which direction you should move.
- Have notes jotted on a pad in front of you so that he or she knows you are prepared.
- Most individuals of stature do not like long meetings, so get to the point once you determine the proper direction.
- If you go or are with others, observe protocol in addressing the person; even if you are on a first-name basis, conduct yourself in a formal manner. In private, be formal until he or she makes a point of letting you know it is not necessary.
- Most people feel that your dress is a reflection of your attitude toward them. It is, therefore, extremely important to dress meticulously for these sessions. Dress is also a measure of success. No one likes to become involved with someone who does not appear successful.
- Be aggressive (but not obnoxious or overbearing), even if it upsets your stomach. If you don't hustle, it won't come to you.
- Prominent individuals will want to help if you are sincere and reasonable.

- Be honest. If prominent individuals find you have misled them, you'll lose not only them but also other individuals with whom they're in contact.
- Read a good book on how to be a lobbyist.

## Cultivating Other Prominent Persons

Many times you will want your project to become favorably known to other prominent individuals who are in a position to help, particularly if you wish repeated funding. To accomplish this, here are several useful ideas.

- Host a workshop in which prominent individuals can be used as keynote speakers or speakers/trainers for particular sessions. An action-reaction effect is created by this method: prominent individuals draw media and media draw prominent people. Always follow up a session like this with a personal meeting with the individual. Your relationship now takes on a different meaning.
- Use publicity. Every time publicity is generated for a prominent individual by their involvement with your project, you are actually receiving double publicity, as well as establishing a "track record" for your project. Newspaper coverage will eventually result in magazine articles and television coverage. Local cable outlets often repeat their public service programs frequently throughout the week and, of course, a tape can preserve this "good news" and be shared with small groups and even individuals as easy as you can say VCR.
- Try lobbying. Why do you spend an enormous amount of time developing a rapport with prominent individuals? It is basically known as elementary politics, lobbying or the "theory of exchange." Simply explained, the theory is based on the maxim, "one good turn deserves another." It must be strongly emphasized, however, that your organization is held in high esteem because of the quality performance of its staff and is respected because of its work and ability to produce. Without this record of accomplishment, even prominent individuals will not help.

- Include prominent individuals and your Board of Directors. Having prominent people on your board is especially invaluable at funding time. If you had to decide between two projects for funding that were fairly close, one with the strong support of influential people and one without, which would you support?

## Project Management and Administration

Once the grant is funded, the real work begins. That for which you worked so hard in the grant writing process will now come to pass. But, as the old Chinese proverb says, "Be careful what you wish for, as it may come true." Whether your project is ultimately deemed successful from the point-of-view of the funding source, in terms of products and deliverables, may depend on how well you communicated with them during the project period.

Overall, the funding source-government or foundation-wants the recipient of their funds to be responsible and deliver on the project's promises. This means treat the money and the subject matter with care, follow the law, produce as promised and in summary, stick to the plan.

Proper stewardship of grant monies is vital to you and the funding source. Periodic progress reports will likely be required (quarterly is reasonable), but you may be asked for monthly reports. Clarify the nature of these reports ahead of time and build them into your project plan.

The same advice applies to the final report, which may be required within the time period of the contract or sometimes within a specified period (i.e., 90 days) after the expiration of the grant. This final report includes both narrative material as well as final fiscal information.

*Here are a few more elements of project management to keep in mind:*

- At the beginning sound financial record keeping that will allow you to survive any audit, even one that may come up to three years later.
- Advance payments are highly unlikely, so be prepared at the

beginning of your project to pay salaries and/or have a sound credit relationship with personnel and suppliers for up to 60 days.

- Clarify expenditures to see if they are allowable costs before you sign on the dotted line. For example, purchasing equipment and property in general must usually be approved in advance, often in the contract; independent expenditures are usually not allowed if they are to be charged to the project.

- Facilities must be as promised and available for site visits, planned and unplanned. Substituting facilities, changing locations and so on usually require prior approval, as do changes in the names and/or roles of principal investigators and key project staff.

- Make sure your organization is adhering to all legal matters and responsibilities of being a contractor, government or not.

- Establish procedures for project income and clarify who owns copyrights and income through royalties.

From what you have read in this chapter, there should be no doubt that people, on your side and on the side of the funding source, are extremely important during the course of the project. These parties can help your cause, but they can as easily hurt your chances of completing a successful project. The wrong person bearing the wrong attitude or delivering the wrong message can undo the good written work of many others. Proceed with caution and, when in doubt, let your written reports make the case for you.

An interesting methodology for project evaluation, both at the grant writing stage and the project as it progresses, has been developed by the U.S. Department of Education's "Fund for the Improvement of Post-Secondary Education" (FIPSE). Even if your project is not related to education topics, their techniques can be helpful in your grant writing. Your grantor may well require periodic reports on the progress of your project; developing such evidence during the grant writing stage will make it easier to collect this data during the execution of the project, so it should be a consideration from the grant writing stage onward.

For example, what would count as solid quantitative and qualitative evidence that your project had succeeded or failed? It may be difficult within the term of the grant to assess accomplishment of long-range objectives, but there might be several short-term indicators or milestones that you can identify. Using the FIPSE techniques of formative and summative evaluation in the preparation of your grant and the design of your project could be a valuable tool.

FIPSE publishes a bibliography of books and articles on program evaluation to assist you with evaluation design. These references define formative and summative evaluation techniques; address evidence, measurement and sampling questions; and discuss the immediate and long-range outcomes you can expect, based on project objectives. This bibliography is available on FIPSE's website, http://www.ed.gov/offices/OPE/FIPSE/biblio.html.

# *Summary*

Just writing a great grant is not limited to setting words on paper; conducting thorough reviews, seeing that it is presented correctly and on time and finding people to help you move the grant through the review procedure are important parts of the process. Having a support team made up of regular staff and volunteers can help you in the grant writing task just as they do in the day-to-day operations of your program; and having influential people on your Board of Directors can help after the grant has been submitted. Finally, planning ahead for the time that the grant is awarded and the project is underway will ensure the ultimate success of the grant writing process: receiving the funding for your project!

CHAPTER 12

# Looking Back, Looking Ahead

◆ **After learning about how our just-submitted proposal was viewed by the funding source, what questions should we ask about future funding?**

◆ **How do I know if my funding source is good for just one year or more than one year?**

◆ **If my application is not funded, what should I do to help my chances in the future?**

Now that you've done your homework on your program's needs and have drafted your proposal, be sure to take time to focus on long-term future funding before submitting it to your prospective funding source(s). Funding for the first year is ok, but you really want to have a guarantee of future funding so that your program can continue and evolve, taking your original idea and improving it to contribute to your program's and organization's success. In-hand with this long-term perspective comes the necessity for continual improvement -always look to the future to enhance and improve your chances for continued funding with your current grantor, as well as to identify new sources of funding.

Learn how you can obtain extended and/or future funding from your current fund grantor and stay ahead of the game by keeping track of legislative mandates and the political pendulum, doing research to identify and network with private organizations, and maintain and expand your joint venture coalitions for future grant writing success. And never forget that you will need to properly administer your program as you proposed, which means you'll have to work smart at the continual improvement process. This chapter covers some of the situations you'll need to keep an eye on for long-term funding success, including keys on how to build long-term funding into your first proposal, as well as proposal pitfalls and how to recover from them if you don't get funded.

## Future Funding

This oft-neglected area of the grant proposal is sometimes the most important to funding sources and is the key to your organization's long-term program success. Covering all facets of your proposed program with direct and peripheral services dependent upon a successful program is important. This will have been covered in your proposal. For example, if you are asking for computers for classrooms and teacher training, the funding source may be interested in how you intend on paying for the upkeep and upgrades of this equipment once the original grant money has been spent. Always re-visit your original RFP and see if it asks about future funding or at least what your agency's long-range plan is. This element used to be required in most private (foundation and corporate) funding applications but it is becoming the fashion for government-funded projects as well.

In this section you must think in future terms and devise a plan to keep the program going, even if you are only asking for one-time funding. If you are asking General Motors for a van to shuttle kids to your program, who will pay for the gas and upkeep? If you open a senior center, what is needed to keep it open? If you have been able to reclaim an environmentally threatened wetland, what can you do for other similar sites in your region?

There are several ways to approach these issues and other problems that simply can't be solved or serviced in a single funding year. We could divide this topic into several parts-maintenance money, new or second phase funding and support to duplicate your pilot project in other needed areas. Review the RFP and/or ask your funding source if any of the following types of funding are available, and appropriate, for your program.

## Maintenance Money

If your original project requires making organizational plans to assume the costs of maintaining project operations, indicate how much you will need and where the additional funds will come. For example you might say, "Board of Directors member and gas station owner John Q. Public has pledged to donate free gas and regular tune-ups for the van." Or you might say, "The local college will donate one half-time secretary to act as billing for our new clinic." Identify these funding sources in advance and then seek the dollars to close the gap from a traditional funding source.

## New or Second Phase Funding

Consider that after completing a successful first project year, you may well want to begin considering how your original idea could and should be expanded to move beyond the initial goals to address new or advanced objectives. Building on the thorough documentation of accomplishments from your first phase, the funders who planted the first financial seeds are likely and appropriate sources for supporting post first-year funding of the original project, or to follow through on first-year findings and observations. Once you have built a sense of stewardship and competence in meeting the original goals and objectives, and doing so in a proper fiscal manner, you are indeed the preferred vendor of similar and advanced services. A good time to raise this possibility is about three months before the deadline for applications for the next year or during a face-to-face or phone-to-phone meeting with your contract monitor. If you are encouraged, or not discouraged, develop a concept paper, or an invited pre-proposal, and test the waters. Get guidance on "scope," both in terms of work and money and strike while the iron is hot.

## Support to duplicate your pilot project in other needed areas

This is the most simple of the future funding concepts. Your approach has proven to work in one locale, and now you demonstrate the need for using your proven strategies and tactics in other documented needy areas. Make sure that you deliver the same good detail as you did in year one's application, document the need and invite the right joint venture partners.

# *Proposal Pitfalls: Life after Rejection*

In nearly every grant writer's career, some proposals will not be funded. How can you ensure this never (or seldom) happens to you? In some cases, you can't. Perhaps the political nature of the review process excluded you—an unknown from your perspective and an uncontrollable fact of life. Maybe the funding source already had in mind the organization they would fund and everyone else's proposals went by the wayside. This doesn't mean that you didn't give it your best shot and now is not the time to give up on grant writing. Seek new sources, make sure you've done your homework as we've discussed throughout this book, revise your proposal and submit it to these new sources... perhaps even more than one funding source, depending on the technical funding specifications of the RFP.

If your proposal is not funded, contact the funding prospect and find out why. Learn from the source all that you can and incorporate what you've learned in your next proposal effort. It might be a good idea to ask your contact to help you review the programs you chose as having the best fit with your organization and project. Ask them what one or two related programs best fit your organization and your already identified project needs. These targeted programs are the ones on which you should seek further information.

Every grant applicant is due some feedback from a failed or unfunded proposal. What kind of feedback, when and in what detail will vary, depending on the funding sources. Some organizations will have reviewers prepare numerical and narrative comments and will organize these useful comments and forward them to applicants. This is the best-case scenario. More likely it is either a quantitative (numerical) score or a brief qualitative (word-based) commentary. If you get neither, ask for some sort of feedback such as taking notes from a telephone interview with a funding source spokesperson that will allow you to probe as to what generally separated successful proposals from unsuccessful ones.

## *Summary*

Grant funding sources are usually trying to make a long-term difference in a community. As a grant writer and fundraiser, you should always plan for the future funding of any program you propose. This way you're ensuring your program's long-term contribution to the community based on the funding source's interests in your type of program. Since grant writing is a process of continual improvement, successful grant writers are constantly researching, fundraising, networking and submitting proposals. Because you also act as your organization's internal monitor of the program, carefully managing expectations of your boss, subordinates and program volunteers, your job is full of challenges. However, these challenges are well worth the effort since grant writers who get programs funded also gain increasing organizational and community-based support. Your grant writing skills will take your career into a new direction, growing and evolving every day. The exciting and worthwhile rewards of the successful grant writer are yours for the asking. As the marketing line for Nike says, "Just Do It."

# *Glossary*

*The following terms are most (new ones are invented every day) of those commonly used in contracts and grants literature, regulations, and announcements. They are in alphabetical order by first word of phrase or letter of acronyms and abbreviations.*

**ABSTRACT** - A summary of your grant proposal.

**ACC** – Annual Contribution Contract

**ACIR** – Advisory Commission on Intergovernmental Relations (conducts studies on Federal, State, and Local governments)

**ACTION** – A federal anti poverty agency from the Great Society

**ACTUAL COST** – The amount paid for an asset (see asset), not its resale value or worth. An item's cost can also include the freight charges and installation cost.

**ADA** – Americans with Disabilities Act

**ADAMH** – Alcohol, Drug Abuse, and Mental Health Block Grant

**AFDC:** Aid to Families with Dependent Children

**AFL–CIO:** American Federation of Labor–Congress of Industrial Organizations

**AID:** U.S. Agency for International Development

**ALLOCATION** – A distribution of funds among grant recipients, arrived at by applying a formula to specific program funds available.

**ALLOTMENT** – An amount of funds received by a grant recipient.

**ANNUAL REPORT** – Yearly publication focusing on financial, program, and governance information of a corporate giving program or foundation. Annual reports usually describe the grant–maker's priority funding areas, grant making policies and procedures, guidelines for grantseekers, and programs that received grants in that year. Financial pages list assets, income, granted funds, and operating expenses. Granted funds may be categorized by program area (such as education, scientific research, youth services), and specific organizations as well as by amounts.

**AOA** – Administration on Aging

**APPROPRIATION** – Funding levels are established for programs; follows authorizations in legislation.

**AUDIT** – To inspect the accounting records and procedures of a business or organization in order to verify whether or not they are accurate and complete. An internal audit is done by a member of the organization whose records are being inspected. An independent audit is done by someone outside of the organization.

**AUTHORIZATION** – legislation which creates and establishes a program as well as establishing a funding ceiling; precedes appropriation. In many cases, the authorization legislation is multi-year. The full authorized amount is rarely appropriated.

**BALANCE** – The amount shown in an account, normally the difference between a debit and a credit.

**BALANCE SHEET** – A financial statement that gives a snapshot of the property owned by a company and of claims against that property as of a certain date.

**BLM** – Bureau of Land Management

**BLS** – Bureau of Labor Statistics (information on wages and price indexes and occupational projections)

**BOG** – Basic Opportunity Grants (Basic Educational Opportunity Grants)

**BUDGET** – One's estimate of income and expenses over an interval of time, whether daily, weekly, monthly, annually, etc.

**BUREAU** – Referring to a particular department, agency or office, usually (but not always) referring to a particular task or duty performed by government agents in that office or department.

**CAPITAL GRANT** – Grant to provide funding for buildings, construction, or large pieces of equipment rather than program or operating expenses.

**CAPITAL IMPROVEMENT** – Something that improves an asset's value and extends its life.

**CATEGORICAL GRANT** – A grant given to support an activity in a specific category such as health, the arts, education, transportation, public safety, etc. Some categories may be broader than others, i.e. health–adolescent pregnancy prevention, or general, i.e. health–senior citizens.

**CBD** – Commerce Business Daily

**CD** – Community Development "Block" Grants

**CDC** – Center for Disease Control

**CETA** – Comprehensive Employment and Training Act (Labor). Replaced by JTPA.

**CFDA** – Catalog of Federal Domestic Assistance

**CFR** – Code of Federal Regulations

**CHALLENGE GRANT** – Grant contingent on the recipient's raising additional funds from other sources. For example, a  corporation might award an organization $1 for every $3 in new money raised from individuals. See also Matching gift.

**CHARITABLE CONTRIBUTION** – See Deductible Contribution.

**CJCC** – Criminal Justice Coordinating Center

**COG** – Council of Governments; Substate Regional Planning Agency

**COLLABORATION FUNDING** – A set of partners have come together to achieve a common goal or vision, usually from different organizations. This can include both public and private partners, government agencies, even individuals.

**COMMITTED FUNDS** – That portion of a corporate or philanthropic budget that has already been allocated or pledged to organizations, groups, or specific programs.

**COMMUNITY FOUNDATION** – A public charity supported by combined funds contributed by individuals, foundations, nonprofit institutions, and corporations. A community foundation's giving is limited almost exclusively to a specific locale, such as a city, a county or counties, or a state. Although it seeks funds to be held as an endowment, with the income used to make grants, a community foundation accepts funds from donors who authorize principal to make grants, in whole or in part.

**COMMUNITY REINVESTMENT ACT** – Passed by Congress in 1977, the Act requires that certain federal agencies use their regulatory powers to help meet the credit needs of the communities they serve, including low–income neighborhoods.

**COMPANY-SPONSORED FOUNDATION** – See Corporate Foundation.

**CONSTRAINT** – A restriction produced by a formula that is applied to allotments. Constraints are generally used to ensure maximum or minimum funding levels for recipients or limits on year–to–year changes in funding levels.

**CONTRACT** – An agreement between two or more parties that creates an obligation to do or not to do something.

**CONTRACT AWARD** – The amount one receives to perform a service for or delivered finish goods to an end user; the individual or business receiving this award is legally bound to perform an exact function resulting in a result.

**CONTRIBUTIONS COMMITTEE** – A committee, usually drawn from a corporation's board, executive staff, and employees, sometimes including outside members, that is charged with determining policy and overseeing the corporation's philanthropic activities. The committee may also oversee philanthropic programs other than direct grants, such as employee involvement and loaned executive programs.

**CONTRIBUTIONS POLICY** – A statement that outlines the parameters of a corporate or philanthropic activity, usually drawn up and approved by the board or its contributions committee.

**COOPERATIVE VENTURE** – A joint effort of one or more grant–makers or a governmental unit. Each partner may participate through sharing information, technical resources, funds, research, etc.

**CORPORATE CONTRIBUTIONS** – A general term referring to charitable contributions by a corporation. It is usually used to described cash contributions only, but may also include other items, such as the value of loaned executives, products, and services.

**CORPORATE FOUNDATION** – A private philanthropic organization set up and funded by a corporation. Although corporate foundations are subject to the same rules and regulations as other private foundations, they often do not have substantial assets of their own, but depend on funds paid by the corporation to the foundation each year.

**CORPORATE GIVING PROGRAM** – A philanthropic program operated within a corporation. The program may be managed through a department of its own or through a community affairs (or similar) department.

**CORPORATION** – A legally created artificial person, chartered by the federal or a state government, for the purpose of doing business in the place of a real person or goup of persons and which is separate and different from them. This entity is legally treated as a real person but with a potentially longer life span and the ability to sell off parts of it through stock transfer.

**COST–SHARING FACTOR** – A data element that explicitly reflects the share of program costs to be financed with federal funds. See also Matching Rate and Reimbursement Rate.

**CPI** – Consumer Price Index

**CSC** – Civil Service Commission

**D & B** – Dun & Bradstreet (a financial rating service)

**DEA** – Drug Enforcement Administration

**DEDUCTIBLE CONTRIBUTION** – A contribution (gift) to a charitable cause that is allowed as a deduction from taxable income by the Internal Revenue Service. Corporate contributions to social programs and organizations are in some cases assumed as business expenses.

**DEMINIMUS** – A provision that eliminates grant payments to grantees whose formula allotment is below a specified amount.

**DEPRECIATION** – The wearing out of plant equipment, machinery, etc. and which reduces taxable income.

**DIRECT COSTS** – Program related costs

**DISSEMINATION:** Refers to how you will inform others of your project and its outcome.

**DOC** – U.S. Department of Commerce

**DOD** – U.S. Department of Defense

**DOE** – U.S. Department of Energy

**DOJ** – U.S. Department of Justice

**DOL** – U.S. Department of Labor

**DOT** – U.S. Department of Transportation

**DS** – U.S. Department of State

**EA** – Energy Assistance (Low Income) Block Grant

**EARMARKING** – See Set-asides.

**ED** – U.S. Department of Education

**EDA** – U.S. Economic Development Administration

**EDGAR** – Education Department General Administrative Regulations

**EEOC** – Equal Employment Opportunity Commission

**ELIGIBILITY** – Conditions which must be met by an applicant for a grant or loan.

**ELIGIBILITY FACTOR** – A data element that reflects conditions grant recipients must meet in order to be eligible to receive grant funds.

**EMS** – Emergency Medical Service

**EMT** – Emergency Medical Technician

**ENDOWMENT** – Stocks, bonds, property and funds given permanently to a foundation so that it may produce its own income for grant making purposes. Also a gift of money or property from one to another, usually of a government agency or private foundation to another organization or an individual. It can also mean the permanent fund from which these gifts are drawn.

**ENTITLEMENTS** – Programs that provide benefit payments for individuals whose eligibility is determined by law.

**EO** – Executive Order

**EPA** – Environmental Protection Agency

**ESE** – Elementary and Secondary Education Block Grant

**ESEA** – Elementary and Secondary Education Act

**EVALUATION** – A systematic process designed to reduce uncertainty about the effectiveness of a project and its results.

**EXPENDITURE RESPONSIBILITY** – Grants by private foundations to traditional nonprofit organizations churches, schools, medical facilities, and other publicly supported agencies are presumed to be charitable and require no extra documentation for the Internal Revenue Service. Grants to any other type of organization, another private foundation, a profit-making business, a civic league, labor organization, and so on—require the private foundation to exercise additional "responsibility" to be certain the funds are "expended" in an acceptable manner. Specifically, the foundation must ensure that the grant is used solely for the purpose for which it was made, must obtain complete reports from the grantee on how the funds were spent, and must report in detail to the Internal Revenue Service on any such expenditures.

**FAPRS** – Federal Assistance Program Retrieval System

**FAA** – Federal Aviation Administration

**FBI** – Federal Bureau of Investigation

**FCC** – Federal Communications Commission

**FDA** – Food and Drug Administration

**FDIC** – Federal Deposit Insurance Corporation

**FEASIBILITY STUDY** – An analysis and projection of future income, expenses and profitability of business or investment.

**FEDERATED DRIVE** – A joint fund raising effort on behalf of several nonprofit organizations. Usually run by an organization that is itself nonprofit. Contributed funds are distributed to its member organizations according to its own criteria.

**FEMA** – Federal Emergency Management Agency

**FHA** – Federal Housing Administration

**FHLMC** – Federal Home Loan Mortgage Corporation ("Freddie Mac")

**FHWA** – Federal Highway Administration

**FIPSE/FIPE** – Fund for the Improvement of Post–secondary Education

**FISCAL CAPACITY FACTOR** – A data element that reflects the ability of a government to generate revenues from its own economic resources, subject to its taxing authority.

**FLOW-THROUGH-FUNDS** – Corporate contributions to corporate foundations that are grant–making, not for endowing the foundation permanently. Most corporate foundations depend on these funds each year rather than on income produced from endowment.

**FMC** – Federal Management Circular

**FNMA** – Federal National Mortgage Association ("Fannie Mae")

**FORM 990** – Annual tax return that private foundations (including company–sponsored foundations) must file with the Internal Revenue Service. A similar form may also be filed with the appropriate state offices. Includes information about the foundation's assets, income, operating expenses, contributions, paid staff and salaries, name and address of a person or persons to contact, program funding areas, grant–making guidelines and restrictions, and grant application procedures.

**FORMULA** – A prescribed method for (1) distributing funds among grant recipients to finance (completely or partially) eligibility for funding. It is a structured mathematical statement, i.e., algebraic equation; it specifies the data element(s) used to make the allocation or reimbursement (see Reimbursement Rate) and the relationships between the data elements (e.g., if they are to be multiplied, divided, added, or subtracted).

**FOR PROFIT/PROPRIETARY FOUNDATION** – A nongovernmental, nonprofit organization with funds and a program managed by it's own trustees and directors, established to further social, educational, religious, or other charitable activities by making grants. A private foundation receives its funds from, and is subject to control by, an individual, family, corporation, or other group of limited number. In contrast, a community foundation receives its funds from multiple public sources and is classified by the Internal Revenue Service as a public charity.

**FOUNDATION BOARD OF DIRECTORS** – Governing and policy–making body of a foundation, (A company sponsored foundation's board members may include members of the corporation's board, members of the contributions committee and the contributions staff, members of the community and others not affiliated with the corporation.)

**FR** – Federal Register

**FRAUD** – One's intentional misrepresentation or deception of or about an action or activity that causes loss to another party.

**FTC** – Federal Trade Commission

**FUND ACCOUNTING** – An accounting system which establishes accounts for segregating revenues and other resources, together with all related liabilities, obligations, and reserves, for the purpose of carrying on specific activities or attaining certain objectives in accordance with special regulations. Fund Accounting, in a broad sense, is required to demonstrate compliance with the requirements for which the funds were raised and "granted."

**FY** – Fiscal Year (example FY '02 = July 1, 2002 – June 30, 2002, FY1, FY2, etc.)

**GAO** – General Accounting Office. A major evaluator of federal funding efforts but in a traditional audit fashion as well as in terms of meeting program goals.

**GNMA** – Government National Mortgage Association ("Ginny Mae")

**GNP** – Gross National Product

**GPO** – Government Printing Office

**GOALS** – Goals are the vision for your project, or the "ends."

**GRANT, GRANTS-IN-AID** – An assistance award in the form of dollars, product(s) and/or technical assistance. There are three general categories of Grants: Categorical, Block, and Revenue Sharing and several subcategories

    **Categorical** – Grants allocated for a single purpose within a specified time (see previous listing).

    **Project** – Grants for a specific program and purpose, nationwide/regional competition.

    **Formula** – Grants to states on a proscribed basis; the state may distribute "these" funds based upon a state plan—these funds are termed "pass–through".

    **Block** – Consolidation of categorical funds into a single flexible grant program for distribution to the states.

    **General Revenue Sharing** – Distribution of federal funds, formula (mathematical) state, counties and municipalities for their use with few restrictions.

    **Special Revenue Sharing** – This program was the precursor of Block Grants.

    **Block Grants** – As designed, Categorical Grants were blended into several single Multi–functional Grants which were distributed to states and local governments.

**GRANTS-IN-AID** – Such aid is defined as resources provided by the federal government in support of a state or local program of governmental service to the public. This includes:

a)  Direct cash grants to state or local governmental units, to other public bodies established under state or local law, or to their designees (e.g., federal aid for highway construction).

b  Outlays for grants–in–kind such as purchases of commodities distributed to state or local governmental institutions (e.g., school lunch programs).

c)  Payments to nonprofit institutions when:

   (1)  The program is coordinated or approved by a state agency (e.g., the Hill–Burton hospital construction program).

   (2)  Payments are made directly because of provisions of a state plan or other arrangements initiated by a state or local government (e.g., federal aid for higher education).

   (3)  Payments are made with the explicit intent of augmenting public programs (e.g., community action programs).

d)  Payments to regional commissions and organizations that are redistributed at the state or local level or provide public services.

e)  Federal payments to state and local governments for research and development that is an integral part of the state and local government's provision of services to the general public.

**GRANT CONTRACT** – A statement, signed by both grant–maker and grant recipient, describing how the grant is to be used and what reporting is required.

**GRANTEE** – Person/Organization who receives a grant.

**GRANTOR** – Organization who gives a grant to a Grantee

**GSA** – General Services Administration. The federal agency that cares for government property, buildings, vehicles, etc.

**HHS** – U.S. Department of Health and Human Services

**HMO** – Health Maintenance Organization

**HOLD HARMLESS PROVISION** – This provision guarantees that a grant recipient will not receive less funding than it did under a previous program or under a preceding formula. Hold Harmless Provisions are used to protect a recipient's funding levels when substantial changes are made to an existing program or formula. They are sometimes also referred to as grandfather provisions.

**HRA** – Health Resources Administration

**HUD** – U.S. Department of Housing and Urban Development

**IHS** – Indian Health Service (federal), division of HHS

**INCENTIVE FACTOR** – A data element that is used to reward a grant recipient's performance. For example, the Work Incentive Program offers a bonus allotment to those state recipients that encourage placing job trainee graduates into higher wage jobs.

**INDIRECT COSTS** – See Overhead.

**IN–KIND CONTRIBUTION** – A corporate or government contribution that is not in cash. Such a contribution may take a variety of forms: for example, a donation of used office furniture or equipment, access to the company's computer to keep mailing lists or financial records, supplying printing services, office space, or the professional services of employees.

**INFORMATION AND REFERRAL** – The function of providing to the public current information on organizations, agencies and services offered throughout a jurisdiction or area, but not necessarily provided by the same organization operating the Information and Referral, sometimes called I & R, service.

**INSTITUTIONAL DEVELOPMENT/CAPACITY BUILDING** – Grant-makers thatinvest in institutional development or capacity building grants are usually seeking to strengthen the organization so it can better achieve its mission. These types of grants can pay for board and staff training, recruitment, new software and hardware, management, financial audits, salary assessments, and development/fundraising efforts, and can include anything that will promote organizational growth. These grants are often awarded for two years or more. INVESTMENT – Money or property spent to acquire property or other assets to produce income.

**IPA** – Intergovernmental Personnel Act

**IRS** – Internal Revenue Service

**JOINT VENTURE** – A project undertaken by more than one investor acting as one organization.

**JTPA** – Job Training Partnership Act (Labor Department) (successor to CETA)

**LEAA** – Law Enforcement Assistance Administration

**LWCA** – Land and Water Conservation Act

**LOCAL SHARE** – Resources (Financial or Nonfinancial) a grantee must provide in relation to the grantor's share in order to receive a grant.

**MAINTENANCE OF EFFORT PROVISION** – A grant condition where the recipient (a) maintains the same contribution to a program from its own resources as in a prior period, or (b) agrees that federal funds will be used to supplement, and not supplant, funds from other sources.

**MATCHING GIFT** – A grant by a corporation that matches an amount contributed, usually by an employee, to a nonprofit organization. It may be an exact match of funds or a ratio match, such as $3 given for every $1 contributed by an employee. See also Challenge Grants.

**MATCHING REQUIREMENT** – The grant recipient's share of program costs, or the rate at which a recipient must finance program costs from its own resources. This matching is a condition for receiving federal grant funds.

The match may be a hard or a soft match, depending on the conditions of the grant. A hard match means the recipient must provide its share of the match with dollars appropriated from its own sources. A soft match means the recipient may provide in–kind contributions, such as rent–free office space which equals the dollar value of the required match.

**MCH** – Maternal and Child Health Block Grant

**MDTA** – Manpower Development and Training Act. Preceded CETA.

**METHODS OR WORK PLAN** – Describes the steps to be taken to achieve the desired results. The format of this section may be in narrative, outline, graphs or chart forms.

**MINIMUM ALLOCATION** – A guarantee to each grant recipient of a funding level that equals a minimum specified level, either in absolute dollar or percentage terms.

**MOA** – Memorandum of Understanding

**MSA** – Metropolitan Statistical Area


**NASA** – National Aeronautics and Space Administration

**NCI** – National Cancer Institute

**NEA** – National Endowment for the Arts

**NEH** – National Endowment for the Humanities

**NEPA** – National Environmental Policy Act

**NHLI** – National Heart and Lung Institute

**NIA** – National Institute on Aging

**NIAAA** – National Institute of Alcohol Abuse and Alcoholism

**NICHD** – National Institute of Child Health and Human Development

**NIEHS** – National Institute of Environmental Health Sciences

**NIE** – National Institute of Education

**NIH** – National Institutes of Health

**NIMH** – National Institute of Mental Health

**NIOSH** – National Institute of Occupational Safety and Health

**NLRB** – National Labor Relations Board

**NONPROFIT** – A term describing the Internal Revenue Service's designation of an organization whose income is not used for the benefit or private gain of stockholders, directors, or any other persons with an interest in the company. A nonprofit organization's income is used to support its operations. Nonprofits can be public or private.

**NPS** – National Park Service

**NSF** – National Science Foundation

**NTIS** – National Technical Information Service

**OAA** – Older Americans Act

**OBJECTIVES** – Objectives are measurable within the context of your project. They are the "means" by which you will work toward the goal. Objectives relate clearly to your work plan, budget, and statement of need.

**OBLIGATIONS** – The amount of grant funds awarded by the federal government to a grant recipient during a given period; obligations incurred require that the recipient make federal payments during the same or a future period.

**OFCCP** – Office of Federal Contract Compliance Programs

**OHD** – Office of Human Development

**OJT** – On–The–Job Training

**OMB** – Office of Management and Budget; a unit of the Office of the President

**OMB CIRCULARS** – Uniform policies and rules to be followed in the administration of federal programs.

**OPERATING EXPENSES** – All sums spent on programs, salaries, fundraising, general administration, and operations.

**OPM** – Office of Personnel Management

**ORG** – Office of Research Grants (National Institute of Education)

**OSHA** – Occupational Safety and Health Administration

**OVERHEAD** – Also called in–direct costs, this is a fiscal arrangement whereby the grant receiving organization earns monies in addition to direct costs, for their services in the area of payroll and personnel services, staffing, utilities, and other services that create the environment for the project staff to complete their assignments. Overhead rates vary from under ten percent to 100 per cent depending on the operational costs documented by the grant receivers.

**PAYOUT REQUIREMENT** – The Internal Revenue Code requirement that all private foundations, including corporate foundations, pay out annually in grants and contributions the equivalent of (approximately) 5 percent of the value of their investment asset.

**PERCENTAGE CLUBS** – Groups of corporations in specific locales that make yearly charitable contributions or grants that total a set percentage of their pre–tax net income.

**PHS** – U.S. Public Health Service

**PILOT FUNDING** – Pilot projects are those projects undertaken as a test. Usually pilot funding is a bit of a gamble on the part of the grant-maker, a trial to see if a particular approach will succeed in addressing that problem.

**PILOT PROJECT GRANT** – A grant to fund a first–of–its–kind program in one place to determine how well it works and if it might be replicated elsewhere.

**PHS** – U.S. Public Health Service

**PLANNING GRANT** – Grant that funds the planning process of a program. It might, for example, support surveys to determine the scope of a program or needs it should address.

**PLEDGE** – A commitment to contribute a certain amount of money, or specified assets, either at one time or over a period to time, to a particular organization.

**POT** – The funds earmarked as a subset of the total amount of funds to be allocated by formula. A pot is used when funds are subdivided, and each subdivision is allocated to recipients by a separate formula.

**PPBS** – Planning–Programming–Budgeting System

**PRE–TAX NET INCOME** – A corporation's annual net income before it has paid taxes. The Internal Revenue Service allows corporations to deduct contributions to charitable organizations, up to 10 percent of the corporation's taxable income.

**PRINCIPAL INVESTIGATOR/PROJECT DIRECTOR** – The overall leader of a grant project. Investigator used in academic settings.

**PROGRAM GRANT** – Grant earmarked to fund a specific project or program activity of an organization rather than for general operating expenses.

**PROGRAM OFFICER** – Staff member in a government, foundation, or corporate contributions office who is responsible for screening grant applications, researching the organization or program seeking funds, reviewing proposals, and making recommendations about grants, often in a particular area.

**PROGRAM-RELATED INVESTMENT** – A loan made by a foundation to a nonprofit organization for a project related to the foundation's stated purposes and interests.

**PROJECT GRANT** – An amount of money given to complete a specific project by a certain time. The funds are normally paid in stages as phases of the project are completed.

**PROPOSAL** – Written request (in a format determined by the grant-maker) for a grant or contribution. Usually outlines why the grant is needed, the need or purpose it will serve, the plan for meeting the need or purpose, the amount of money needed, and background (general and financial) about the applicant.

**PROXY** – A substitute generally used when the statistics necessary to directly measure the need for, or cost of, a service are not available. It is usually a related series of data.

**PRO RATA REDUCTION** – An equal, across–the–board reduction applied to all recipients. If sufficient funds are not available to provide a formula–determined level of funding, then a pro rata reduction may be applied.

**PSRO** – Professional Standards Review Organizations

**PUBLIC CHARITY** – Charitable organizations (those designated under Section 501 (c) (3) by the Internal Revenue Service) qualify as public charities, private operating foundations, or private foundations. A public charity as defined in Section 509 (identified by the Service as "not a private foundation") normally receives a substantial part of its income, directly or indirectly, from the general public or from government. The public support must be fairly broad, not limited to a few individuals or families.

**RANN** – Research Applied to National Needs

**R&D** – Research and Development

**REGIONAL ASSOCIATION** – Membership organization of grant–making groups, such as foundations and corporate contributors, based in a specific area; may be citywide, statewide, or regional in scope. Associations provide a variety of member services (workshops, conferences, monitoring of relevant legislative activity, publications) according to members' needs. Association budget are supported by member dues.

**REIMBURSEMENT** – In some programs, the recipient must incur the program costs before claiming available federal aid. In such cases, the federal government guarantees a Reimbursement Rate to recipients. This is a fixed dollar amount per unit of service or a specified percentage share of the total costs for delivering a specific kind of funds. Fixed reimbursement per unit of service is linked to the number of units of service; percentage rates of costs are linked to service costs (which may vary among recipients).

**RESEARCH FUNDING** – A grant made for a specific and clearly defined purpose, to test a hypothesis, or to undertake research. These grants are most often awarded to an academic institution and directed toward a particular staff member.

**RESTRICTED GRANT**– Grant that is to be used for certain defined purposes or within a certain time, as determined by the grant–maker.

**RESTRICTED INCOME** – Contributions designated for a specific purpose.

**RFB** – Request For Bid (used with contracts)

**RFP** – Request For Proposal

**RFQ** – Request For Qualifications

**RPA** – Regional Planning Agency

**RSVP** – Retired Senior Volunteer Program (federal), division of ACTION

**SBA** – Small Business Association

**SBIS** – Small Business Investment Company

**SCORE** – Service Corps of Retired Executives, division of ACTION

**SEC** – Securities and Exchange Commission

**SECTION 501(c) (3)** – Internal Revenue Code section that defines exempt organizations – those organized and operated exclusively for religious, charitable, scientific, literary, educational, or similar purposes. Many foundations restrict their grant–making to 501(c) (3) organizations, with the single exception of the "testing for public safety" category, are deductible as charitable donations for federal income tax purposes.

**SEED FUNDING** – Assists with the establishment of a new organization or project. This type of grant is generally given to a small project at an early stage of its development. The organization usually needs to undertake additional planning and development efforts to expand further. The purpose of seed money is to nurture a project or organization through its formative stages.

**SET-ASIDES** – A prescribed percentage or dollar amount of grant funds that is earmarked for a specific purpose, at the national or at the state level, and may not be used for other purposes.

**SF–424** – Standard Form 424; U. S. Government Grant Application Form

**SHARE** – Each grant recipient's percentage share, not its dollar allotment, resulting from a formula allocation.

**SITE VISIT** – Fact–finding visit by a grant–maker to an organization that has applied for or received funding. It may also be a visit to the area(s) and institution(s) that are affected by the grant request.

**SOCIAL AUDIT** – An examination of a corporation's actions and use of resources as they affect both employees and the communities and society in which it operates.

**SOFT MATCH** – In–Kind Contributions

**SSA** – Social Security Administration (federal), division of HHS

**SSI** – Supplementary Security Income (federal)

**SMSA** – Standard Metropolitan Statistical Area.


**TAX–EXEMPT** – A classification granted by the Internal Revenue Service to qualified nonprofit organizations that frees them from the requirement to pay taxes on their income. Private foundations, including endowed company foundations, are tax–exempt; however, they must pay a 2 percent excise tax on net investment income.

**TC** – Treasury Circular

**TECHNICAL ASSISTANCE** – Operational, financial planning, legal, or other management assistance.

**TERRITORIES** – The Commonwealth of Puerto Rico, the Virgin Islands, the Marshall Islands, Guam, the Trust Territory of the Pacific Islands, and American Samoa.

**TOTAL COST FACTOR** – A data element that directly measures total program or project costs.

**TREAS** – Department of the Treasury

**TVA** – Tennessee Valley Authority


**UMTA** – Urban Mass Transportation Administration

**UNIT COST FACTOR** – A data element that reflects the cost per workload unit, such as per pupil expenditures.

**Unrestricted Income** – Contributions received for general operating purposes

**USC** – United States Code

**USDA** – United States Department of Agriculture

**USGS** – United States Geological Survey

**USIA** – United States Information Agency

**USPS** – United States Postal Service


**VA** – Veterans Administration

**VISTA** – Volunteers in Service to America (federal), division of HHS


**WEIGHTS** – These are relative proportions, such as 50 percent, 20 percent, and 30 percent, which sum to 100 percent. Weights are often used with the data elements in an algebraic expression to denote their degree of importance (relative value) in achieving program objectives.

**WORKLOAD FACTOR** – A data element that measures directly, or is a proxy for, the quantity (number of units of service) to be provided, such as the number of educationally deprived youth.


**YTD** – Year to Date

**YTM** – Year to Month

# AUTHORS NOTE

Dr. Daniel M. Barber is a professor of public policy and a former chair of the Graduate Center for Public Policy and Administration at California State University and the founder and CEO of Grantwriters.com. Born in Chicago, Illinois and raised in West Virginia, he earned his bachelors and masters degrees in journalism and urban studies and his doctorate in public administration.

While a graduate student at the University of Miami, Dr. Barber began his grant writing career addressing a number of environmental and transportation issues. In 1971, he was selected as the first Executive Director for the South Florida Regional Planning Council. In that capacity, he expanded, through grants and contracts, the Councils' initial membership base of three counties and a relatively small budget, to a roster of seven counties and over 10 times the original budget. He later held the assignment of Assistant Director of the Illinois Office Manpower and Human Development, where responsibilities included multi-million dollar grant programs in employment and training, community services and economic opportunity.

Dr. Barber is also the author of Citizen Participation in American Communities (Kendall/Hunt - 1981) and has served as Project Director and Principal Investigator for numerous state and federal grants and research projects servicing a diverse selection of community-based, governmental and educational organizations throughout the United States. This extensive background, along with materials developed for courses taught at major universities and numerous community colleges, helped to test and improve the unique advice used in this book. He has also served as a consultant for leading non-profit organizations and is in demand throughout the nation as an expert trainer on grants and intergovernmental relations for government and industry.

Honors and prestigious appointments include Pi Alpha Alpha The National Honor Society in Public Affairs, Phi Delta Kappa, Sigma Delta Chi, Orange Key (University of Miami), Institute for Educational

Leadership ^ Educational Policy Fellow, and service as a research associate for the National Academy of Science and National Research
Council.

With the founding of Grantwriters.com, Dr. Barber has been instrumental in developing a wide variety of web-based training materials
including the Grantwriters.Com Online course, books, diskettes and
mini-guides. In his five years as service as the Director of the Graduate
Center for Public Policy and Administration, he organized one of the
first graduate level grant writing courses in the country. Dr. Barber has
been a faculty member at California State University, Long Beach since
1975 and has helped to oversee a nationally accredited and highly
acclaimed program for training public service professionals.

# *Index*

# FINDING FUNDING:
## The Comprehensive Guide to Grant Writing

Dear Colleagues:

Thank you for your recent purchase of **FINDING FUNDING: The Comprehensive Guide to Grant Writing**. We sincerely hope that you have joined the ranks of those who found this publication to be a useful guide to grant and proposal writing. This book and its accompanying diskette were developed with a broad cross section of users in mind and hopefully is leading you step-by-step through the preparation of a successful grant application, and meeting the terms and conditions required by the funding source. The additional feature of this book is the computer diskette with its hundreds of funding sources, sample letters, forms, budgets, model timetables, pert charts, and examples of time-saving "boiler plate."

I hope you will recommend **FINDING FUNDING** to your friends and associates. For additional copies of **FINDING FUNDING** and/or the Finding Funding Document Diskette, please use the form below or visit either of our websites **www.bondstreetpublishing.com** or **www.grantwriters.com** and use our secure on-line credit card processing. While visiting our websites be sure to look at our wide range of special topic Mini Guides, our unique Grantwriters.com Online Course, our Custom Source Reports, and other research services.

Daniel M. Barber

---

### ORDERING INFORMATION

You may purchase additional copies at $39.95 each plus $4.00 shipping and handling (S&H). Additional diskettes at $9.95 each plus $2.00 S&H. We are pleased to offer quantity discounts for governmental agencies, community based and nonprofit organizations, schools and colleges.

### SHIPPING INFORMATION

Name _____

Address _____

City _____ State _____ Zip _____

Telephone _____ E-Mail _____

Books: _____ @ $39.95 = _____ Diskettes: _____ @ $9.95 _____

Total Purchase _____ + sales tax _____ Total Enclosed _____

**Bond Street Publishers • 1261 Hackett Avenue, Long Beach, CA 90815**
*CA residents add 8% tax*

---